Trapped in the War on Terror

TRAPPED
in the
WAR
on
TERROR

IAN S. LUSTICK

UNIVERSITY OF PENNSYLVANIA PRESS

Philadelphia

10 9 8 7 6 5 4 3 2 1

Published by
University of Pennsylvania Press
Philadelphia, Pennsylvania 19104-4112

A Cataloging-in-Publication record is available from the Library of Congress

ISBN-13: 978-0-8122-3983-6
ISBN-10: 0-8122-3983-0

For Terri

CONTENTS

PREFACE   ix

Chapter 1
THE IMPERATIVE OF TRIAGE   1

Chapter 2
PERCEPTIONS OF THE TERRORIST THREAT   8

Chapter 3
MEASURING THE TERRORIST THREAT:
WHAT IS THE EVIDENCE?   29

Chapter 4
THE CABAL, THE INVASION OF IRAQ,
AND THE ORIGINS OF THE WAR ON TERROR   48

Chapter 5
THE WAR ON TERROR WHIRLWIND   71

Chapter 6
FREEING AMERICA FROM THE WAR ON TERROR   115

NOTES   147

INDEX   177

PREFACE

A specter haunts America: the specter of terrorism. The list of potential catastrophes is endless—a dirty radioactive cloud over Manhattan, hoof-and-mouth disease wiping out American cattle herds, bombs against a few tunnels or bridges bringing our transport system to a halt, smallpox unleashed on an airplane spreading almost immediately and unnoticeably throughout the country. As imagined disasters multiply, the scale of perceived danger inevitably outruns confidence in our defenses.

The government's loudly trumpeted "War on Terror" is not the solution to the problem. It has become the problem. The War on Terror does not reduce public anxieties by thwarting terrorists poised to strike. Rather, in myriad ways, conducting the anti-terror effort as a "war" fuels those anxieties. By stoking these public fears and attracting vast political and economic resources in response to them, the War on Terror encourages, indeed virtually compels, every interest group in the country to advance its own agenda as crucial for winning the war. As a result, widening circles of Americans are drawn into spirals of exaggeration, waste, and fear.

The immense costs of the War on Terror, the self-inflicted wounds we suffer from it, and its permanently perceived inadequacy in comparison with the threats it forces us to imagine are more destructive of our national life than the damage terrorists are likely to inflict on us and our society. The War on Terror's record of failure, with its inevitable and spectacular instances of venality and waste, will humiliate thousands of public servants and elected officials, demoralize citizens, and enrage taxpayers. The effort to master the unlimited catastrophes we can imagine by mobilizing the scarce resources we actually have will drain our economy, divert and distort military, intelligence, and law enforcement resources, undermine faith in our institutions, and fundamentally disturb our way of life. In this way the terrorists who struck us so hard on

September 11, 2001, can use our own defensive efforts to do us much greater harm than they could ever do themselves.

Above all, we need clarity. There is and will continue to be a terrorist threat, emanating not only from Muslim extremists abroad but also from Timothy McVeigh-type fanatics at home. This threat will, in time, produce some attacks and some casualties. In the world as it is, this prediction is as easy to make as the prediction that in the future airliners will crash and that disgruntled former employees will murder former coworkers. The question is not how any of these or other bad things can be absolutely prevented but how we can most effectively reduce their frequency and seriousness. Counterterrorism policies and programs are therefore important. They can and should be carefully designed and implemented. An undisciplined, spiraling, and hysterical War on Terror to forestall every catastrophe our best minds and our cleverest script writers can imagine, however, is itself more damaging and dangerous than the terrorist threats it is supposedly combating.

During the Cold War, America adapted to the ever-present threat of nuclear incineration. One reason we could do so is that the threat was clear, easy to understand, and emanated from a distinct and specific place, the Soviet Union. Accordingly, we were able to fashion a strategic posture and culture of nuclear deterrence. Safety was achieved, or at least an acceptable level of assurance of safety, because the Soviets were convinced that we were convinced that an attack by either of us on the other would mean the annihilation of both. As bizarre as this doctrine of mutual assured destruction was, it played an unchallengeable role in securing the peace and protecting the world from the disasters piled up in missile silos, in bomb bays, and onboard submarines.

Ironically, against far weaker enemies and a far less awesome threat, we may today find it much more difficult to achieve the level of security, or a comparable sense of safety, that we managed to establish during the Cold War. The fundamental challenge we faced in our fifty-five-year confrontation with the Soviet Union was to remain steadfast against a horrifying but clearly visible threat. In 1947 George F. Kennan's famous "X" article provided subsequent administrations with the fundamental intellectual framework for assessing and countering the Soviet threat in a sustainable manner.[1] Kennan argued that the United States could be safe without "rolling back" communism and thereby risking a world war with the Soviet Union. If we were willing to commit the resources

and mobilize the steely patience necessary to contain Soviet expansionism and deter Soviet nuclear weapon use, we could not only survive but
prosper and emerge victorious following the collapse of a communist
economic and political system unable to compete with ours.

In the aftermath of 9/11 the challenge is different. It is to act pru-
dently in the face not of a clearly locatable threat but of intractable
uncertainty about painful, even catastrophic possibilities that may lurk
almost anywhere, including within our own borders. What are the real
reasons for the War on Terror? In this book I analyze its self-reinforcing
dynamics, using that analysis to suggest a way out of the trap of the
War on Terror, and then advance a sustainable approach to the threats
we face from al-Qaeda and others who would use massive violence
against our citizens. Franklin Roosevelt famously told us that the only
thing we really have to fear is "fear itself." If we can master the fear of
terrorism that leaves us in the grip of the War on Terror, we can then
fashion strategies to achieve genuine, if, as in the Cold War, incomplete,
psychological and military security. A crucial element in this strategic
posture will be to save ourselves from the self-inflicted disasters that,
apart from the Vietnam War, we mostly managed to avoid during the
long twilight struggle with the Soviet Union.

I am exceedingly grateful to the many people who helped me bring the
ideas in this volume to fruition. Although they cannot be assumed to
agree with the analysis and arguments put forward here, they have been
willing to take an interest in the questions I raise. First among those
to be thanked are Barry Mann, Executive Director of the Annenberg
Center for Medical Education at Lankenau Hospital in Wynnewood,
Pennsylvania, and Mark Ingerman, Chief of Infectious Diseases and
Preventative Medicine at the hospital. The first opportunity for airing
the analysis elaborated in this book was in the symposium they organized and moderated, "Terrorism, Bioterrorism, and Hospital Preparedness: A Commemoration of 9–11," held on September 11, 2005, at
Lankenau Hospital.

Michael Delli Carpini, Dean of the Annenberg School of Communications at the University of Pennsylvania, provided important encouragement and support. Several University of Pennsylvania students
responded enthusiastically and skillfully to requests for research assistance. They include Daniel Issacs, Michael Grosack, Adam Porroni,

and Mihaela Popescu. Todd Wakai of *TV Guide* provided prompt and professional assistance in accessing data about airings of movies and shows on national television. I benefited immensely from conversations about my analysis with colleagues at the Solomon Asch Center for Study of Ethnopolitical Conflict at the University of Pennsylvania, especially Clark McCauley and Paul Rozin. Special thanks is due to Jena Laske at the Asch Center for research support and editorial advice. I am particularly grateful for readings of portions of the manuscript by colleagues and others who were able to respond under significant time pressures in the midst of their very busy schedules. These include Ruth Ben-Artzi, Susan Brandon, Nelson M. Kasfir, Evan Lieberman, Bernard Lustick, Terri Lustick, Dan Miodownik, Brendan O'Leary, Peter Sharfman, Jeff Weintraub, and Leo Wiegman. Peter Agree at the University of Pennsylvania Press was a terrific support throughout the process of conception, writing, and editing of the volume, wise in his counsel and patient in his approach. I am also very grateful to Erica Ginsburg for her meticulous editorial work.

I dedicate this book to my wife, Terri, whose passions I share, whose insights and encouragement were indispensable, and whose love and support I cherish always.

The Americans took the bait and fell into our trap.
—Seif al-Adl (al-Qaeda's Security Chief)

Chapter 1

The Imperative of Triage

In the anxious months following the al-Qaeda hijacking attacks and the anthrax mail-letter attacks of 2001 I was asked by the Behavioral Science unit of the FBI Academy in Quantico, Virginia, to help organize a conference bringing together social scientists and law enforcement and intelligence officials. The purpose of the meeting was to help those charged with thwarting future terrorist attacks to understand the kinds of decisions they would need to make and to identify best practices for organizing and coping with what seemed an overwhelming and terrifyingly threatening new reality. In small-group discussions one theme repeated itself. Law enforcement officials on the front lines of the counterterrorism offensive told of being inundated with tens of thousands of tips coming from alarmed citizens and from their own surveillance networks, about suspicious activities that might presage a terrorist attack or preparations for an attack. Subsequently the Justice Department's inspector general reported that within just one week of the 9/11 attacks, the FBI had "received more than 96,000 tips or potential leads from the public, including more than 54,000 through an Internet site it established for the PENTTBOM [Pentagon, Twin Towers Bombing] case, 33,000 that were forwarded directly to FBI field offices across the country, and another 9,000 tips called into the FBI's toll-free 'hotline.'"[1]

An awful aspect of the human condition is that far more things appear necessary to do than there are resources to do them. Governments, as well as people, struggle with this problem by being rational. In some more or less systematic fashion they try to use what they have to get what they want. Seldom, however, has the American government or the American political system as a whole reacted to a problem more irrationally than it has in responding to the attacks of September 11,

2001, with the War on Terror. The result has been not only waste on a colossal scale and camouflage for a host of selfish and destructive projects by well-positioned zealots but the emergence of a War on Terror that is itself a more fearsome enemy than the terrorists it was putatively designed to fight. A key element in this failure was the calculated and enforced refusal by our national leadership to think systematically and publicly about the post-9/11 threat or allow others to do so.

How, I asked one official at the conference, did he manage to decide which tips to investigate and which to put aside as lacking sufficient credibility or importance? The response was staggering. "We chase down every tip, sir. Any one might be the next World Trade Center attack." No one around the table acted surprised. I responded that such a policy would be utterly impossible to sustain. As a practical matter some rules would have to be devised to separate significant leads from hoaxes, errors, or inaccurate or wildly speculative suggestions. At the very least, rules for separating promising from unpromising leads would be necessary if sufficient resources would be able to be devoted to the truly important ones. But my analysis was rebuffed. The fear of being identified after another attack as the person responsible for having ignored the tip that would have prevented it was simply overwhelming. Despite the commitment of more than a third of all FBI special agents to the antiterrorism campaign, this attitude virtually paralyzed the agency's initial response to the problem.[2]

The simple truth is that whenever scarce resources confront multiple demands for their use, triage of some sort is necessary. No matter how powerful the commitment was to "chase down every lead," the FBI was forced to ignore most tips and choose only some to investigate. Looking back on the period immediately after 9/11 responsible officials told *New York Times* reporters that National Security Agency eavesdropping had been streaming thousands of items for follow-up to the FBI and that the "unfiltered information was swamping investigators." Virtually all these tips "led to dead ends or innocent Americans."[3] Within one year the FBI had received more than 400,000 tips from the public. Of these, 85,000 were classified as "lead worthy" and sent to field offices or legal departments for investigation.[4] This means that some kind of triage technique, whether crude or sophisticated, conscious or unconscious, resulted in the Bureau's effectively ignoring nearly 80 percent of the information it received from the public.

"Triage" is originally a medical term referring to the task of categorizing patients in an emergency. Those who would benefit most crucially from immediate attention must be distinguished from those who would benefit from attention but would not suffer in some vital way from a delay. A third group consists of those so severely injured that attention, immediate or not, would be unlikely to improve their prospects. This kind of ruthless concentration on the principle of efficiency in the use of resources is always difficult and painful. The task is particularly challenging when policy "doctors" are faced with calls to solve problems unlikely to be problems at all *but,* that if they *are* problems, could be catastrophic in their consequences if not attended to immediately. Consider how difficult medical triage would be if every agitated and distraught person on one hundred stretchers physically appeared to be perfectly normal, but if each were convinced that he or she was about to die as a result of surreptitious processes that could be prevented only by the skilled care of the entire team of doctors with excellent understanding of pathologies unseen but believed to be at work.

This hypothetical predicament is similar to the reality the United States has brought itself to *feel* it is facing in the War on Terror—an impossibly large array of desperate demands for protection against readily imagined but unseen threats of catastrophe. The FBI and others operating at the tactical level may have developed some protocols for vetting possible leads. At the political level, however, the country is still suffering from a frenzied response to the specter of terrorist threats to the homeland. This national thrashing about in response to the any-moment possibility of disastrous attacks is so counterproductive that its consequences far outweigh the damage done to American interests and assets on September 11, 2001.

What has become apparent with time is that without a disciplined understanding of the threat and its scale, and given the immense wealth of the country that could be dedicated to national security, there are few rational limits on the scale of the resources we could be convinced should be dedicated to thwarting possible terrorist attacks. If we do not systematically evaluate threats, we will end up worrying about all conceivable vulnerabilities. By this logic, our resources will be the only limit to investments in our security, leading to a frenzy of impossibly huge outlays. Without a clear idea of what threats we actually face and what we can realistically do to cope with them, our country could be driven to sharp cuts in our standard of living and in the life chances of tens of millions of our citizens, cuts justified by fears that otherwise we might be exposed to some horrifying calamity at the hands of murderous terrorists armed with weapons of mass destruction (WMD).

Thus we find ourselves trapped in the War on Terror. There are two general kinds of explanations for this sorry, terribly dangerous state of affairs, one generous and the other cynical.

Let us take a generous approach to the question. We may imagine that well-meaning and genuinely frightened· and patriotic Americans, from ordinary citizens to high-ranking officials, are simply doing their best to rapidly improve America's readiness and defenses. When the task of preparing for this protean, all-azimuth threat of terrorism, however, is combined with an appreciation of the complexity, interdependence, and relative openness of our vulnerable society, careful planners would find it difficult to reject *any* suggestion for spending on counter-terrorism measures or preparedness training. We could then attribute the immense inefficiencies in the country's response to terrorism and the pervasive sense that our efforts are inadequate to the deep intractable character of the objective threat. Indeed it would be irrational, given our limited information and the scale of possible threats, to aspire to some sort of genuine triage. Perhaps, when dealing with the possibility of multiple large-scale disasters, it is simply impossible or unwise to try to distinguish real threats that *could* be mitigated with prudent policies, from real threats that *could not* be mitigated no matter what we might do. Instead we should seek to render ourselves invulnerable to all conceivable threats. Aside from the palpable impossibility of such a task, such an effort abandons the principle of triage and the principle of rationality itself. It would mean, in other words, abandoning efforts to distinguish (1) real threats that we might thwart if we try, from (2) nonexistent but potential threats that could be mitigated, if they were to become real, by policies we might adopt, from (3) nonexistent threats that could not be mitigated by our policies even if they were in fact real. This is a logic based on perceptions, not the reality, of a problem of absolutely overwhelming proportions. It is indeed a logic that can and does help explain the irrationalities of the War on Terror we shall explore in the coming pages.

More cynically, we might explain our predicament as the result of separate, interconnected plots by dedicated factions. From this perspective, particular key interest groups and individuals were clever and ener-getic enough to realize that the paranoia unleashed by the 9/11 attacks could be exploited for their own purposes. These players were suffi-ciently well placed to lead the political system toward beliefs, fears, and fantasies that would systematically favor their projects, their organiza-tions, and their careers. This line of analysis gives pride of place to the neoconservative "cabal" nested within the civilian hierarchy of the Pentagon and their primary patrons, Vice President Dick Cheney and Defense Secretary Donald Rumsfeld. It also emphasizes the key sup-porting role played by large military contractors, parts of the organized Israel lobby, and Republican partisans. This network of experienced politicos and ideologically committed zealots spent the first year of George W. Bush's presidency pushing the cabal's blueprint for a force-ful, "heroic" foreign policy of worldwide American engagement and supremacy and specifically for an invasion of Iraq.

This cabal's agenda had been set forth in high-profile articles and manifestos circulated in the late 1990s. Well before 9/11 and quite apart from the threat of al-Qaeda terrorism, this tightly knit network of for-eign policy and national security policy makers, publicists, and political leaders had advocated a war to topple Saddam Hussein's regime in Iraq as the cornerstone of what was often described a neo-Reaganite policy. Its main elements would be the unilateral use of American military and economic power to establish U.S. hegemony on a quasi-imperial basis. The neoconservatives and their allies were stymied, however, by opposi-tion to what was viewed as reckless abandonment of settled principles of U.S. foreign and national security policy by Secretary of State Colin Powell, the uniformed military, and most of the intelligence commu-nity.

The attacks of 9/11 turned the tide. Joining the war in Afghanistan that was necessitated by Taliban assistance to al-Qaeda to the invasion of Iraq that the cabal had always wanted, the "supremacists" convinced the president, and much of the country, that the apparently quick, cheap, and satisfying victory in the war in Afghanistan could be re-peated in Iraq. They did not need to convert most Americans, or even many Americans, to their vision of a global American empire; instead they inflamed national anxiety by focusing on prospects for al-Qaeda-type terrorists to strike the American homeland with weapons of mass destruction, delivered to them by countries described as belonging to the "Axis of Evil." As the bloody and expensive debacle in Iraq drags on, it remained an absolute political imperative for the war's architects to maintain a high level of fear of terrorist attacks against the homeland. Only by maintaining and accentuating such fears and linking them to the outcome of the war could Bush be reelected, the political reputation of the neocons be saved, and the broader interests of the conservative movement with which they are associated be protected.

In reality neither the generous nor the cynical argument can by itself explain the trajectory of American politics and policy since 9/11. By combining them, however, we can see how the War on Terror trap was set, how it has closed on us, and how we can escape. For the threats we face, however difficult, are not so overwhelming or unusual as to render our rational faculties irrelevant. Clearheaded analysis, sticking to evidence and logic, can provide a reasonable, prudent, and realistic basis for combating the mortal adversaries we do face while ensuring that we do not become, as those adversaries intend, our own worst enemy.

The War on Terror itself, not al-Qaeda or its clones, has become the primary threat to the well-being of Americans in the first decade of the twenty-first century. My fundamental conclusion is that the War on Terror is vastly out of proportion to the actual problems we face from terrorists and terrorist groups. The real tasks before us following 9/11 are fundamentally mismatched to the instrument supposedly designed to accomplish those tasks. To explore the War on Terror and its roots I first establish how the American government, opinion leaders, and ordinary citizens perceive the threat and challenge of terrorism to the homeland. Then I evaluate those perceptions in light of available evidence that unmasks massive exaggerations in our assessments of the likelihood of terrorist attacks capable of inflicting levels of destruction at or above that experienced on September 11, 2001. I will then ask how to account for the immense gap in the assessment of the scale of the threat and the evidence of its existence. The answer to this question involves identifying the ruthless and calculated manipulation of post-9/11 anxieties that set off the spiral toward an extravagant and self-destructive War on Terror. I account for that campaign as itself a result of the very structure of the problem as it was framed, naturally and uncalculatedly, by the top leaders of the country and intellectual elites from across the political spectrum. The engine for sustaining this war, a struggle defined by a constantly receding, never identifiable horizon, is then named. Today our system of government encourages virtually every American interest group, lobby, political party, and industry to redefine its particular vested interest as an objective crucially necessary for the accomplishment of the goal that has been blessed with an infinite willingness to expend resources—victory in the War on Terror.

The organization of the book is simple. The next chapter establishes the dimensions of the War on Terror as measured by the actions of our government and the beliefs of our citizens. In Chapter 3 I compare the vast scale of the War on Terror to actual evidence for the significance of terrorist threats inside the United States. I argue that the War on Terror bears, in its scale and in its particulars, no systematic relationship to any discernible threats. In three subsequent chapters I explain this gigantic misappropriation of resources and suggest the means for escaping from the trap the War on Terror has become.

Chapter 2

Perceptions of the Terrorist Threat

Since September 2001 the possibility of more terrorist strikes on U.S. soil has generated immense fear in the minds of Americans. How justified is that fear? Does it correspond to the real threats our country faces? To what extent does it represent a diabolical legacy of 9/11—Americans trapped within a humiliating, costly, and essentially impossible effort to secure themselves against the terrors of their own imaginations?

Americans are clearly frightened of catastrophic terrorism. Despite the absence of any attacks in the four years following September 11, 2001, they believe they have a right to be scared. Although the government tells citizens not to be frightened, it also regularly advises them to be "vigilant." When the respected 9/11 Commission finished its work, it reinvented itself as the Public Discourse Project and endorsed the America Prepared campaign. With the heading "Homeland Security Starts at Home," flyers and newspaper advertisements urged every American household to make a family emergency plan in case of terrorist attack, gather and store necessary supplies, and consult government agency Web sites to learn about what to expect and how to cope with different kinds of attacks. Media attention, popular entertainment, and government actions, ranging from creating enormous budgets for finding and fighting domestic terrorists to conducting foreign wars and implementing radical new surveillance measures, have filled the lives of Americans with images and information suggesting the imminence, omnipresence, and potency of terrorist threats. According to Department of Homeland Security standards, the entire country, at every moment since the establishment of its threat warning system, has lived under "Threat Condition Yellow—Elevated," meaning "significant risk of terrorist attacks." In New York City, and occasionally elsewhere, the official threat condition has risen to "orange," meaning "high risk of terrorist attacks," but at no time, and in no part of the country, has the threat condition been said by the government to be less than "elevated."

WHAT DO AMERICANS BELIEVE ABOUT
THE THREAT OF TERRORISM?

Political scientists typically analyze public opinion, attitudes, and beliefs by dividing the citizenry into three categories. At the top are the political elites. These men and women are the leaders of society, not necessarily in government and not necessarily elected. They speak and are heard regularly by millions if not tens of millions of Americans or have direct, regular, and unmediated access to those who do. They are senators, representatives, cabinet secretaries and deputy secretaries, military commanders, media moguls, corporate executives in Fortune 500 companies, op-ed columnists at America's leading newspapers, television journalists, famous evangelists, popular radio talk-show hosts, heads of regulatory agencies, leading attorneys, university presidents, and Nobel Prize winners. To the extent they speak out on political questions, celebrities from the entertainment and sports industries, best-selling authors, and self-help gurus all have political influence. Although masses of ordinary Americans may see the president on television, hear snippets from commentators, or tune in to talk shows featuring arguments about politics, members of the elite communicate most directly, systematically, and importantly with another category of the population, known as the "attentive public." Composing roughly 5 percent to 15 percent of the population, members of the attentive public are people with the education, time, interest, and verbal skills to participate as engaged listeners with respect to elites and as sources of trusted opinions, interpretations, and facts for their families, religious communities, friendship circles, and coworkers.

Members of the attentive public include editorial writers at medium- and small-town newspapers, professors, teachers, and other "experts" interviewed on current affairs by local media outlets, talkative and well-informed barbers, ministers, priests, and rabbis, opinionated employers, civic leaders, bloggers, and so on. Opinions of masses of Americans arise, crystallize, and change in some complex process involving their exposure to the sound bites and slogans they may hear directly from the elite and their frames of reference. The definitions of problems, categories of analyses, and boundaries of "acceptable" opinion that mold their beliefs, however, are strongly shaped by the views of members of the attentive public with whom they regularly interact, either in person or via the media. Of course, influences also travel from the mass toward the elite, so that opinion leaders in the attentive public may find they have to fine-tune their arguments to avoid alienating their audiences or reducing their own credibility. Elites may need to make adjustments when confronted by obdurate and widespread criticism from segments of the attentive public associated with important constituencies or by the difficulties they may experience running against the grain of mass-level attitudes and expectations.

Let us therefore consider the perceptions and treatments of the War on Terror at each of these levels of public opinion—elite, attentive public, and mass. Of course leaders do not always, or perhaps even usually, say publicly exactly what they think privately. Most politicians, most of the time, say what they do because they believe it is right, proper, or useful to say it. This is the settled view of a long list of the most distinguished political philosophers in the western tradition, including Plato, Machiavelli, Hobbes, Rousseau, Madison, and Marx. It is also the working assumption of most political analysts and pundits. In any event, it is the only reliable principle for interpreting political speech by leaders, since their innermost thoughts, even if they are known to the speakers, simply cannot be known by anyone else.

With this principle in mind we can learn a great deal about how terrorism is effectively viewed by the American political system by examining what leaders say about it, both when they are speaking to the attentive public and when they address the mass public. However disingenuous or feigned those speeches may be, what is said is put on record, and it is what the leader may be inferred to be ready to defend. Certainly, the way a leader talks about terrorism may reflect his or her assessment of what interlocutors and the public care about and what they may be able to understand. At minimum, however, "terror talk" shows that even if speakers do not genuinely believe in what they say, they have judged it advisable to appear to believe it, understanding the impact that that appearance will have on various constituencies and on their own reputations.

In the first five years of George W. Bush's presidency, the president seldom spoke before the kind of small audiences we could easily categorize as representing the attentive public. When he did, however, after September 2001, he focused almost exclusively on terrorism and the War on Terror. In one such speech delivered on October 6, 2005, to the National Endowment for Democracy, he signaled his assessment of the enormous scale of the problem by comparing it directly to the nation's struggle in World War II ("Once again, we're responding to a global campaign of fear") by describing the enemy in apocalyptic terms as a "great evil" and as a "mortal danger to all humanity"; by urging his audience to join with him to "recognize Iraq as the central front in our war on terror"; and by categorizing the War on Terror as a "global ideological struggle," implying its equivalence to the total political, cultural, economic, and military commitment made by Americans in their Cold War struggle with the Soviet Union.[1]

Although it is the president with his "bully pulpit" who is primarily responsible for communicating the government's views to the general public, other top officials play important roles in molding the perceptions of the attentive public. That the War on Terror has stood at the top of the government's agenda in its communications with that crucial stratum is compellingly evident from speeches by top administration officials to think tanks and private organizations focused on world affairs. Based on information on the official White House Web site, in 2003, 2004, and 2005 six speeches were given by high-ranking administration officials at the Hudson Institute, the American Enterprise Institute, the Council on Foreign Relations, and the Heritage Foundation—three by Vice President Cheney (one of those in tandem with Defense Secretary Rumsfeld), one by Condoleezza Rice when she served as national security adviser, and one by Steven Hadley in his capacity as national security adviser. It is instructive that although the organizations involved did not specifically request it, the topic of terrorism was the focus of each of these speeches—either the direness of the threat, the progress of the War on Terror, and/or the contribution of the war in Iraq to the War on Terror.[2] In 2005 the Heritage Foundation on its Web site listed dozens of videotapes of major events held at its headquarters—speeches, symposia, panel discussions, and so on—from 2001 through 2004. Of these events, twenty-two pertained in some way to economic affairs. One was about nuclear weapons. Far and away the most prominent topic was terrorism—the focus of thirty-six different events in this four-year period.[3]

This pattern of dominance of the elite-attentive public discussion by concerns with the terrorist threat and the War on Terror is apparent not just in the agendas and event listings of think tanks; as I discuss in Chapter 5, these subjects were dominant features of the 2004 presidential election campaign as well. But terrorism dominates the agenda even apart from political campaigns. In recent years perceptions of the enormity of the terrorist threat have overshadowed all other problems top government leaders think they face, at least as reflected in the regularity with which speeches by those officials focus on that topic. For example, in the three years between October 2002 and October 2005, high-ranking Department of Defense officials gave 562 speeches with some version of the word "terror" in their titles. That means they gave 36 percent more speeches about terrorism than about Secretary of Defense Rumsfeld's signature theme (transformation of the military), 22 times more speeches about terrorism than about nuclear weapons, 43 times more than about proliferation, and 51 times more than about ballistic missile defense. Even more speeches in this time period by Defense Department officials featured the word "Iraq" in the title (1,483), but of course the war in Iraq was regularly described by the administration, and was so treated on the Defense Department's Web site, as the "central front" in the War on Terror.[4]

In February 2006, when John Negroponte, the director of national intelligence, reported publicly for the first time to the Senate Select Committee on Intelligence, he could not have made it clearer that the administration perceived that the War on Terror was its highest priority and that it wanted the country to perceive that it was the administration's highest priority. To emphasize the central and overwhelming importance of the War on Terror, Negroponte spoke on behalf of every top official in the intelligence community, each of whom was present— General Michael V. Hayden, principal deputy director of national intelligence; Robert S. Mueller, director of the Federal Bureau of Investigation; Porter J. Goss, director of the Central Intelligence Agency; General Michael D. Maples, director of the Defense Intelligence Agency; Charles Allen, chief intelligence officer, Department of Homeland Security; and Carol Rodley, principal deputy assistant secretary of state for intelligence and research. "Let me begin," Negroponte told the committee, "with a straightforward statement of preoccupation shared by all of us sitting here before you: terrorism is the preeminent threat to our citizens, Homeland, interests, and friends. The War on Terror is our first priority and driving concern."[5]

Thus ever since the attacks of September 2001, when the administration has sought to communicate its views directly to molders and shapers of opinion in American life, it has portrayed terrorism as the most important challenge facing the country and the problem with which the national leadership is most fully and consistently engaged.

Of course top leaders in the Bush administration also bring this message to the general public directly. Consider the president's State of the Union speeches, delivered annually to a joint session of Congress and broadcast live on all the main television networks. In his first State of the Union message, early in 2001, President Bush declared education was his "top priority."[6] His speech mentioned education 7 times. Taxes and tax relief, another high priority, were mentioned 31 times. Only one reference to terrorism appeared in the speech, but after 2001, terrorism and the War on Terror dominated these highest-profile presidential messages to the government and nation. From 2002 to 2006 the president's State of the Union speeches included a total of 11 mentions of education, 3 mentions of unemployment, 62 mentions of taxes, 91 mentions of Iraq, and 122 mentions of terrorism.[7]

The president's weekly radio broadcast is another, less formal, but more regular way for him to communicate his perceptions about the challenges he perceives to be facing the country. A White House list of the topics of these weekly messages reveals a similar pattern. After September 11, 2001, terrorism and Iraq came to overshadow virtually all other concerns. In 2001 the topic listings included ten mentions of the economy and seven mentions of taxes, but the average number of mentions for these topics in the years following 2001 dropped 50 percent, to eight per year. In 2001 seven presidential radio broadcasts were devoted to education compared with an average of only one reference to education or the No Child Left Behind program over the next four years, from 2002 to 2005. By contrast, while seven radio addresses in 2001 (all *after* 9/11) were devoted to terrorism and/or Iraq, in each subsequent year an average of eleven presidential radio addresses included the words "Iraq" or "terrorism," an increase of more than 50 percent.

Public opinion is molded, however, not simply by the messages delivered to it by government leaders but also by the members of the attentive public, whose views are much more regularly, intimately, and compellingly shared with ordinary citizens. The attentive public plays a key role in shaping and stabilizing mass opinion. Its definition of the problem of terrorism as the dominant imperative for American national security, and of the solution as a long and expensive "war," are transmitted to wider audiences by experts, talking heads, and commentators who provide the national media with quotable wisdom on national security and foreign policy questions. The vast majority of the American attentive public appears to operate now with a deeply ingrained perception that the country is engaged in a necessary and systematic long-term War on Terror. The key point to recognize is the extent to which this influential stratum of the American polity takes the scale and importance of the threat of terrorism against the United States for granted. This threat's existence and the imperatives deemed to be associated with it are assumed and undiscussed, thereby forming part of the basis upon which all other issues, including how to prosecute the War on Terror, are considered.

The media and the shelves of our libraries are thus filled with arguments, including criticism of how the War on Terror is prosecuted, that nonetheless establish its rationale and scale as unquestionably appropriate. A typical example of this kind of message appeared in the *San Diego Union-Tribune* as an analysis entitled "Four Years After 9/11, War on Terror Slogs On." The author of this piece, published to coincide with the fourth anniversary of the attacks on September 11, 2001, was former Special Forces Officer Brian Michael Jenkins, senior adviser to the president of the RAND Corporation, one of the most prominent defense and foreign policy consulting firms in the country, whose contracts are predominantly with the United States government. Jenkins's assessment is grim. He compares the War on Terror to World War II and the Cold War. "Like the Cold War," he says, "the current contest could easily last decades." While complaining that the effort has lacked focus and perhaps become bogged down in Iraq, and that Muslim hostility toward America had increased, he nevertheless noted the absence of subsequent attacks on the American homeland and disruption of al-Qaeda in Afghanistan as evidence of some success in the long-term struggle that had, in effect, only just begun.[8] In his book criticizing the government's fiscal irresponsibility in the War on Terror, Joshua S. Goldstein nonetheless gives full support to the War on Terror as a necessary campaign to "remake the world and America's place in it."[9] Paraphrasing President Bush, he describes it as "worldwide in scope, open-ended in time, the War on Terror is a desperate struggle to save American cities from destruction."[10] Despite his fiscal concerns, Goldstein recommends spending on the order of $120 billion more per year than was already being spent in 2004 to achieve victory.[11]

The National Opinion Ballot of the Foreign Policy Association (FPA) conveniently captures the perceptions of the attentive public. With its national network of World Affairs Councils, the FPA is the country's largest organization dedicated to enhancing knowledge and discussion of foreign affairs among American citizens. Every year it circulates the National Opinion Ballot among members of the attentive public, targeting those with foreign policy interests. Each year it reports data gathered from more than 30,000 responses to the survey. For example, in 2003 the FPA summarized the results of the ballot as follows:

There is support for the United States:

- taking the lead internationally, but not acting unilaterally;
- increasing efforts in "nation building" in Afghanistan;
- pressuring the Saudis to root out terrorist elements;
- requiring American oil companies operating in Nigeria to pay for environmental damage they have caused;
- engaging China, but at the same time maintaining U.S. security commitments to Taiwan; and
- ratifying the Convention on the Elimination of All Forms of Discrimination Against Women.

There is opposition to the United States:

- encouraging Taiwan's independence;
- continuing U.S. farm subsidies and tariffs on imported agricultural products; and
- withdrawing U.S. forces from Afghanistan in the near future.

Other views that were revealed include:

- A preemptive policy frightens the whole world.
- The Afghans should do their own "nation building."

- The United States should support Saudi reforms and Prince Abdullah.
- The United States should try to facilitate a reunification between China and Taiwan.
- Taiwan potentially could influence the mainland toward becoming a more democratic government.[12]

This summary is probably a reasonably accurate index of the American attentive public's views in 2003 on the range of foreign policy issues as those issues were defined within the national discourse on international affairs. It is more revealing, however, to examine questions that were included in the survey, and those that were not. In 2003 and 2004 not a single question was asked about whether respondents believed there was a major terrorist threat, whether there needed to be a global and sustained "War on Terror," or how likely it was that the United States would experience another major terrorist attack. Instead, the questions on the ballot were framed within a general context described, in 2004, as the "U.S. struggle to fight a global war on terrorism." Respondents were then asked a variety of specific questions about what techniques or policies were being, or might be, more or less successful in prosecuting this war. In other words, the carefully worked-out nonpartisan production of these polls regarding the most critical foreign policy issues facing the country did not result in the posing of questions about the War on Terror. From this pattern of absence it is obvious that in the minds of those producing the polls, and most probably in the minds of respondents (who appear not to have objected to the absence of such questions), the imperative for a "War on Terror" is a background assumption, a belief not deemed appropriate, itself, for discussion or likely to produce significant differences of opinion among respondents.[13]

In October 2005, Daniel Yankelovich, one of America's leading pollsters, reported the results of his Public Agenda surveys, a collection of data every six months organized to create the Confidence in U.S. Foreign Policy Index. A central feature of the survey consists of twenty goals with respect to which respondents are asked to award grades for U.S. foreign policy from A to F. In its spring 2005 poll 58 percent of the public gave the government A's or B's for "giving the war on terrorism all of the attention it deserves" while 54 percent did the same for "hunting down anti-American terrorists." These were the third and fourth best sets of grades awarded across the twenty foreign policy goals. Again, what is of most interest, however, is the absence of an option allowing the respondent to indicate that he or she thought the government should not be engaged in a war on terrorism or that hunting terrorists should not be classified as a "foreign policy" problem. The effect, especially instructive because it was unintended, of posing such loaded questions is to reinforce the narrow boundaries of thinking about terrorism by the American public. Indeed, the Yankelovich poll also asked respondents if they worried that "terrorists may obtain biological, chemical, or nuclear weapons to attack the United States," reporting that a whopping 88 percent did worry about this.[14] Such polls do not just reflect the conceptions of the pollsters or the opinions of those polled. They contribute to creating and reinforcing perceptions of the scale of the terrorist threat and the need for a War on Terror.

It is assumed without debate or public questioning that terrorism is a problem of the sort that must be addressed by a "war." The War on Terror has thus achieved the status of a background narrative. It is used by members of the attentive public as the source for categories, questions to be considered, and criteria for evaluating options, when opinion leaders communicate about terrorism with the great mass of the American public. Again, consider the wording of polls done by the Pew Research Center for the People and the Press. Beginning in October 2002, just one year after the 9/11 attacks, Pew began asking a question in its regular surveys that it continued to ask through 2005: "Do you think the war in Iraq has helped the war on terrorism, or has it hurt the war on terrorism?" The Pew surveys showed that beginning in October 2002 respondents believed the Iraq war was helping the War on Terror. These respondents significantly outnumbered those who believed the opposite. Perceptions shifted, however. In the summer of 2004 Americans appeared to be evenly divided on the question. In July 2005 a substantial plurality (47 percent) believed the Iraq war hurt the War on Terror, compared to 39 percent who said they thought it helped.[15] We will shortly consider surveys dealing directly with general public perceptions of the terrorism threat. At this point, the important thing to note is not change in the public's assessment of the contribution the Iraq war makes to the War on Terror. Much more important is the unquestioned assumption implied in both the questions and answers to these various surveys that virtually every national policy, including American operations in Iraq, must be evaluated on the basis of whether or not they contribute to victory in that war.

Editorial opinion in the newspapers of mid-sized American cities is another marker of the extent to which those who communicate their opinions directly to the American public perceive the country as engaged in a War on Terror. Using the Lexis-Nexis search engine it is possible to survey the topics of editorials state by state. Under Florida, for the period including 2001–5, a Lexis-Nexis search showed a total of 345 locally published articles written by newspaper editors. Of these, 4 referenced drugs or the war on drugs; 8 mentioned Cuba; one mentioned China. Meanwhile, 10 mentioned Iraq; 25 mentioned terrorism or the War on Terror. The same kind of search located 906 editorials in Iowa. Of these, 62 mentioned drugs or the "War on Drugs." Only 38 editorials mentioned farming or agriculture. China was mentioned 6 times. However, 74 editorials mentioned terrorism or the War on Terror and 70 mentioned Iraq. In Maine this search found 119 editorials including 24 that mentioned terrorism or the War on Terror and 20 mentioning Iraq, compared with 4 that mentioned fish, fishing, or lobster; 1 referring to China, and zero mentioning drugs or the War on Drugs.[16]

This pattern prevails in red as well as blue states, where spirited debate over government policies and spending priorities in the prosecution of the counterterrorism effort is common. Leaving aside exhortations to action or praise of the government and military for their conduct of the War on Terror, the vast majority of the *criticisms* of the this campaign are nonetheless crucially based on the presumption of the authors that the audience does not question, and need not be persuaded, of the appropriateness of a national "war" against "terrorism." What is at issue in virtually all of these criticisms is how that war should best be fought.

How do ordinary American citizens perceive the threat of terrorism and the War on Terror itself? Since September 2001 numerous polls have been conducted asking Americans, with slightly different wordings of the question, how likely they thought a major terrorist attack in the United States was in the next few months. It is instructive to note, as a measure of the political pulse of the American people, that every major polling organization has focused substantial and regular attention on public opinion regarding the threat of terrorism, asking questions that were hardly, if ever, asked before September 2001. A number of these surveys were sponsored by such media organizations as CBS News, NBC News/*Wall Street Journal*, ABC News/*Washington Post*, CNN/*USA Today*/Gallup, and Fox News/Opinion Dynamics between October 2001 and August 2005. The percentage of those surveyed believing a terrorist attack on the United States homeland was either "somewhat likely" or "very likely" has fluctuated between 80 percent and 40 percent, averaging approximately 70 percent over nearly four years.

In the immediate aftermath of the July 2005 bombings in London, a CBS News poll found that more Americans spontaneously identified terrorism as the second most important problem facing the nation (after the war in Iraq) while also indicating that fully 94 percent of Americans believed "there are terrorists inside the United States planning attacks."[17] Reflecting fears raised directly after the London subway bombings, a *Newsweek* poll carried out in August 2005 found that 82 percent of respondents deemed it "likely" or "very likely" that "Islamic extremists will carry out major terrorist attacks against U.S. cities, buildings, or national landmarks in the near future," while 40 percent were "somewhat worried" or "very worried" about the possibility that "someone in your family might become a victim of a terrorist attack." A CNN/*USA Today*/Gallup survey in July 2005 found that 53 percent of respondents believed the federal government was "not doing enough to prevent acts of terrorism on mass transit systems, such as subways, buses, and trains," though only 35 percent held that view of government policies regarding terrorist attacks on airplanes. Instructively, only 2 percent and 5 percent, respectively, thought the government was doing "too much."

The degree to which the public is willing to sacrifice as part of its commitment to the War on Terror is also evident in the responses to a series of detailed questions included in a survey by the Center for Survey Research and Analysis at the University of Connecticut. This survey focused on American public attitudes toward renewal of the PATRIOT Act, including various restrictions and infringements on traditionally protected civil liberties and rights to privacy. Seventy-seven percent of respondents favored renewal of the PATRIOT Act, though most of these favored some amendments to it. Sixty-nine percent favored provisions of the act that "enable courts to authorize federal law enforcement agents in criminal investigations to monitor the names, dates, and addresses of Internet communications." Fifty-three percent favored the act's provisions that require "libraries to turn over records in terrorism investigations and prevents the libraries from revealing to the patrons that these records have been turned over to the government," though only 23 percent favored granting the government permission for secret searches of the homes of U.S. citizens. A Fox News/Opinion Dynamics poll reported that in July 2005, 64 percent of respondents were willing to give up "some personal freedom in order to reduce the threat of terrorism"; 63 percent supported a "shoot to kill" policy with regard to suspected terrorists if the police thought it necessary. A CBS survey in July 2005 found strong support for increased government video surveillance as part of the War on Terror. Seventy-one percent answered "good idea" in answer to the following question: "Some people think installing video surveillance cameras in public places is a good idea because they may help to reduce the threat of terrorism. Other people think this is a bad idea because surveillance cameras may infringe on people's privacy rights. What do you think? Would you say that it is a good idea or a bad idea to install surveillance cameras in public places?"[18]

Among the trends apparent in these polls is a decline in American public approval for President Bush's conduct of the War on Terror along with continued high but jaggedly declining levels of fear of imminent terrorist attacks. The polls also suggest that public perceptions are sufficiently entrenched and sufficiently sensitive to evidence of an increased terrorist threat that very sharp increases in concern can be triggered by specific events. These are not just the beliefs of the Americans responding to these polls. These polls also, perhaps more reliably in light of the cost of undertaking these surveys, underline the conviction of these polling organizations that the American public is interested in this subject, perceives it as vital, and wants to track its own views about whether the terrorism threat is increasing or decreasing and how well the government is doing in the War on Terror.

Consider two other measures of national perceptions of the scale and relative importance of the "specter of terror": national funding levels for counterterrorism and the prominence of terrorism as a primary feature of plot lines in popular entertainment. These measures are especially significant because they also constitute powerful stimuli for the concerns they reflect. In other words, increasing funding for counterterrorism naturally encourages those who may wish to receive federal grants to highlight, feel more strongly about, or treat as more salient than they otherwise might have the concerns about terrorism that they do have. It is reasonable to expect that to the extent that images of terrorism and imminent threats of destruction wreaked by terrorists permeate popular culture, those who have those concerns will find less reason to question them while those who might otherwise not suffer from these anxieties will more likely develop them.

Federal funding levels for counterterrorism are an excellent indicator of America's overall judgment of the scale of the terrorist threat and its importance relative to other challenges.[19] Funding levels change as a function of opinion and perception at all three levels of public awareness—leaders, including senators and representatives as well as officials within the executive branch; the attentive public, which shapes and enforces the contours of debate over these measures; and mass opinion, associated with expectations about upcoming elections that exert a powerful, if lagged, influence on political leaders.

The Bush administration claimed in early 2006 that overall, since 2001, it had "more than tripled spending devoted to non-defense homeland security."[20] In October 2004 the White House announced the signing of the 2005 Homeland Security Appropriations Bill with a 6.6 percent increase for Homeland Security compared to enacted funds for 2005.[21] In 2005 the administration advanced a budget for 2006 with a total of $41.1 billion for the Department of Homeland Security, described as "an increase of seven percent over the enacted FY 2005 funding, excluding Project BioShield."[22] Of course, calculations are tricky because of changing and complex categories. Nevertheless, the records show a clear pattern of steady and substantial increases in spending on homeland security.

Let us look more closely at some of these expenditures. In 2004 the White House described FBI Director Mueller as having already "transformed the FBI into an organization dedicated to making the prevention of terrorist attacks its first priority." Yet the FY 2005 budget for the FBI still featured increases "in funding over 2004 for counterterrorism investigations by $60 million and provided $357 million for counter-terrorism enhancements."[23] In its FY 2006 budget, the Office of Management and Budget (OMB) organized its substantive programs under three broad categories—Economic Opportunity, Protecting America, and the Compassionate Society. "Winning the War on Terror" appears as the first priority within the Protecting America category. In each year since 2001 this imperative has dominated the administration's portrayal of the threats the country faces. In its overall description of the 2006 budget in the Protecting America category, OMB emphasized that it was increasing spending in the fight against possible biological and chemical terrorist attacks, including $1.7 billion to the National Institutes of Health "to support both the basic research that leads to breakthroughs in scientific knowledge, and applied research and development that converts that knowledge into effective countermeasures such as vaccines and treatments"; a $22 million increase to the Department of Homeland Security (DHS) for biological countermeasures; $53 million more for "for chemical agent research and development" in DHS; a $223 million increase for Department of Defense (DOD) efforts to boost "agent detection, early warning, decontamination, and medical countermeasures for chemical and biological threats"; and $44 million to DHS "to implement a new prototype system for early warning and protection of the nation's water system."[24]

One year later, in February 2006, the president's FY 2007 budget made headlines for the depth of cuts to Medicare and a host of domestic spending programs. Such cuts, however, were not applied to the War on Terror. Over and above amounts slated for hurricane relief, the Department of Homeland Security was granted between a 5 percent and 7 percent increase, depending on the method of calculation. The single largest component of the War on Terror—the wars in Afghanistan and Iraq—was slated to cost another $120 billion on top of an overall 5 percent increase in funding for the Department of Defense. With funding for the National Institutes of Health frozen, the president's budget actually reduced spending in some health research areas so as to increase spending on bioterrorism- and bio-security-related research.[25]

Of course these and other actual and projected increases are on top of consistently large and increasing levels of funding that began their rise immediately after September 11, 2001. Thus did OMB's FY 2006 justification note that its investments in the War on Terror were building on previous efforts, including "$17 billion in grants to assist State and local homeland security efforts" over the previous four years. It is also important to note that Congress has generally responded to presidential budget requests regarding the War on Terror by appropriating *more* money than requested. For example, in September 2005, Congress expressed strong interest in beefing up border security and made adjustments in the Homeland Security budget that directed funding for border patrol activities to be increased by $618 million. Coupled with some reductions elsewhere, congressional action resulted in a net increase of $335 million.[26]

The funding levels for the War on Terror are so high, so widely distributed through the government, and so rapidly changing that reliable total figures for the cost of the War on Terror are difficult to calculate. If we concentrate just on federal funds it is possible to get some idea of the financial scale of the campaign and the trends exhibited by this spending.

As I have stressed, the administration has urged the country to share its view of the wars in Afghanistan and Iraq as integral parts of the global War on Terror. True to this conception, the OMB's first category of budgetary expenditures for "Winning the War on Terror" lists the requirements for supporting American forces in Afghanistan and Iraq in order "to ensure Iraqis and Afghans are fully capable of defending themselves and their new societies against the forces of terrorism."[27] Therefore, we must begin by estimating the total and continuing annual cost of our military presence in Afghanistan and in Iraq. In an independent analysis of the current, long-term, direct, and indirect costs of the Iraq war, Nobel Prize-winning economist Joseph E. Stiglitz and Harvard scholar Linda Bilmes concluded that the total costs of the war, compared with costs incurred by the U.S. government had the war not been launched, would probably be more than $2 trillion. This conclusion was based on assumptions that U.S. troops will remain in Iraq for four more years, but at decreasing levels, and that the federal government will have to bear interest costs on loans made to finance the war, sharply higher recruitment costs for the armed forces, the cost of equipment replacement, the costs of health care for injured veterans, and tax revenues lost as a result of reduced years of productive labor by servicemen and -women killed and wounded in the war.[28]

The Office of Management and Budget refused to comment on the Stiglitz-Bilmes study, preferring to focus strictly on month-to-month "operating costs." But even if the indirect expenditures and "opportunity costs" (the technically correct way to assess economic choices) are ignored, the overall scale of American expenditures on the war-in-Iraq aspect of the War on Terror is enormous. According to an October 2005 report by the Congressional Research Service, the total cost of the Iraq war to American taxpayers had reached $251 billion. The report calculated a total expenditure of $82 billion for operations in Afghanistan and $24 billion for enhancements in base security attributable to the wars in those countries for a total of $357 billion through fiscal year 2005.[29] During the same period, expenditures only on activities falling within the purview of the Department of Homeland Security rose at an average annual rate of approximately 25 percent.[30] At least until after the hurricanes Katrina, Rita, and Wilma in September and October of 2005, these resources, totaling $171 billion, were overwhelmingly focused on the War on Terror. The two War on Terror conflicts and expenditures within the Department of Homeland Security have cost $528 billion over four years, equaling approximately 16 percent of all U.S. government discretionary spending during that period.[31] A good marker of the vast importance given to counterterrorism by the country's executive and legislative leadership is that a conservative estimate of the average amount spent annually by the federal government on the War on Terror is nearly 80 percent higher than average annual federal spending on education, declared by President Bush upon taking office in 2000 to be his highest spending priority.[32]

Opinion polls, budgets for fighting terrorism, and attention to the topic by politicians and other opinion leaders show that the American political system consciously believes, or at least acts as if it believes, that al-Qaeda-type terrorist attacks against targets inside the United States are not just a major problem but a challenge of overwhelming and immediate importance. Gauging the overall American perception of the terrorist threat also means trying to assess the psychological and cultural embeddedness of these beliefs. To what extent have such beliefs become natural, even commonsensical, parts of popular culture?

The entertainment industry opens a valuable window into American popular culture. It includes television networks, Hollywood moviemakers, and mass-market-oriented publishers of books and magazines. As an industry it responds to public beliefs, prejudices, worries, and fascinations by incorporating them into the narratives offered in television shows, films, novels, and feature articles. Firms in this industry are profit oriented; they have a powerful interest in sensing just what topics their potential audiences find arousing and convincing and what topics they find boring or irrelevant. The prominence of terrorist enemies and fears of terrorism within plot lines used by the mass media is thus a valuable measure of public perceptions.

Immediately after the World Trade Center and Pentagon attacks, Hollywood was reluctant to exploit terrorism plot lines. Release of the Arnold Schwarzenegger film *Collateral Damage* was postponed because it featured Colombian terrorists bent on attacking the United States. But after a delay the film was released and both Hollywood and the television networks plunged aggressively into the preparation and distribution of films and television dramas depicting threats of catastrophic terrorism against the United States and the intrepid efforts of American heroes struggling to overcome bureaucratic incompetence to protect the homeland against terrorist enemies. This genre of film included *The Sum of All Fears,* featuring the destruction of Baltimore by a nuclear bomb smuggled into the country by terrorists; *Face of Terror,* about a Palestinian terrorist bomber in Spain; *Antibody,* about an international terrorist with access to a nuclear detonator; *American Heroes: Air Marshal,* about a jetliner hijacked by terrorists with ambitious plans; *When Eagles Strike,* about terrorists who kidnap an American senator; and *Blast!,* about terrorists who take over an oil rig to detonate an electro-magnetic bomb over the United States.

That films of this type are likely to continue to be released is suggested by the number of potboiler novels about terrorists and catastrophic terrorist attacks by authors whose past works have regularly been turned into movies. For example, a quick survey of a typical bookshelf in Philadelphia International Airport revealed that of thirty-five paperback novels for sale to travelers waiting to board their planes, seven shared fundamentally the same plot—imminent disaster at the hands of maniacal terrorists that might still be thwarted by courageous counterterrorist action. These 20 percent included Tom Clancy's *Splinter Cell,* Michael Crichton's *State of Fear,* Dan Brown's *Deception Point,* James Patterson's *London Bridges,* and Robert Ludlum's *The Lazarus Vendetta.*

Made-for-television movies on these themes were also plentiful. These included *Winds of Terror* (2002), about a biological weapon attack on the United States; *Operation Wolverine: Seconds to Spare* (2003), about terrorists hijacking a train to release enough poison gas to destroy a large American city; *The President's Man 2: A Line in the Sand* (2002), about a secret agent's effort to foil terrorists constructing a nuclear weapon;

Smallpox 2002: Silent Weapon (2002), about a bioterrorist smallpox attack; *The Pilot's Wife* (2002), about the terrorist bombing of a 747 airliner; *Counterstrike* (2003), about terrorists with a nuclear weapon who hijack the *Queen Elizabeth II* luxury liner; *Critical Assembly* (2003) in which a nuclear bomb produced by students is stolen by terrorists; and *Tiger Cruise* (2004), about a navy ship's reaction to the 9/11 attacks. Of all the made-for-television movies and theatrical releases dealing with terrorist themes in recent years, however, there is probably no movie that has had a wider viewership than *Dirty War* (2004), an extremely realistic docudrama depicting Middle Eastern terrorists who detonate a radioactive "dirty bomb" in London. Produced by the BBC and originally aired in Britain, the film was then delivered to HBO in the United States, which broadcast it repeatedly in early 2005.

It became difficult for television viewers to avoid repeated exposure to depictions of their country as living beneath a sword of Damocles, protected only by the uphill battle of a few heroic special agents working against the odds to thwart the designs of brilliant and ruthless terrorists. Viewers have been presented with reruns of older movies featuring terrorist attack plots; documentaries on terror and terrifying topics including Osama bin Laden, 9/11, and bioterrorism; as well as made-for-television movies about terrorism. At the same time, well-established television shows (such as *Law and Order*) have regularly devoted episodes to terrorism topics while networks have scrambled to develop new shows as vehicles for this and related themes. In one two-week period chosen at random from the summer season (the first two weeks of July 2005, Philadelphia metropolitan viewing area), viewers with cable access had at their disposal the following options, usually aired more than once: *Executive Decision* (a 1996 movie about Islamic militants hijacking an airliner); *JAG* (an episode of the show about the investigation of a Marine found on a terrorist's boat); an episode of *Law and Order* in which a man murders a neighbor, thinking he is a terrorist; *Meeting Osama bin Laden*, a documentary featuring personal interviews; *Tenchi Muyo in Love*, a movie about time travelers who find terrorist bombers; an episode of *The District* in which police and the FBI in Washington track down multiple terrorists; an episode of *The West Wing* in which the president approves assassination of a terrorist leader; and an episode of *Walker, Texas Ranger* in which a bomb is planted by Middle Easterners. During the regular viewing seasons of the past few years, television viewers have been treated to half a dozen new shows about terrorism and/or specialized military, intelligence, and law enforcement agencies fighting terrorists. These programs have included *The Agency* (CBS); *NCIS* (CBS); *Threat Matrix* (ABC); *Alias* (ABC); and most popular of all, *24* (Fox). The entire 2005 season of *24* was devoted to a story line involving a sleeper cell of Middle Eastern terrorists in the United States that unleashes a nuclear-tipped missile against a major American city.[33] Meanwhile, in December 2005 the Showtime cable channel presented a miniseries about Islamic terrorists in the United States entitled *Sleeper Cell*. As Michael Ealy, the star of the show, put it: "This show is about the reality of the Beast that we're fighting right now, on many fronts."[34]

CASSANDRA AT THE GATES VERSUS THE BOY WHO CRIED WOLF

Although it officially went out of business when its report on the 2001 attacks was completed, the 9/11 Commission has continued to operate as a private watchdog group. Drawing on its bipartisan composition and the trust Americans have generally placed in its findings, former Congressman Lee Hamilton and former New Jersey Governor Thomas Kean now lead the 9/11 Public Discourse Project. The group has issued repeated frightful warnings of terrorist attacks that could occur for which the country would still be unprepared. In late 2005 it condemned the president and the Congress for not implementing all of its original recommendations and issued a "report card" evaluating government performance in fourteen areas related to homeland security. These grades included one F, three D's, one C-, and four C's.[35] In an official statement Hamilton and Kean expressed their frustration. "We believe that the terrorists will strike again. If they do, and these reforms have not been implemented, what will our excuses be? While the terrorists are learning and adapting, our government is still moving at a crawl."[36] In joint appearances on radio and television news programs Kean and Hamilton decried what they viewed as a lack of attention to the threat of terrorism in Washington. "It's not a priority for the government right now," said Kean, "God help us if we have another attack."[37] Indeed the group has repeatedly offered the view that it is simply a matter of when, not if, there will be another attack of massive dimensions.

In Greek mythology Cassandra, the daughter of King Priam of Troy, was blessed and cursed by the god Apollo. Blessed with the power to see catastrophes before they happened, she was cursed by her audience's automatic refusal to believe her. In the fable about the boy who cried wolf, the boy exaggerates the threat of an attack by the wolf so often that when the wolf really does arrive, no one listens to his warning, and no one is prepared. In the first story, the public loses by not believing in dire warnings that are accurate. In the second, the public loses because it believed too easily in dire warnings that are false. From the 9/11 Commission to every politician and pundit who rages against what they describe as the flagrant inadequacy of the War on Terror, there is no shortage of warnings. But are these Cassandra-type warnings—truths that we, the audience, are doomed never to appreciate? Or are they equivalent to the little boy's repeated, frightening, false, and ultimately destructive warnings of wolf attacks that are in fact not about to occur? Absent the gift of prophecy, we can judge our true circumstances only by carefully looking at the evidence, the task to which we now turn our attention.

Chapter 3

Measuring the Terrorist Threat: What Is the Evidence?

There is very little evidence, hard or soft, that "terrorist groups with global reach" are operating in the United States with plans to use deadly force either catastrophically or non-catastrophically in attacks against American targets. The fact that there is little evidence for the threat, however, does not mean it does not exist. As Secretary of State Rumsfeld put it with regard to the search for weapons of mass destruction in Iraq, "absence of evidence does not constitute evidence of absence."[1] Indeed, I argue that violent attacks on our citizens, on our soil, by non-state actors must be treated as not only possible but plausible and as a problem requiring attention; the question is how much attention compared to the attention we should devote to the vast array of other challenges and opportunities the United States faces. To answer this question we must weigh the evidence of the threat terrorists now pose, searching not, of course, for certainty but for an assessment based on an unblinking appreciation of the dangers of underestimating the threat as well as a sober appreciation of the impossibility of eliminating risk from our lives. Based on that assessment we can then ask whether a "war" against the threat we do find is or is not the appropriate strategy for coping with it.

Let us begin by putting the American obsession with terrorism—a titillation sometimes referred to as "terror porn"—in a wider but readily recognizable context. I remember particularly enjoying a Seinfeld routine that mimicked local television news broadcasts. The script went something like this: "Experts now say that an everyday product in your refrigerator right now is likely to kill you unless you immediately take the simple steps needed to save yourself. Stay tuned for details after these messages."

The humor draws on self-recognition by Americans of how rampantly their attention is coerced by hyped but ultimately trivial "threats." Media outlets use the threats to compete for viewership or readership without expensive investments in new programming. The result has been a parade of exaggerated amplifications of health- or security-related rumors or of extremely low probability but potentially catastrophic events.[2] The list of fears that have afflicted Americans or have been wildly if briefly exaggerated by the mass media runs the gamut—mercury in the water, radon in the air, pesticides in apple juice, pins in Halloween candy, auto accidents caused by cellphone use, cancer caused by cellphone use, secondhand smoke, shark attacks, cyber porn, road rage, skin cancer from sunshine, calcium deficiency due to sunscreen, SARS, the shortage of flu vaccine, and so on.

Of course none of these bubbles of fear are manufactured from nothing. They tend to appear after a widely reported real event. The media then frames the incident as part of a pattern by noting other instances of this particular kind of personal catastrophe. Such reporting produces disproportionate fears by viewers or readers that this particular disaster might actually happen to them or their families. Fears and worries then peak, fade, and retreat to some more or less reasonable level, making way for the next publicly reinforced worry. The point is that for brief periods hyperbolic treatments of particular possibilities of personal catastrophe produce levels of attention to that specific "problem" that may range from unwarranted worry to near panic.

As a community of 300 million people, Americans are thus familiar with cycles of unwarranted fears. We are accustomed to exposure to a world in which an endless list of terrible things that really can, demonstrably, occur are made known to us by a media machine that can discover and sensationalize even the rarest and most unlikely of negative events. In the previous chapter we have seen that by almost any measure the United States has become obsessed with the threat of terrorism. As one astute analyst observed early in 2004, anti-terrorism had "become the animating principle of nearly every aspect of American public policy."[3] The intense and pervasive fear of terrorist attacks has indeed not only transformed our national priorities and the terms of national political debate but has also provided rationales for war and even shaped the contours of popular culture. One indication that the American public may fairly be described as "obsessed" with terrorism and the War on Terror is the scant attention directed by the government, experts, or by the public to measure the actual extent of the terrorist threat facing the country.

So how great *is* the threat of terrorism in the United States and how does the scale of that threat compare to the immensity of the perception of that threat? As the saying goes, "it is an ill wind that blows no good." However much civil libertarians may fault our government's post-9/11 expansion of its surveillance practices inside the United States, this unprecedented comprehensive effort to scour our society for terrorist threats, sleeper cells, individuals with possible connections to terrorist groups, or individuals with sympathies with the aims of terrorist groups can greatly assist us in our effort to weigh the evidence for the presence of a serious terrorist threat. In service to this campaign our society has been rendered more transparent to law enforcement than ever before. Although federal officials have occasionally acknowledged infringements on norms of privacy and the hardships suffered by innocent people as a result of mass arrests of suspects, government spokespersons have regularly defended these practices. They justify more monitoring of more speech and behavior of more Americans with fewer judicial constraints than ever before by appealing to the extreme nature of the threat of catastrophic terrorism.

In the language of science and medicine the government much prefers to avoid "false negatives" (real terrorists not apprehended) even if that means accepting an extremely high rate of "false positives" (apprehension of many people innocent of any connection to or knowledge of terrorist activities). For my purposes this zealous and even ruthless approach to uncovering any hint of terrorist activity or sympathy for terrorists is extraordinarily useful, indeed invaluable. Why? Because as measured by arrests, indictments, and convictions, the results of such a thorough, not to say paranoid, hunt for terrorist threats can be expected, if anything, to *overstate* the actual scale of the terrorist threat present within our borders. In other words, by basing our assessment of the terrorist threat present inside the homeland on the results of the constant scouring of the country by the FBI and other agencies laser-focused on the War on Terror I can be confident I am giving every benefit of the doubt to the argument *contrary* to that advanced here.

When hundreds of prisoners captured in Afghanistan were declared "enemy combatants" the executive branch ordered that they be held at Guantanamo Bay Naval Base and elsewhere. Enemy combatants are held without charge or effective access to the courts, and with no oversight of the interrogation methods used, as long as military authorities judge it advisable. The original definition of an enemy combatant as approved by the Supreme Court in the case of Yaser Esam Hamdi was "someone carrying a weapon against American troops on a foreign battlefield." The government has sought, and appears to be operating with, a much broader definition, however. According to a *New York Times* report, a Defense Department order issued in 2004 defined an enemy combatant as anyone "part of or supporting Taliban or al-Qaeda forces or associated forces." In December 2004 a federal judge posed three hypotheticals to the Justice Department official representing the government in a case brought by Guantanamo detainees following the intervention of the Supreme Court. Her questions were designed to identify the limits the government imagined there might be in its discretion to designate someone as an enemy combatant. The judge asked about "a little old lady in Switzerland who writes checks to what she thinks is a charitable organization that helps orphans in Afghanistan but really is a front to finance al-Qaeda activities . . . a resident of Dublin who teaches English to the son of a person the CIA knows to be a member of al-Qaeda . . . a *Wall Street Journal* reporter, working in Afghanistan, who knows the exact location of Osama bin Laden but does not reveal it to the United States government in order to protect her source." Brian D. Boyle, the Justice Department representative, replied that under the government's definition the military would have the right to detain each of these individuals as enemy combatants.[4]

In November 2002 President George W. Bush signed into law the Homeland Security Act. This act authorized the most comprehensive federal government reorganization in almost sixty years. It combined dozens of agencies and offices staffed by approximately 169,000 employees into a new cabinet-level Department of Homeland Security. One year earlier, the USA PATRIOT Act had substantially increased law enforcement authority and access to intelligence information about suspected domestic terrorists. With little or no judicial supervision, American citizens were exposed to roving wiretaps, federal government investigation of their borrowing habits at public libraries and their browsing patterns on the Internet, as well as searches of their residences and monitoring of patterns of telephone use without notification.

The authority of the FBI to investigate the private lives of American citizens surreptitiously for possible connections to terrorism has increased enormously. One practice is the issuance of "national security letters." In the 1970s such letters were only rarely issued and only in connection with the investigation of foreign persons. Via such a letter the government could demand that the recipient use his or her occupational or other status to access confidential records of communications and activities by others. In the post-9/11 War on Terror, however, such letters have been used to investigate American citizens. Each letter can lead to the collection of information about, among other things, "where a person makes and spends money, with whom he lives and lived before, how much he gambles, what he buys online, what he pawns and borrows, where he travels, how he invests, what he searches for and reads on the Web, and who telephones or e-mails him at home."[5] Former Attorney General John Ashcroft issued directives that encouraged the FBI to use these letters aggressively. For example, once a person's name was established as interesting, any contacts that others may have had with that person, whether consequential or incidental, can constitute a basis for investigating them. Such links could arise simply from the fact of having visited the same Web site or having checked into the same motel on the same evening. Persons in similarly incidental contact with those persons then become targets for investigation. The number of implicated persons quickly explodes as each activity traced touches dozens or hundreds of other people whose casual contacts then radiate out to touch thousands more. Combined with advanced data-mining techniques, this practice can quickly lead to the collection and permanent retention of intimate information on thousands or even tens of thousands of American citizens from one initial "person of interest."

Over the last several years an average of thirty thousand such letters have been issued annually, with no judicial or legislative oversight. In one case made public by the *Washington Post* a manager of digital records for Connecticut libraries was directed to surrender "all subscriber information, billing information and access logs of any person" who used a specific computer in one particular library."[6] By going public, this one national security letter recipient defied an absolute and permanent injunction contained in these documents that forbids their recipients from ever revealing their content to anyone. Indeed even congressmen have expressed frustration by the FBI's refusal to grant them full access to the texts of the letters.

Leaks by government whistle-blowers in late 2005 also revealed widespread use of high-tech National Security Agency techniques for intercepting and monitoring phone calls and e-mails by Americans. As a result of secret directives signed almost every six weeks by President Bush since 2001, the vaunted capacities of the super-secret National Security Agency to intercept, file, and analyze electronic signals of all kinds have been applied to eavesdropping on telephone calls made by Americans. Targeting mainly, but not exclusively, international calls, these directives freed the NSA from having to secure judicial approval, either prior to the eavesdropping or afterward, from the surveillance court that was specially created for that purpose.[7]

Taking into account the powers granted the executive branch under the Patriot Act, the widespread and routinized use of national security letters, and the scope of largely unfettered NSA surveillance of electronic communications within our borders, we do not need more details about these or other, still unannounced, techniques of surveillance and investigation to establish one key point. As a result of the War on Terror the conversations and many of the activities of all American citizens are, or can be, subject to surveillance by law enforcement agencies driven to find terrorists or persons who might be suspected of terrorist sympathies.

Of course processing and interpreting this information requires vast increases in manpower. While comparable information about personnel policies within the National Security Agency is unavailable, the FBI is more open about its allocation of agents. According to the FBI's report to the 9/11 Commission in the fall of 2001, 4,000 FBI agents, equaling 67 percent of all those who had been assigned to criminal investigations, were reassigned to counterterrorism.[8] In this report, filed in April 2004, the FBI described counterterrorism as the Criminal Investigative Division's top priority. Following the surge into counterterrorism immediately after 9/11, the FBI implemented a program to train all its agents in counterterrorism techniques. Since 2001 hundreds of new hires or reassigned and retrained FBI employees have been assigned to terrorism-related intelligence analysis and translation tasks. In its report to Congress in 2004 the FBI indicated it had "increased the number of Special

Agents assigned to terrorism matters by 111 percent, the number of intelligence analysts by 86 percent and the number of linguists by 117 percent."[9] In 2005 the number of FBI special agents permanently assigned to counterterrorism was reported as 2,398, meaning about one out of every five FBI agents. This total exceeds even the number of those assigned, from both the FBI and the Drug Enforcement Agency, to investigate all forms of drug-related crime.[10] Additionally, the FBI established Field Intelligence Groups in its field offices staffed by 1,450 employees, with plans in 2004 alone to add 300 more intelligence analysts to these offices.[11] By doubling the number of its Joint Terrorism Task Forces and granting security clearances to thousands of law enforcement officers, the FBI has sought to coordinate its contribution to the War on Terror with "our 750,000 partners in state and local law enforcement."[12]

In March 2005 Attorney General Alberto Gonzales summarized the FBI's record by reporting to Congress that its counterterrorism effort "more than tripled" since September 2001, "from 9,340 cases pending and received in the field to over 33,000 in FY 2004."[13] One result of escalating investigative and law enforcement of counterterrorism activities by the FBI, the border patrol, immigration authorities, and other agencies has been the detention of more than 1,000 unnamed persons suspected of terrorist activities. After 9/11, 5,000 "persons of interest," mostly residents with expired visas, were held indefinitely in maximum security facilities. Many more have been interrogated and others held in confinement as material witnesses.[14] In addition, 83,000 more suspects have been confined and interrogated outside the borders of the United States, including 14,500 reported as still in custody in November 2005.[15]

What has been the result of these massive expenditures of time, money, and personnel? What has been gained by the removal of so many constraints normally associated with protection of American civil liberties? How great a contribution to the reduction of terrorism has resulted from the removal of most constraints against the sharing of information by the CIA and NSA with domestic law enforcement agencies such as the FBI? Answers to these questions would first require reliable and stable statistics indicating the amount of terrorism in the United States or numbers of terrorist attacks against U.S. targets. This obviously significant kind of data, however, so central to tracking the scale of the terrorist challenge and our record in trying to defeat it, is peculiarly difficult to come by. Beginning in 1985 the State Department published a global report on significant acts of international terrorism by type, target, country, and casualties. These reports did not break down the data to show how many of the terrorist attacks occurred within the United States. We know, however, and President Bush himself has emphasized, that since September 11, 2001, no one has been killed by an act of terrorism on American soil.[16] One reason such data are not readily available may be because they would show two trends contrary to the assumptions of the War on Terror: (1) that there is no statistical evidence of a terrorist threat in the United States itself; and (2) that the war in Iraq, with its many American military and civilian casualties, vastly *increased* the number of Americans killed as a result of the kind of actions labeled as "terrorism" in the State Department reports. What is clear is that after the annual report in 2004 showed a sharp uptick in terrorism worldwide, especially in Iraq, the State Department suspended the practice of issuing these statistical reports, shifting responsibility to a new National Counter-Terrorism Center. Official statistics released in 2006 used categories that made comparison with previous years impossible.[17]

Nevertheless, government officials have stepped forward on occasion to provide information about the number of terrorism-related legal actions it has taken, in part to argue that the national counterterrorism effort is both justified and successful. When John Ashcroft stepped down as attorney general on January 28, 2005, he said that an al-Qaeda nuclear terrorism attack on the United States was the "greatest danger" facing the country and that "from time to time" the government had uncovered evidence of efforts by terrorists to develop such a capacity.[18] Press reports of his remarks commented that he offered no evidence or illustrations for his assertions. It is noteworthy, however, that the government did informally accuse one person, Jose Padilla, of plotting a related kind of attack with a radiological weapon—a so called "dirty bomb." After keeping Jose Padilla in a military brig in solitary confinement for three and a half years, however, the government turned his case over to civilian authorities. Formal charges leveled against him not only did not include accusations of participation in plotting a nuclear or radiological attack, but the indictment omitted any claim that Padilla had planned to attack Americans on American soil. Attorney General

Alberto Gonzales refused to explain why his department dropped the charge of radiological terrorism.

In his farewell speech Ashcroft did say, however, that "more than 375 people have been charged in terror-related prosecutions in the United States since the 2001 attacks, with 195 either convicted or entering guilty pleas." This represents a bold and important claim and was repeated regularly by President Bush. To most Americans it seemed as if this were a claim that perhaps these 375 individuals, but certainly the 52 percent found guilty, were involved in dangerous terrorist activities that could well have resulted in significant or even catastrophic terrorist attacks on American soil. If true this would indeed have represented solid evidence of a need for a large-scale counterterrorism program, if perhaps not quite the vast and all-encompassing War on Terror waged by the government.

Six months after Ashcroft's speech, however, the *Washington Post* published an extraordinarily detailed analysis of all the cases included in the totals of 375 indictments and 195 convictions the attorney general had provided. The *Post* examined the data and found, in fact, only 39 convictions for terrorism and national-security related crimes since September 11, 2001. Why 39 instead of 195? In order to claim the larger figure Ashcroft had included 156 cases of convictions or guilty pleas involving, not terrorism or national security but making false statements, usually in connection with visa or immigration law violation. A clear indication of the lack of seriousness of the crimes involved in these convictions is that the median sentence for those found guilty was just eleven months. Indeed, the *Washington Post* found "no demonstrated connection to terrorism or terrorist groups" for 180 of the 375 people charged. Only fourteen people convicted of terrorism-related crimes were found by the *Post* to have links to al-Qaeda. As an example of the inflation of the statistics, the *Post* reported that "the prosecution of 20 men, most of them Iraqis, in a Pennsylvania truck-licensing scam accounts for about 10 percent of the individuals convicted—even though the entire group was publicly absolved of ties to terrorism in 2001." Justice Department officials responded to analysis by denying any attempt to exaggerate the importance of their terrorism investigations, but they did not dispute any of the details included in the *Post*'s story.[19]

Since the spring of 2005 there have been a scattering of highly publicized terrorism-related indictments, and some convictions. The latter may be added to the total of thirty-nine relevant, if not necessarily weighty, cases referred to above. These more recent prosecutions are often hailed as the discovery of al-Qaeda "sleeper cells." The sleeper-cell metaphor was borrowed from anticommunist campaigns in the early and mid-twentieth century. The image is of groups of devoted and highly skilled terrorists, appearing as normal and loyal U.S. citizens, operating silently within American society, waiting for the signal or the opportunity to strike. Indeed, despite expert opinion suggesting that the fears of such undiscovered networks are wildly exaggerated,[20] the image of sleeper cells has itself struck deep roots in the imagination of the American public. As noted previously, in 2005, the cable channel Showtime broadcast a miniseries entitled *Sleeper Cell.* The synopsis of the first episode read: "Darwyn Al-Hakim is a Muslim ex-con who has just been released from prison and finds his way to an Islamic extremist named Farik, who recruits him to join a terrorist sleeper cell planning an attack in Los Angeles."[21]

Government prosecutors have made two substantial claims to have uncovered al-Qaeda-type sleeper cells. The cells involved small groups in suburbs of Buffalo and Detroit. In the first case the government declared that a group of American citizens of Yemeni extraction living in Lackawanna, New York, was operating as an al-Qaeda sleeper cell. In the summer of 2002 the CIA called the group "the most dangerous terrorist cell in the country," and concerns about the activities of the group are reported to have been an important factor in the decision to raise the color-coded national threat level from yellow to orange in September of that year. The men and their families vociferously protested their innocence, claiming that they had traveled to Pakistan to participate in Islamic religious retreats organized by the devotional Tabligh movement. They later admitted, however, to having traveled to Pakistan and Afghanistan in the spring of 2001 at the urging of a radical preacher and veteran of Muslim campaigns in Afghanistan and Bosnia. The group did arrive at an al-Qaeda training camp and met with Osama bin Laden himself. After a short time at the camp, however, members of the group decided against joining al-Qaeda and left for home. Immediately following the attacks on September 11, one of them contacted the FBI to offer his assistance. The government chose to treat the group as an active sleeper cell and arrested five of them in September (a sixth was arrested in Bahrain). Threatened with thirty years' imprisonment on various charges if they did not plead guilty to "material support to terrorism," the defendants accepted the plea bargain and were each sentenced to seven to ten years in prison.[22]

The story of the Detroit sleeper cell began the week after the 9/11 attacks with a mistake by federal agents. In that period thousands of Muslims throughout the country were detained as suspects in the just-launched War on Terror. In Detroit, agents searching for one man found three other men in the apartment they thought was his. In these men's possession were false identity papers, cassette tapes of (pacifist) Muslim fundamentalist messages, and a video of Middle Eastern tourist sites. Prosecutors accused the men of "conspiring to help terrorists" and announced they had "cracked an 'operational combat cell' of Islamic terrorists."[23]

After an eighteen-month investigation of this case, four men were brought to trial. Two were convicted by a jury of supporting terrorism, two were acquitted of that charge, three (including one self-confessed grifter) were convicted of document fraud. Soon after the convictions were handed down, however, the Justice Department launched an inquiry into the behavior of Richard Convertino, the lead prosecutor in the case, for suppressing exculpatory evidence, including testimony, photographs, and expert analysis by military intelligence officers. A year later the convictions regarding conspiracy to help terrorists were overturned by a federal judge at the request of the Justice Department itself. In 2006 Convertino was himself indicted for conspiracy, perjury, and obstruction of justice in connection with his handling of the case.[24]

It is significant that both the Lackawanna and Detroit groups were "discovered" as sleeper cells in the more or less hysterical aftermath of the 9/11 attacks. No evidence in either case was presented pointing to the operation of these groups as sleeper cells and in each case retrospective, dispassionate analysis has led virtually all informed observers to conclude that neither of these groups fit the template. It may therefore be said with confidence that despite the greatly enhanced transparency of American society for law enforcement and intelligence agencies of the U.S. government, the immense resources devoted to the search for hidden terrorist networks inside the country, and opportunities presented for prolonged, if not infinite, interrogation of suspects under the terms of the PATRIOT Act and other measures described above, not one authentic sleeper cell has been found inside the United States since September 2001. Indeed, when the president's assistant for homeland security and counterterrorism, Frances Townsend, was asked whether in light of the absence of attacks since September 2001 the government still believed there were sleeper cells present inside America, Townsend avoided citing evidence or even belief that such cells existed, replying only that law enforcement and intelligence personnel were acting on the assumption that sleeper cells are present in order to "target them."[25]

Since June 2005, when the *Washington Post* published its authoritative accounting of the results of War on Terror investigations and prosecutions, there have been a few notable arrests and convictions. Just as the "dismantling" of the Detroit sleeper cell was hailed by then Attorney General Ashcroft as evidence that the War on Terror was working, so too have these individual cases been characterized officially as triumphs of and justifications for the War on Terror.[26] Three other cases were referred to by Ashcroft along with those in Detroit and Lackawanna. They involved a group of seven men in Portland, Oregon, an arms dealer from Britain arrested in New Jersey, and a University of Idaho graduate student. The Portland men were found guilty early in 2004 not of plotting terror attacks inside the United States but of planning to travel to Afghanistan to fight alongside the Taliban.[27] The arms dealer was an elderly Indian man from London who tried to scam buyers in the United States with a dud missile only to find that he was the victim himself an elaborate sting operation. The graduate student's arrest was hailed by Idaho Governor Dirk Kempthorne as "proof that terrorists are hiding in the heartland." The student, Sami al-Hussayen, was described by Ashcroft as part of "a terrorist threat to Americans that is fanatical, and it is fierce."[28] Accused by prosecutors of providing "material support" to terrorism, al-Hussayen turns out only to have donated money on behalf of a rich uncle to Islamic charities and to have volunteered his computer skills to help the charities. The Idaho jury acquitted him of all charges.

One success in the government's War on Terror appears to have been a conviction in June 2003 of an Ohio trucker, Iyman Faris, an American citizen of Kashmiri birth who turned himself in to authorities in March 2003. Faris admitted visiting an al-Qaeda training camp in Afghanistan, meeting Osama bin Laden, and carrying out preliminary "casing" work in the United States to provide information relating to a possible attack on the Brooklyn Bridge using a blowtorch. After pleading guilty Faris was sentenced to twenty years in prison. No conspiracy charges were made and no others were accused of participating with Faris in a sleeper cell.[29] Another conviction was secured against Ali Al-Tamimi, an American citizen and cancer researcher with a Ph.D. in computational biology from George Mason University who was sentenced to life in prison without parole plus seventy years for telling a small group of Muslims shortly after September 11, 2001, that they should go to Afghanistan to fight with the Taliban. Al-Tamimi protested his innocence based on his right to free speech. The judge announced she considered the sentence "very Draconian" but explained that she had no choice under congressional sentencing guidelines.[30] Four months later another Virginia man, Ahmed Omar Abu Ali, was convicted of joining al-Qaeda while in Saudi Arabia and planning to assassinate President Bush. Abu Ali maintained his innocence. The conviction was based on a videotaped confession given to Saudi police. Abu Ali was arrested while studying at an Islamic university in Medina. His lawyers argue that the confession was false and elicited by mistreatment and torture. On August 31, 2005, with FBI chief Mueller at his side, Attorney General Gonzales voiced concern that some Americans had begun to doubt whether or not there really were "homegrown" terrorists in the United States. "Today," he said, "we have chilling evidence that it is possible."[31] Gonzales was referring to a six-count indictment handed down against three African Americans and one Pakistani permanent resident who spent time together in a California prison and plotted to "kill infidels by attacking U.S. military facilities, an Israeli consulate building, the El Al Israeli airline, and Jewish synagogues in the Los Angeles area."[32] Upon release from prison they purchased guns and were conducting gas station robberies when they were arrested. Another well-publicized conviction was of Sheik Mohammed Ali-Hasan al-Moayad, a well-known Yemeni cleric arrested in a sting operation in Germany, extradited to the United States, and charged with funneling money to al-Qaeda and the Palestinian group Hamas. Moayad protested his innocence but had once boasted of being Osama bin Laden's personal spiritual adviser. The judge threw out most of the evidence brought by the government, but in July 2005 a Brooklyn jury found him and his assistant guilty, not of plotting or supporting terrorism in the United States but of "conspiring to provide material support and resources to foreign terrorist organizations." He was given the maximum sentence—seventy-five years in prison.[33]

A much higher-profile case was that of Sami al-Arian and seven others put on trial in June 2005 for racketeering, conspiracy, and organizing financial support to an extreme Palestinian organization implicated in many violent acts of terrorism in Israel. While hailed by some at the outset as "a trial with more important national security implications than any since the Rosenbergs," the charges against the former South Florida University professor and his co-defendants did *not* include accusations that they carried out, aided, or planned terrorist attacks inside the United States or that they were in touch with al-Qaeda or other global terrorist organizations.[34] The government spent five months presenting its case. Al-Arian's lawyer refused to put up a defense but instead simply invoked al-Arian's First Amendment rights to freedom of speech and assembly. In December 2005 the jury acquitted al-Arian of supporting a foreign terrorist organization and deadlocked on the other less serious charges.

Another case that drew widespread attention in the spring of 2005 neither came to trial nor even resulted in an indictment. The episode nevertheless illustrates the strong desire of government officials to justify the scale of the War on Terror with discoveries of homegrown threats. It also shows the rigor with which government agencies are combing through the daily activities of vast numbers of people in search of anything even resembling a terrorist threat. The case came to national attention in early April 2005 when the *New York Times* featured prominently an article under the headline "Two Girls Held as U.S. Fears Suicide Bomb."[35] Both of the two sixteen-year-old girls were long-time (illegal) residents of the United States. One was the child of Bangladeshi immigrants. The other was born in Guinea. In March the two were taken to a detention facility in Pennsylvania, strip searched, and interrogated for two weeks without parents or lawyers present or knowing where they were.

According to documents obtained by the *New York Times*, the FBI considered the two girls as an "imminent threat to the security of the United States." The government was worried the girls were planning to become suicide bombers. They first came to the FBI's attention while its agents were monitoring postings in an Islamic-oriented chat room. Although their thoughts about issues of Islamic law and custom were not incriminating, when agents posing as youth counselors searched their rooms they found a school essay and a drawing that seemed to the FBI to indicate a plan to become suicide bombers. A month and a half later, however, the *New York Times* published another, smaller, article reporting that after six weeks in detention the girls had been "quietly released and officials have declined to comment on the case."[36]

One case that has revealed some contact between a Muslim American citizen and al-Qaeda in Pakistan is that of a Lodi, California, laborer of Pakistani descent, Hamid Hayat. He was under surveillance while returning from Pakistan to the United States by plane at the end of May 2005. The FBI questioned him for two weeks about his contacts with al-Qaeda in Pakistan. After failing a lie detector test, Hayat reportedly admitted that he had trained in an al-Qaeda camp run by his grandfather in Pakistan, and although he had no orders to carry out terrorist attacks in the United States, he volunteered to do so, specifically against supermarkets and hospitals. He was arrested, charged with "providing material support to terrorists," and imprisoned without bail.[37] His father, an ice cream truck driver, was also arrested and charged with making false statements to the FBI.

The younger Hayat was indicted on one charge of providing material support to terrorists, but at his trial the government's case was held up to substantial ridicule in the press. By all accounts the accused is a weak-willed and unintelligent individual whose first language is Pashto and who understands English poorly. Videotapes of the "confessions" of the father and son showed "befuddled and uncomprehending" men wrapped in blankets, with heads down, nodding or answering questions in monosyllables.[38] They were described by a *San Francisco Chronicle* reporter as responding to questions with "answers that had been previously suggested by the agents—who did most of the talking."[39] The government's case was further weakened by its reliance on the testimony of an informer paid $250,000 by the FBI to infiltrate the Lodi Muslim community. The credibility of this informer was brought into question by evidence that several of his assertions, including the claim to have observed Osama bin Laden's right-hand man, Ayman al-Zawahiri, at the Lodi mosque in 1999, were false. After lengthy deliberations, the juries cleared the father but convicted the son.

It is instructive that in his 2006 report to the Senate Select Committee on Intelligence, Director of National Intelligence John Negroponte made specific mention of this and only this case to illustrate the War on Terror's importance in thwarting terrorism inside the homeland. Equally instructive was the substantial exaggeration Negroponte included in his characterization of Hamid Hayat's arrest. Reflecting the government's strong desire to provide evidence of the threat it portrays itself as combating, he cited the case as an "example" of a "homegrown" jihadist cell, rather than the arrest of one individual charged with having trained in an al-Qaeda camp. Despite the absence of evidence that anyone was involved in a plot of any kind, apart, perhaps, from Hamid Hayat himself, Negroponte spoke of "a network of Islamic extremists in Lodi, California [that] maintained connections with Pakistani militant groups, recruited US citizens for training at radical Karachi madrassas, sponsored Pakistani citizens for travel to the US to work at mosques and madrassas, and according to FBI information, allegedly raised funds for international jihadist groups."[40]

The government has registered some convictions on charges of fundraising for foreign groups appearing on its list of terrorist organizations, but the record reveals a string of high-profile false arrests followed by de-escalated indictments, failed prosecutions, and sometimes what appear to be rather desperate efforts to trumpet some sort of accomplishment in the War on Terror. The truth is that in the four and a half years since 9/11, the government has assiduously investigated virtually any Middle Easterner in the United States who could in any way have been suspected of being associated with terrorism. As measured by the number of terrorists apprehended, the results have been meager. "Of the 80,000 Arabs and Muslim foreign nationals who were required to register after September 11, the 8,000 called in for FBI interviews, and more than 5,000 locked up in preventive detention, not one stands convicted of a terrorist crime today. In what has surely been the most aggressive national campaign of ethnic profiling since World War II, the government's record is 0 for 93,000."[41] In March 2005 a classified FBI assessment of the domestic terrorist threat that was leaked to the media matched this assessment. Its crucial finding was that "to date, we have not identified any true 'sleeper' agents in the US . . . US Government efforts to date also have not revealed evidence of concealed cells or networks acting in the homeland as sleepers."[42]

Instead of being reassured by this finding, many people involved in the law enforcement effort, including top-echelon leaders, find themselves frustrated, embarrassed, and confused. Assuming there is a large and dangerous terrorist threat, they work hard, with a sincere desire to serve their country and protect its population. Yet since 9/11 they have convicted virtually no one of posing a serious terrorist threat. It is in response to this predicament, and to critics suggesting that failures to find terrorists arise from stinginess, incompetence, or an overall lack of seriousness in the prosecution of the War on Terror, that President Bush declared, in a speech marking four years since the 2001 attacks, that the United States (and its allies) had prevented ten serious al-Qaeda plots since then: "Overall, the United States and our partners have disrupted at least ten serious al Qaeda terrorist plots since September the 11th, including three al Qaeda plots to attack inside the United States. We've stopped at least five more al Qaeda efforts to case targets in the United States, or infiltrate operatives into our country. Because of this steady progress, the enemy is wounded—but the enemy is still capable of global operations."[43]

The president gave no details about the plots he had in mind. The *Washington Post* rushed to press the White House for details. The newspaper reported that "after scrambling all day and debating how much could be disclosed" the White House produced a list. Only three of the alleged plots targeted the United States. One was the case of Padilla, though as explained above these accusations were, after a short period, dropped by the Justice Department. The other two involved plane hijackings and attacks to have been carried out in 2002 and 2003. The *Post* quoted unnamed intelligence sources as saying these reports originated from the captured al-Qaeda leader Khalid Sheik Mohammed, who had masterminded the 9/11 attacks and told his interrogators about ideas he had had before 9/11 to launch additional attacks against Los Angeles and an East Coast target. The seven foreign plots said to have been foiled included bombings in London and attacks on Heathrow Airport, ships in the Persian Gulf, and on Western interests in Pakistan.[44] Pursuing the story further, the *Post* quoted a former CIA officer involved in counterterrorism during the years in question as commenting that the president had made the ten plots "sound like well-hatched plans," but he didn't think they fell into that category. Other intelligence sources insisted on anonymity but told the *Post* reporters "that the White House overstated the gravity of the plots by saying that they had been foiled, when most were far from ready to be executed. Others noted that the nation's color-coded threat index was not raised from yellow, or elevated risk of attack, to orange, or high risk, for most of the time covered by the incidents on the list."[45]

In what was widely interpreted as an attempt to distract the country from criticism of his authorization of warrantless spying on Americans, President Bush retold the story of one of the "plots" on this list five months later. In a speech on February 9, 2006, he announced that the tallest building in Los Angeles, the Library Tower, had been the target of al-Qaeda linked terrorists in 2002.[46] The president explicitly used his retelling of the alleged plot to try to keep American perceptions of the terrorist threat fresh in their minds. "We cannot let the fact that America hasn't been attacked in 4½ years since September the 11th lull us into the illusion that the threats to our nation have disappeared. They have not."[47] Indeed CNN immediately reported the speech in tones that corresponded to the president's obvious desire to highlight the threat of al-Qaeda terrorists to deliver another 9/11-type blow against America and implied the effectiveness of the War on Terror.[48] The fact that the president very much wanted to provide evidence of the presence of a terrorist threat in the United States in 2006 but could do no better than recycle a "plot" that intelligence experts had already debunked as unserious is proof of how scanty the evidence is for a potent terrorist threat inside the United States.

One thing must be clear if the argument I am making is to be understood. I am *not* maintaining that any of those individuals the government has charged of breaking the law are innocent of those charges of which they were convicted. Nor am I arguing that these prosecutions and investigations are inappropriate or unwarranted (though they may be in some cases). Nor am I arguing that there is absolutely no terrorist threat present within the United States. My primary concern is to establish the enormous scale of resources devoted to the search for domestic terrorists, the virtual nonexistence of constraints on the conduct of investigations and the gathering of evidence, and the disposition of authorities to err on the side of arresting and charging the innocent so as to maximize the probability of discovering the guilty. On these facts alone I can now confidently assess the meager results of the counterterrorism hunt inside the United States.

What we see is striking—the near total absence of evidence of al-Qaeda sleeper cells or of sophisticated groups of Muslim extremists planning or preparing for attacks of massive destruction inside the borders of the United States. One clear and dangerous, but *non-Muslim*, threat *was* uncovered. In April 2003, right-wing extremists William Krar and Judith Bruey of Tyler, Texas, were found to be in possession of a large cache of fully automatic machine guns, remote-controlled explosive devices disguised as briefcases, sixty pipe bombs, and the materials necessary to build a large cyanide bomb.[49] Krar was eventually sentenced to eleven years in prison, and Bruey to five. Government success in thwarting this plot, however, was not claimed as a victory in the War on Terror. Although the local FBI office issued a brief statement in May 2004 mentioning the War on Terror's contribution to apprehending the pair,[50] neither then Attorney General Ashcroft, nor the Department of Homeland Security, nor President Bush has ever mentioned this case as an example of a victory in or justification for the War on Terror.

The following chapter explains why the government has not portrayed this success as a War on Terror victory. I argue that the War on Terror was born out of a very specific set of political imperatives requiring the terrorist threat to be from violent Muslim extremists, not from violent Christian extremists. In the concluding chapter I consider the implications of the existence of terrorist threats, whether from Muslims, Christians, or anyone else, and argue for a sustainable, winning strategy to cope with those threats. But the plain fact is this: if there are such threats, their magnitude is without doubt vastly *smaller* than the scale of the War on Terror. It is this gross discrepancy, between available evidence of terrorist threats, on the one hand, and the immensity of the War on Terror, its pervasiveness within American society, and its spiraling cost, on the other, that I wish to explain.

Chapter 4

The Cabal, the Invasion of Iraq, and the Origins of the War on Terror

America's counterterrorism effort has a life of its own. Americans are not in charge of the War on Terror; the War on Terror is in charge of us. The array of slogans, bureaucracies, lobbying strategies, wars, budgets, contracts, books, television shows, films, cottage industries, and academic centers that makes up the War on Terror has come to operate as a self-organizing, self-perpetuating whirlwind—a veritable hurricane of public policies and private ambitions that feed on one another and on the impossibility of any outcome we could know as "victory." We are disoriented, drowning in red ink, distracted from crucial domestic and foreign policy problems, and led astray into counterproductive disasters, most notably in Iraq. We are not protagonists in a struggle against a terrorist enemy. Instead, the instrument we created for our protection has become our enemy, an adversary potentially more dangerous than al-Qaeda, Iraq, and the rest of the Axis of Evil ever were.

We are all familiar with the idea of vicious cycles, of self-strengthening, reinforcing feedback loops. In the natural world avalanches, tornados, hurricanes, and whirlpools arise from widening chain reactions in which effects become ever more powerful causes of bigger effects. In the social world we see the same kind of dynamic when seemingly irresistible forces, sometimes unleashed from small and even ordinary events, produce fads, riots, or even revolutions.

Each of these phenomena is based on the formation of a vortex—a spiral of self-generating change that overwhelms the trajectories of individual objects or the decisions of individual people. Two elements are necessary to form a vortex in any domain. First, some structural features must be arrayed to form huge reservoirs of potential energy. Thus tornados are enabled by masses of hot, humid air located underneath masses of cold air. A stock market collapse is enabled by a superabundance of stockholders with unredeemed profits and the diffuse perceptions of disappearing opportunities to realize those profits. Yet the mechanisms that can unleash this kind of accumulated power do not operate without some triggering event. Something apart from the structural conditions themselves must set the processes in motion that combine to form the powerful vortex. Conditions that make tornados possible do not produce them unless a moving front or some other event punctures the layer of stable air separating the cold mass above and the hot, humid mass below. Nor do overheated markets always collapse, but under the right conditions an appropriate signal or series of signals or shocks can jolt the normal pattern of ups and downs in trading toward a steep and even cataclysmic descent powered by ever-increasing numbers of sellers trying to lock in profits and then avoid or cut losses.

Just what is responsible for creating the vortex of the War on Terror? The actions of a very specific, energetic, well-organized, and well-positioned group provided just the right sort of impetus. This group transformed the national response to the 9/11 attacks from a rational and direct reaction to a serious, specific threat (al-Qaeda) to a crusade for the implementation of its own long-cherished blueprint for a new kind of America and a new kind of American role in the world.

THE CABAL

In the 1840s a small but single-minded and powerful group of American politicians and activists engineered the annexation of Texas and the Mexican war as vehicles for the western and southern expansion of the United States. This group was known contemporaneously, and is now known to historians, as the "junto."[1] The group responsible for launching the War on Terror and giving it the particularly expansive cast that I shall describe has an identical profile and has played a very similar role. Composed of leading conservative Republican politicians along with neoconservative activists, intellectuals, and journalists with overlapping strategic objectives, this junto or "cabal," as it has often and appropriately been labeled, was united behind a vision of achieving American hegemony abroad and conservative ascendancy at home.[2] This group had long seen an American war of liberation against Saddam

Hussein's regime as the practical basis for coordinated action, viewing it as the linchpin for achieving its overall goals.

The most active participants in this movement were politicos organized formally within the Project for the New American Century (PNAC), whose chairman, William Kristol, is also editor-in-chief of the *Weekly Standard*, the magazine universally regarded as the neoconservative movement's mouthpiece.[3] Participants included high-ranking figures within the Defense Department, the White House, and the State Department, as well from outside the formal boundaries of the government.

The cabal ruthlessly exploited the attacks on the Pentagon and the World Trade Center to advance their agenda, but that agenda had been made very clear well before September 11, 2001. William Kristol and Robert Kagan published an informal manifesto of the PNAC in the Council on Foreign Relations journal *Foreign Affairs* in the summer of 1996. "Conservatives," they warned, "will not be able to govern America over the long term if they fail to offer a more elevated vision of America's international role." The role they described for the United States was to establish a position of "benevolent global hegemony" and to preserve it "as far into the future as possible." The dual purpose of the muscular use of American hyper-power would be "to destroy the world's monsters" and to "manage empire." To implement this post-Cold War vision, to overcome the electoral advantages of Clinton-style platforms of multilateralism abroad and social democracy at home, Kristol and Kagan called for "a true 'conservatism of the heart'" that would "emphasize both personal and national responsibility, relish the opportunity for national engagement, embrace the possibility of national greatness, and restore a sense of the heroic." They claimed their "neo-Reaganite foreign policy . . . would be good for conservatives, good for America, and good for the world. . . . Deprived of the support of an elevated patriotism, bereft of the ability to appeal to national honor, conservatives will ultimately fail in their effort to govern America."[4]

Two other key PNAC documents include a formal statement of its purposes issued in June 1997 and a widely publicized letter delivered to President Clinton in January 1998. These documents bear the signatures of virtually all of the Republican hawks and neoconservatives who seized control of U.S. foreign policy after 9/11. The former document echoed the Kristol and Kagan article in *Foreign Affairs*: it called for a "Reaganite policy of military strength and moral clarity" and demanded "a military that is strong and ready to meet both present and future challenges; a foreign policy that boldly and purposefully promotes American principles abroad; and national leadership that accepts the United States' global responsibilities."[5] This statement of principles was signed by Richard Cheney (vice president three years later), I. Lewis Libby (later Cheney's chief of staff), Donald Rumsfeld (secretary of defense to be), Paul Wolfowitz (deputy secretary of defense under Rumsfeld), Zalmay Khalilzad (special envoy to Afghanistan and ambassador to Iraq), Elliott Abrams (national security council adviser for the Middle East, first under Condoleezza Rice and then under Steven Hadley), Paula J. Dobriansky (undersecretary of state for global affairs), and Peter Rodman (assistant secretary of defense for international security affairs).

The letter delivered by the PNAC to President Clinton in January 1998 demanded war in order to remove Saddam Hussein's weapons of mass destruction (WMD) and to remove and replace Saddam and his regime as a crucial first step to transforming the Middle East. "We urge," said the letter, "a new strategy that would secure the interests of the U.S. and our friends and allies around the world. That strategy should aim, above all, at the removal of Saddam Hussein's regime from power . . . [including] a willingness to undertake military action as diplomacy is clearly failing. . . . [T]hat now needs to become the aim of American foreign policy." In addition to the names of many of those who signed the PNAC statement of purpose (such as Rumsfeld, Wolfowitz, and Abrams), names on this letter also included Richard Perle (named chairman of the defense policy board in the first George Bush administration); Richard L. Armitage (deputy secretary of state), John Bolton (undersecretary of state for arms control, later ambassador to the United Nations), and R. James Woolsey, former CIA director and member of the Defense Advisory Board).[6]

The PNAC was also the driving force in Congress behind passage of the Iraq Liberation Act, which escalated American political and economic support for political mechanisms of regime change in Baghdad. Although the PNAC was the single most important organized cluster of activist hawks within the cabal pushing for war in Iraq prior to 9/11, other groups deserve mention as well. The names on their organizational mastheads reveal a kind of interlocking directorate: Dick Cheney, John Bolton, James Woolsey, and Richard Perle have been members of the board of advisers of the Jewish Institute for National Security Affairs (JINSA), an organization long dedicated to a militant U.S. foreign policy anchored in a close military and political relationship with Israel to confront Islamic and/or Arab mobilization with armed force. In a formal resolution in fall 1997 JINSA declared that "the goals of the Palestinians and the goals of the Israelis are incompatible." In light of this contradiction, said JINSA, the United States should stop defining its policy as support for the peace process and adopt instead an anti-terrorist, pro-security posture in support of any retaliatory or preventive actions the government of Israel might adopt against Palestinians. As an overall context for this commitment, JINSA has untiringly advocated increases in American defense spending and programs to establish and consolidate U.S. strategic domination of the Middle East.[7]

In March 1998 JINSA issued a formal resolution warning of weapons of mass destruction in Iraq and calling for the indictment of Saddam Hussein and his chief lieutenants as war criminals. It called on the United States

to provide overt political and financial support for legitimate, democratic opposition to Saddam Hussein in Iraq [including but] . . . not limited to: recognition of a government in exile should one be established, unfreezing of frozen Iraqi assets in the US to provide financial support for democratic Iraqi opposition groups, removing UN sanctions from areas controlled by opposition groups; . . . instituting Voice of Iraq broadcasts to be heard throughout Iraq; [and] instituting a no-fly zone throughout Iraq and a no drive zone where appropriate.[8]

Douglas Feith chaired the board of JINSA before being named Rumsfeld's undersecretary of defense for policy. Along with Perle, Abrams, Dobriansky, and other PNAC figures, Feith was also active in the Center for Security Policy, founded and directed by Frank Gaffney, a neoconservative activist in the Reagan administration long associated with extreme right-wing political groups in Israel who moved from rabid anticommunism to a focus on Iraq and a call to arms against "Islamofascism."

Under the auspices of a similar group based in Jerusalem, the Institute for Advanced Strategic and Political Studies, Feith and Perle contributed to a proposal delivered to Israeli Prime Minister Benjamin Netanyahu in 1996 advising him to declare Israel's refusal to withdraw from the West Bank and Gaza, its abandonment of the principle of trading "land for peace," and its reliance on military and economic power buttressed by close ties with an invigorated, assertive America to render Arab and Muslim opposition irrelevant. In cooperation with the United States, the proposal suggested, Israel would seek to roll back Syrian influence and remove Saddam Hussein from power.[9] The primary drafter of this proposal was David Wurmser, who later served as a special adviser to John Bolton and then as Middle East adviser to Vice President Cheney.

The important point here is that well before September 11, 2001, this cabal was already operating in a disciplined and sustained manner toward extraordinarily ambitious goals. Its members worked in relatively close coordination, facilitated by a clear sense of mission. Its agenda included neo-imperial American power projection abroad, conservative Republican political victories at home, and, specifically, a war in Iraq that would eliminate the regime of Saddam Hussein and transform that country into a model of neoliberal economic growth—a kind of "Klondike on the Euphrates" for well-connected American corporations positioned to buy up privatized Iraqi government assets at bargain basement prices.[10] Central figures in the cabal avoided focusing on terrorism prior to 9/11 in favor of emphasizing the need to "liberate Iraq." But once the attacks occurred in September 2001, they worked with zealous determination to transform fear and anger toward al-Qaeda terrorists into the basis for a very specific kind of War on Terror, a war whose crucial feature would be unquestioned public acceptance of a ruthless Muslim enemy present both at home and abroad that could be neither clearly seen nor permanently defeated. The never-ending story thus set in motion would provide future administrations with ample justification for the wide-ranging use of American military power abroad and executive authority at home. It would also afford presidents and other top officials with plentiful opportunities for displaying heroic leadership, and, most specifically and importantly, it would constitute an effective basis for building public support for an invasion of Iraq.

THE CABAL TAKES CHARGE

Pundits as well as government officials (speaking off the record) agree that in the George W. Bush administration the buck does not stop at the desk of the president; it stops at the desk of the vice president. In the late spring of 2003 I participated in an all-day roundtable discussion among outside experts and high-ranking intelligence officials on American options in Iraq after the overthrow of Saddam Hussein. At the end of the day, the outside experts were asked what they would recommend the United States do with Iraq now that it had destroyed Saddam's regime. The experts were asked, "What would you say if you had three minutes with the vice president?" No one in the room batted an eyelash at the way the question was phrased. Each was to imagine what he would say to the vice president, not the president. The absence of surprise was of course because everyone clearly understood whose opinion counted most, that not of President George W. Bush but of Vice President Richard Cheney.[11]

It is true that in any administration, foreign policy and national security policy are never developed or implemented as a straightforward expression of the views of the president, regardless of his constitutional powers and status as commander in chief. Battles over turf, ideology, and policy instruments normally arise that yield decisions and policies as compromises of repeated struggles among coalitions of high-ranking bureaucrats, advisers, and relevant cabinet secretaries—the "principals." Of course, when a president takes a strong and sustained interest in the details of foreign and national security policy, the importance of bureaucratic infighting can diminish, as was the case in the Nixon, Clinton, and George H. W. Bush administrations. But even under Nixon, policies were often the result of bitter struggles between Henry Kissinger, when he was national security adviser, and Secretary of State William Rogers. Under Carter there were ferocious battles over policies on Afghanistan and Iran between Secretary of State Cyrus Vance and National Security Adviser Zbigniew Brzezinski. Reagan emphasized his intention to end this kind of rivalry by establishing the primacy of his secretary of state, Alexander Haig, and by appointing relatively weak national security advisers. But Reagan went through several advisers, each of whom reached for more power, which led to conflicts with the State Department and the resignation of Haig, who was replaced by George Shultz. Rivalries continued as subsequent advisers Robert McFarlane and John Poindexter took active and energetic roles in sensitive areas such as Iran and Central America. At the end of his second term President Reagan appointed Colin Powell as national security adviser, thereby achieving a degree of balance and coordination among his top foreign policy and national security advisers—a pattern more or less continued under Clinton whose secretaries of state, Warren Christopher and Madeleine Albright, generally did not grapple with national security advisers Anthony Lake and his somewhat more dominant successor, Sandy Berger. George H. W. Bush also took a strong and detailed interest in foreign policy and national security matters, the domain in which he had the deepest personal experience. During his one term in office, Secretary of State James Baker and National Security Adviser Brent Scowcroft worked in relative harmony.[12]

Amid this record of interdepartmental cooperation and rivalry in foreign policy affairs it is difficult, probably impossible, to find a set of conflicts more bitter or extreme than the ferocious struggles that took place in the first year of President George W. Bush's administration. The president was famously ill-informed on issues of foreign and national security policy and notoriously uninterested in detailed policy debates. His national security adviser, Condoleezza Rice, whose expertise on the communist regime in Moscow had been rendered largely irrelevant by the end of the Cold War, adopted a position of "broker" between the forces seeking control over the Bush administration's foreign and defense policies. It appears that her objective was to remain in Bush's good graces by discerning the information he wanted and the sources he preferred receiving it from. The veteran journalist James Fallows noticed the absence of a commanding center in the Oval Office or in the Office of the National Security Adviser. He reported that in months of interviews with officials about decisions leading up to the Iraq war he "never once heard someone say 'We took this step because the President indicated . . . The President really wanted . . .' Instead [he] heard 'Rumsfeld wanted,' 'Powell thought,' 'The Vice President pushed,' 'Bremer asked,' and so on." Fallows described Condoleezza Rice, along with the president, as "conspicuously absent" from accounts of how events unfolded and who determined their course between 9/11 and the invasion of Iraq.[13]

On February 5, 2001, seventeen days after George W. Bush's inauguration, Condoleezza Rice chaired a principals meeting to discuss Iraq. According to Bob Woodward's account of this meeting the focus was mainly on enforcement of the no-fly zone. A week and a half later U.S. and British warplanes struck twenty command-and-control centers in

Iraq, some very near Baghdad. It seemed as if the Iraq liberation hawks had already won the day. Despite appearances, however, the raids did not signal that the president was already committed to war in Iraq or to the agenda of the neocons. Instead the raids appear to have been prompted by genuine concerns within the uniformed military that Iraqi radar and anti-aircraft capability had to be hit hard in order to reduce the risk to U.S. pilots patrolling the no-fly zone.[14]

This false dawn for the group I shall label "the supremacists" did, however, inaugurate a no-holds-barred struggle for control of foreign and national security policy in the Bush II administration. On one side were the pragmatists led by Powell and Armitage at the State Department with allies in the CIA, in the uniformed military, and, outside the government, among the established Republican "wise men" of foreign affairs and national security, such as Brent Scowcroft, James Baker, and Henry Kissinger. Their views were anchored in a prudent approach to the use of American power, belief in the importance but also the limits of military force, the need to use overwhelming force whenever military options were exercised, commitment to achieving a peace settlement based on "land for peace" between Israel and the Palestinians, and an imperative to avoid commitments to wars that would not be supported by a political consensus at home. On the other side were the supremacists, a combination of fervently ideological neoconservatives and big-stick hawks such as Cheney and Rumsfeld.[15] Their primary allies inside the government were their appointees or protégés—Paul Wolfowitz, Douglas Feith, I. Lewis (Scooter) Libby, John Bolton, William Luti, and David Wurmser. Outside the government they drew support from journalists such as Kristol and Charles Krauthammer and from their allies on the Defense Advisory Board, including Richard Perle, Eliot Cohen, and former CIA chief James Woolsey. Their guiding objective was to initiate a war of liberation against Saddam Hussein's regime in Iraq as the path to implementing broader objectives: neo-imperial American ascendancy at the global level, a "heroic" and conservative transformation of American politics domestically, and reinforcement of militant Israeli government policies against compromise with the Palestinians.

Between these two warring factions was the president, ill-informed and relatively uninterested in world affairs. His closest adviser in this domain was Condoleezza Rice, whose infamous slip of the tongue (referring to the president as "my husb . . .") reflected her determined effort to express sentiments and beliefs as close to his as possible.[16] Rice assumed her post as national security adviser with a position on Iraq that could be seen as supportive of either the pragmatists or the supremacists. According to Seymour Hersh's sources, Rice initially viewed Saddam as "a small problem—chump change."[17] In a 2000 *Foreign Affairs* article Rice assured Americans that Iraq need not be seen as a terribly urgent problem. "There need be no sense of panic. . . . the first line of defense should be a clear and classical statement of deterrence—if they do acquire WMD, their weapons will be unusable because any attempt to use them will bring national obliteration." Hawks could find encouragement, however, in another passage from this same article: "Saddam Hussein's regime is isolated, his conventional military power has been severely weakened, his people live in poverty and terror, and he has no useful place in international politics. He is therefore determined to develop WMD. Nothing will change until Saddam is gone, so the United States must mobilize whatever resources it can, including support from his opposition, to remove him."[18]

Beginning immediately after the inauguration in January 2001, Cheney began an unprecedented long series of visits to the CIA. These consultations were focused primarily on Iraq. Cheney repeatedly, personally, and vigorously pressed analysts to rethink or recalibrate judgments that Iraq was not a pressing security threat.[19] Rumsfeld, Perle, and Wolfowitz also focused unswervingly on Saddam as enemy number one. Perle and Wolfowitz maintained close ties with a notoriously weird professor named Laurie Mylroie. In earlier years Mylroie had been a champion of Saddam Hussein's Iraq but later turned full circle.[20] Her widely hyped accusation that Iraq had been behind the 1993 attack on the World Trade Center was notable for the absence of evidence to support the claim and the virtual unanimity of expert rejection of her thesis. From an exchange reported verbatim by Richard A. Clarke, the National Security Council official in charge of counterterrorism, it would appear that Mylroie's wild assertions were received enthusiastically by the supremacists. The setting was a high-level meeting on terrorism held in April 2001. The meeting began with a briefing by Clarke on the urgent need to target bin Laden and al-Qaeda.

Wolfowitz: Well, I just don't understand why we are beginning by talking about this one man bin Laden.

Clarke: We are talking about a network of terrorist organizations called al Qaeda, that happens to be led by bin Laden, and we are talking about that network because it and it alone poses an immediate and serious threat to the United States.

Wolfowitz: Well, there are others that can do as well, as least as much. Iraqi terrorism for example.

Clarke: I am unaware of any Iraqi-sponsored terrorism directed at the United States, Paul, since 1993, and I think FBI and CIA concur in that judgment . . .

Wolfowitz: You give bin Laden too much credit. He could not do all these things like the 1993 attack on New York, not without a state sponsor. Just because FBI and CIA have failed to find the linkages does not mean they don't exist.[21]

Clarke wrote that he "could hardly believe it but Wolfowitz was actually spouting the totally discredited Laurie Mylroie theory."[22] The extent to which Mylroie's theories were exploited by the supremacists was evident in the lead up to the Iraq war when two of her books were graced by fervid endorsements from Perle and Wolfowitz. Wolfowitz described Mylroie's *The War Against America: Saddam Hussein and the World Trade Center Attacks* as arguing "powerfully that the mastermind of the 1993 World Trade Center bombing was in fact an agent of Iraqi intelligence." Mylroie's second book, *Bush vs. the Beltway: How the CIA and the State Department Tried to Stop the War on Terror,* was published in 2004. It was a denunciation of the pragmatists within the Bush administration during exactly the period discussed here. As Perle put it in his blurb on the book jacket: "Mylroie describes how the CIA and the State Department have systematically discredited critical intelligence about Saddam's regime, including indisputable evidence of its possession of weapons of mass destruction [*sic*]."[23]

Perle's resentment of the intelligence community and the State Department stemmed from the fact that until September 2001, the pragmatists had generally prevailed in their bureaucratic war with the supremacists.[24] Repeated efforts to enlist the president in a campaign toward war in Iraq or toward a decidedly belligerent policy toward China had failed. The expensive ballistic missile defense project, another favorite of the supremacists, was also faltering. Despite intense pressure, CIA Director George Tenet and his Middle East specialists held firm against pointing to Saddam as responsible for the attacks on 9/11, as allied with al-Qaeda, or as posing an imminent threat to the United States. On Iraq Powell had directed American policy toward cooperative efforts with the Europeans to redesign the sanctions regime against Iraq. Rules that were punishing ordinary Iraqis while profiting the regime would be replaced with "smart sanctions." In deputies meetings Armitage held his own to restrain Wolfowitz and others from quickly ramping up American financial, political, and military support for the Pentagon's favorite Iraqi opposition leader—Ahmad Chalabi. In a series of these meetings dedicated to Iraq, no agreement could be reached on how to proceed, resulting in a policy paper presented to the principals on August 1, 2001, that reflected the stalemate—a variety of options for pressure but no recommendation for invasion or a decisive alliance with Chalabi for another attempt to overthrow Saddam.[25] The argument continued, leading to regular clashes between Powell and Wolfowitz. Wolfowitz advocated an invasion to seize the southern Iraqi oil fields and use the "enclave" to encourage revolt in the rest of Iraq. Powell considered such ideas "lunacy," but the civilian hawks in the Pentagon fought against efforts to gauge the consequences of less than fully successful military operations in or against Iraq. The President assured Powell he was not about to do anything rash. At the same time he encouraged the supremacists to continue with their "contingency planning."[26]

The attacks on September 11 may not actually have "changed everything," but they most certainly did change the fortunes of the supremacist faction in its struggle with the pragmatists. Before 9/11 it was mired in a losing slugfest with its bureaucratic opponents and saddled with a disengaged president who shared neither its members' sense of urgency nor their zeal for liberal democratic nation-building. After 9/11 supremacists assumed the dominant position in the formulation of American foreign and security policies. They would use that position to focus the entire might of the United States on their chosen objective—a war of liberation in Iraq—as the first and crucial battle in a political war to revolutionize the place of America in the world and of neoconservatives in American politics. Asked how neoconservative ideas had managed so thoroughly to determine the president's foreign policy thinking, Robert Kagan rejected the idea of an intellectual transformation. "September 11

[was] the turning point. Not anything else. This is not what Bush was on September 10."[27]

The attacks on 9/11 had two massively important effects on the bureaucratic battlefield. First, the president's political capital suddenly increased one hundred-fold. Second, the immense gap between the military power of the United States and that of any other nation or combination of nations suddenly became relevant to domestic politics. The implications are worth careful consideration.

The president's first year in office had been lackluster and had failed to inspire enthusiasm even among his supporters. Nor did his initial response to the disaster bode well (continuing to read *My Pet Goat* to schoolchildren and then hopscotching across the country in an airplane whose location was a public mystery). But the opportunities of the office and the occasion quickly overwhelmed the apparent inadequacies of the man. In what was later characterized as the defining moment of his Presidency, Bush stood atop a wrecked fire engine with a bullhorn and responded to cheers: "I can hear you; the rest of the world hears you, and the people who knocked these buildings down will hear from all of us very soon."

Virtually everyone agreed that al-Qaeda, based in Taliban-ruled Afghanistan, was responsible for the attacks. Accordingly, the country stood almost completely united behind American-led military operations in Afghanistan that would cripple al-Qaeda, kill Osama bin Laden, and destroy the Taliban regime. In the months following 9/11 Bush could be confident that virtually any decision he made would be, at least in the first instance, supported by the overwhelming majority of Americans. The president's skyrocketing approval ratings and the preparedness of the country for a decision involving the appearance of decisive action meant that victory for the hawks was within reach. If the neocons could hitch their longing for a war in Iraq to the president's response to 9/11 they could, they thought, virtually ensure that the country would be committed, not only to the liberation of that country but to similar operations in Iran and Syria.[28] A string of successful neoimperial wars would eliminate the remnants of the Vietnam syndrome, relegate multilateralism and the cautions of the Powell doctrine to the dustbin of history, and put the United States well on the way to the New American Century abroad and the permanent conservative majority at home they had dedicated their careers to achieving.

This is the context in which the utter domination of the American military over any combination of military capabilities possessed by other countries, friends or foes, became politically significant. Before 9/11 and absent the Soviet or communist threat, the fact that the U.S. military machine could be expected to achieve outright victory in any military engagement anywhere had little political importance. No politician could mobilize a great deal of support just by waging war for the sake of winning victories. But with a new, fearsome, and strange enemy, the majority of Americans could be, and was, readily convinced that the superiority of the U.S. military was in fact the decisively important factor in the looming struggle to make the world feel as safe for Americans as it had felt prior to September 11, 2001.[29]

A fascinating window into the hawks' victory over the pragmatists following 9/11 has been provided by Richard A. Clarke. As noted above, Clarke was the "terrorism czar" under Clinton whose critique of the Bush administration's blasé attitude toward al-Qaeda before September 2001 captured the attention of the country and of the 9/11 Commission. Soon after becoming national security adviser, Condoleezza Rice reduced the profile of his operation, leading to his departure from the administration. But until November 2001, Clarke had a seat at the table when principals or deputies met on issues of national security.

By all accounts Clarke had maintained a laserlike focus on bin Laden and al-Qaeda and on the threat of a large-scale attack. Although he reports receiving strong support for his efforts from George Tenet at the CIA, Clarke became increasingly viewed as a kind of "Ahab" obsessed with the "white whale" of al-Qaeda. Nevertheless, when *precisely* the kind of attack Clarke had been warning of occurred, Clarke assumed the serious counterterrorist campaign he had long advocated would be a "self-licking ice cream cone . . . Everybody will know what to do . . . there won't be disagreements over policy . . . It's obvious stuff now."[30] To Clarke's amazement, he was wrong. His account of the aftermath of 9/11 shows how forcefully and effectively the supremacists moved to divert the attention of the president, the focus of the administration, and the emotions of the country, from Osama bin Laden and al-Qaeda to a vastly generalized War on Terror that could, and would, include Iraq as its "central front."

Before 9/11 the supremacists had pursued their goals by treating al-Qaeda as a minor irritant, raising the profile of liberationist ideas about

Iraq, denigrating multilateralism of all kinds, and promoting the forward, unilateralist uses of American military power. But as I have indicated, their march toward the New American Century enjoyed only limited success in the first eight months of the administration. They were frustrated. The 9/11 attacks, however, offered them a spectacular opportunity. They nimbly recast their agenda as based on a War on Terror. In this way they sought to exploit the fear and fury of the American people and the unchallenged global supremacy of the American military. But the most significant new element favoring the supremacists was a decisive shift within President Bush himself toward a "Churchillian" definition of his leadership and a vast inflation of the scale of the global responsibilities he came to feel that leadership entailed.

In the first eight months of his presidency George W. Bush showed pragmatism in relations with China and Russia and a readiness to ruffle the feathers of allies accustomed to Clinton-style multilateralism. Mostly, though, he treated foreign policy as a low priority. But his performance had not excited the country. No president eight months into his term had ever had a lower approval rating in the polls than George W. Bush had on September 10, 2001. Within weeks his approval rating was higher than that ever enjoyed by an American president.

What 9/11 provided Bush, aside from a newly available heroic posture and sudden popularity, was the satisfying impetus to see himself as the champion of good in a sacred antinomian struggle against "evil"—a word he used hardly at all in public speeches prior to 9/11 but regularly afterward, leading up to the "Axis of Evil" phrase in the January 2002 State of the Union address.[31] After 9/11 Bush appeared to adopt a view of his presidency as a mission, even a sacred mission, one requiring American military power to transform the world in order to save it.[32] This shift gave the supremacists what they most crucially needed—a president in the market for just the discourse about foreign policy, national security, and the use of military force that they could provide. After all, the centerpiece of the PNAC program was to transform the world; to bring Americans to imagine themselves heroically, as fighting for the good in a world either barbarously ignorant of the value of American supremacy or maliciously antagonistic to it.

There was one problem. It quickly became obvious that the terrorist attacks were the work of al-Qaeda and that al-Qaeda was in Afghanistan. If al-Qaeda were the *only* enemy, then once Afghanistan was liberated and al-Qaeda crippled or destroyed, that could end the justification for the sustained crusade necessary to achieve the New American Century. Since the supremacists had long before decided that a war in Iraq was the first step, it was crucial to define the newly declared War on Terror as requiring an invasion of Iraq.

Key players made the connection quickly: bin Laden—Saddam Hussein—attacking Iraq. Four hours after a third airliner crashed into the Pentagon on September 11, Donald Rumsfeld asked his staff how the United States might be able to "go after Iraq as a response." In Woodward's account Rumsfeld's notes on that day show that he had wondered whether it would be possible to "'hit S.H. @ same time—not only UBL'" and "asked the Pentagon lawyer to talk to Paul Wolfowitz about the Iraq 'connection with UBL.'"[33] Supremacist operatives then went into high gear. On September 12, the CIA said it was certain al-Qaeda in Afghanistan had launched the attacks, but that very day James Woolsey told James Fallows that "no matter who proved to be responsible for this attack, the solution had to include removing Saddam Hussein."[34] Meanwhile, Wolfowitz argued that al-Qaeda could not have acted alone. "Iraq must have been helping them." In a meeting of principals that afternoon Powell countered Rumsfeld's argument that now was the time to "get Iraq," but Rumsfeld responded that the targets in Afghanistan were not significant enough to bomb and that therefore targets in Iraq should be considered.[35] The intensity and immediacy of the supremacists' pressures on the president with respect to Iraq, and his readiness to act on them in the wake of 9/11 is stunningly revealed in a White House conversation Richard Clarke reports having with Bush on the evening of September 12, 2001.

He [the president] grabbed a few of us and closed the door to the conference room. "Look," he told us, "I know you have a lot to do and all . . . but I want you, as soon as you can, to go back over everything, everything. See if Saddam did this. See if he's linked in any way . . ."

I was once again taken aback, incredulous, and it showed. "But, Mr. President, al Qaeda did this."

"I know, I know, but . . . see if Saddam was involved. Just look. I want to know any shred . . ."

"Absolutely, we will look . . . again." I was trying to be more respectful, responsive. "But, you know, we have looked several times for state sponsorship of al Qaeda and not found any real linkages to Iraq. Iran plays a little, as does Pakistan, and Saudi Arabia, Yemen."

"Look into Iraq, Saddam," the President said testily and left us.[36]

In a press conference on September 14, Wolfowitz declared that American policy was "ending states who sponsor terrorism." Within two weeks, Senator Jesse Helms had called for a strike against Iraq. So had William Safire of the *New York Times*. The cover of the October 1, 2001, *Weekly Standard* featured a "wanted" poster of Osama bin Laden and Saddam Hussein.[37] As Hersh notes, in late 2001 a flood of speeches, op-ed pieces, and articles penned by supremacist stalwarts clamored for military action against Iraq under the banner of the War on Terror. "The question in my mind," said Richard Perle, "is: Do we wait for Saddam and hope for the best? Do we wait and hope he doesn't do what we know [*sic*] he is capable of, which is distributing weapons of mass destruction to anonymous terrorists, or do we take preemptive action?"[38]

The bold and immediate conflation of the terrorist threat with Saddam Hussein was sustained over the eighteen months between the 9/11 attacks and the invasion of Iraq. Paul R. Pillar was the CIA's national intelligence officer for the Near East and South Asia at this time. According to him, the "greatest discrepancy between the administration's public statements and the intelligence community's judgments" was with respect to "the relationship between Saddam and al-Qaeda. . . . The reason the connection got so much attention was that the administration wanted to hitch the Iraq expectation to the 'war on terror' and the threat the American public feared most, thereby capitalizing on the country's militant post-9/11 mood."[39]

The crucial rhetorical move was to define the enemy not just as the terrorists themselves or as terrorist groups with global reach, but as states who sponsored, aided, or who *might* aid terrorists. In other words, the War on Terror had to be framed so as to require the use of military force against countries considered rogue states by the supremacists, especially Iraq. Nicholas Lemann's careful study of changing presidential characterizations of the country's response to 9/11 chronicles the rapid implementation of this logic.[40] Just hours after the attacks, at a Louisiana military base, Bush defined the enemy as those directly responsible for the attacks on New York and Washington. "The United States will hunt down and punish those responsible for these cowardly acts."[41] Nine days later, in his address to the nation and both houses of Congress, he described the mission in wider terms but still limited it to al-Qaeda, the Taliban regime that protected al-Qaeda (if it refused to cooperate), and a particular kind of terrorist group. "Our war on terror begins with Al Qaeda, but it does not end there. It will not end until *every terrorist group of global reach* has been found, stopped, and defeated."[42] In his January State of the Union address he upped the ante again. The members of the Axis of Evil were named—Iraq, Iran, and North Korea—and victory in the War on Terror was now said to entail preventing "regimes who seek chemical, biological, or nuclear weapons from threatening the United States and the world."[43] By June, in his speech at West Point, his position had widened and hardened. The policies of containment and deterrence that had been the bedrock of U.S. foreign and national security policy since the late 1940s were "no longer sufficient." The president declared a new doctrine of preventive war against potential enemies: From now on "we must take the battle to the enemy, disrupt his plans, and confront the worst threats before they emerge."[44] But who was the "enemy"? In his September 20, 2001, speech Bush warned every country in the world: "Either you are with us or you are with the terrorists." By thus categorizing all states not actively allied with the United States as potentially within the enemy camp, and by asserting it as American policy to launch preventive war against states deemed threatening, the War on Terror had become something as large, or even larger, than another world war. It had, in fact, been expanded to provide precisely the virtually unlimited justification for using American military predominance that was at the core of the neoconservative/supremacist vision for how to build the New American Century.

The story of how the Iraq war was then engineered is too familiar by now to require more than the briefest retelling here. Phalanxes of zealous advocates radiated out from the Office of the Vice President and the Office of the Secretary of Defense to dominate all policy making relevant to the War on Terror and the question of Iraq.[45] Under the authority of Cheney and Rumsfeld they sidelined, intimidated, relegated to irrelevance, or stifled State Department planning exercises, its development of ties with responsible Iraqi opposition groups, and virtually any activities by intelligence or military analysts regarding what might go wrong in an Iraq war or what might be required in the aftermath of a military victory.[46] The War on Terror's initial focus on al-Qaeda was effectively abandoned. President Bush himself ceased mentioning the name of Osama bin Laden. A series of successors to Clarke as counterterrorism czar resigned over the next six months in protest at the rush to war in Iraq at the expense of a serious antiterrorism effort.[47]

Claiming success for their bold, low-cost military victory in Afghanistan, the supremacist hawks drastically reduced Powell's influence within the administration. By February 2002 the Bush administration's inner circle, already dominated by the supremacists, had made the decision to invade Iraq. Seven hundred million dollars was secretly diverted from funds appropriated for Afghanistan to develop war plans for Iraq.[48] In August, at a Crawford, Texas, meeting of principals, minus Powell, the decision was sealed and the war plan put in motion. Later that month Cheney told the Veterans of Foreign Wars convention: "There is no doubt that Saddam Hussein now has weapons of mass destruction [and that he will use them] against our friends, against our allies, and against us." Early in September Condoleezza Rice described evidence, including specialized aluminum tubes, that had convinced the administration Saddam had nuclear weapons. "There will always be some uncertainty," she said, "[but] we don't want the smoking gun to be a mushroom cloud." These and other such warnings reflected a decision by the supremacists to concentrate the public justification for war on the threat of an Iraqi nuclear attack.[49] Reporting to Douglas Feith in the Pentagon, the newly created Office of Special Plans had been cherry-picking intelligence reports to do just that.[50]

Meanwhile, Army Chief of Staff Eric Shinseki, who doubted the wisdom of banking on a quick and easy military victory in Iraq, was severely reprimanded by both Rumsfeld and Wolfowitz. George Tenet eventually broke under the pressure (or was bamboozled), and wrote a judgment directly delivered to the president two weeks before the Iraq invasion that Saddam's possession of unconventional weapons was a "slam dunk." Powell did manage to delay the war by moving the issue to the U.N., but he too had been fed the cooked intelligence justifying war in Iraq and presented it with all his personal authority to the United Nations Security Council.

Inside the government the political side of the campaign to bring the

The Seattle Public Library
Ballard Branch
Visit us on the Web: www.spl.org

Check out date: 10/15/13

xxxxxxxxx6420

Trapped in the war on terror /
0010056982142　　　Due date: 11/05/13
book

TOTAL ITEMS: 1

Renewals: 206-386-4190
TeleCirc: 206-386-9015 / 24 hours a day
Online: myaccount.spl.org

* *

All locations open Sundays in 2013
Every branch, every Sunday
Details: www.spl.org or 206-386-4636

country to war in Iraq was put in the hands of the White House Iraq Group (WHIG), formed to "educate the public" about the Iraqi threat. It fed to "friendly" journalists (such as Judith Miller of the *New York Times*) the same Office of Special Plans' collection of selected and exaggerated reports used by Cheney, Rice, Wolfowitz, and others. WHIG included Karl Rove, Lewis Libby, Karen Hughes, and Mary Matalin. Within WHIG the long-term political objectives of the neoconservatives for a belligerent, Churchillian foreign policy that would reorganize American politics to favor the Republican right catalyzed the more immediate readiness of Rove and other domestic political advisers to harness the War on Terror for immediate political advantage. After successfully using the War on Terror to achieve Republican congressional gains in the 2002 election, Rove told one reporter that 2004 would work the same way. Voters, he said, "will see the battle for Iraq as a chapter in a longer, bigger struggle, [a]s a part of the war on terrorism."[51] WHIG was extraordinarily successful. One of Richard Clarke's successors, who resigned in 2002, said it most simply: "There's no threat to us now from Iraq, but 70 percent of the American people think Iraq attacked the Pentagon and the World Trade Center. You wanna know why? Because that's what the Administration wants them to think! . . . they're using the War on Terror politically . . . They are doing 'Wag the Dog'!"[52]

Outside the government the supremacist cabal operated mainly through the Committee for the Liberation of Iraq. The CLI was formed in November 2002, featuring Kristol, Woolsey, Kagan, Perle, and PNAC Executive Director Gary Schmitt. The committee accused Iraq of acquiring weapons of mass destruction and of "supporting international terrorism." The committee's declared purpose was to "educate" the American public to the need for war against Iraq. It presented rationales that went beyond the supposed WMD threat to include promotion of "regional peace, political freedom and international security through replacement of the Saddam Hussein regime with a democratic government that respects the rights of the Iraqi people and ceases to threaten the community of nations."[53]

Despite massive antiwar demonstrations in American cities and around the world, the news media accepted the administration's ramp-up to war with only occasional and muted questioning. Polls showed that in March and April 2003 the invasion of Iraq was supported by 65 percent to 75 percent of Americans. Large majorities of Americans had been "educated" to believe that Saddam Hussein had weapons of mass destruction and that he had been directly involved in launching the 9/11 attacks against the United States. WHIG and CLI had done their jobs. The supremacist cabal now had just the war they wanted.

TACTICAL SUCCESS AND STRATEGIC FAILURE

Al-Qaeda's attack on America in September 2001 was unprecedented in this country's history for its savagery, its combined civilian and military death toll, its location in the continental United States, and its targets—preeminent symbols of American economic and military power. No matter who had been president in that fateful month, no matter what his or her ideological predilections, a determined, vigorous response to the attacks would have been undertaken. With Europe and even most Muslim states expressing sympathy for the victims of the attack and for the United States as a whole, with American military power unrivaled on the planet, and with al-Qaeda openly flaunting its alliance with the Taliban regime, it was just as inevitable that our response would include military action in Afghanistan. But the launching of a generalized War on Terror was not inevitable; nor was a division of the world between those ready to accept American hegemonic leadership and military unilateralism and those unprepared to do; and nor was an invasion of Iraq. That these became driving elements of the War on Terror, indeed that the response took on the dimensions of a "war" against an invisible and essentially undefeatable enemy, was not at all inevitable.[54] It was due instead to the particular motives, political manipulations, talents, and plans of a small but extraordinarily confident and well-positioned group.

This zealous group of highly ideological and ambitious officials seized the opportunity they saw in September 2001 to take command of U.S. foreign and national security policy, to mold the War on Terror in the image of their long-cultivated vision of an American neo-imperial order, and to prove that vision's efficacy by invading Iraq. Victory in Baghdad, according to their plan, would destabilize authoritarian orders throughout the Middle East and set in motion the kind of cascade toward liberal democracy that followed rapidly in Eastern Europe after the fall of the Soviet Union. With an apparent triumph in Afghanistan in 2002 and what seemed like a quick and relatively clean victory in Iraq in March 2003, the cabal had reason to think it was on a roll toward achieving the much broader aims of the New American Century.

By the end of 2003, of course, it was clear to all that the mission in Iraq had not been accomplished. Beyond the looting, the destruction of Iraq's infrastructure, a ballooning insurgency, the refusal of American companies to invest in the Iraqi economy, rapidly growing numbers of American and Iraqi casualties, and incipient civil war, there was one more enormous casualty. The disaster in Iraq dealt a fatal blow to the supremacist fantasy of an American public so satisfied and inspired by victory in Mesopotamia that the big stick of American military power could then readily be used against other high-value targets on the road to American hegemony, especially Syria and Iran. When Iraq became an argument for staying at home rather than for expanding American domination abroad, the neo-supremacist boom turned into a bust. Perle had already resigned from the Defense Advisory Board under a cloud of suspicion regarding favors for companies with which he was involved. The Office of Special Plans was closed. Wolfowitz and Feith left the Pentagon. Libby resigned under indictment from his post in the Office of the Vice President. Rice kicked Bolton out of the State Department into the United Nations—a post he accepted after a bruising and humiliating confirmation fight.

The supremacist cabal not only failed; it failed catastrophically. Afghanistan and Iraq were not a prelude to shock and awe victories over other rogue states. There was no Middle Eastern cascade toward liberal democracy. America's standing in the Arab and Muslim world dropped precipitously. Middle Easterners showed no more readiness to accept Israeli rule of the West Bank than they ever had. Under the canopy of the War on Terror the neoconservatives and their allies had sought to use wars for Kabul and Baghdad to build a robust public commitment to global American hegemony, heroically achieved and proudly maintained. Instead, the prestige of neoconservative ideas and the personal political clout of those most closely associated with the Iraq war plummeted. Contrary to the supremacists' expectations about the invigorating results of victory in Iraq, wide segments of American public opinion, including important parts of the administration's Republican base, reacted to high casualties, a yawning credibility gap, and severe strains on the military by shifting toward a "fortress America" kind of isolationism, including support for building walls along the northern and southern borders of the country and other severe anti-immigrant measures. George W. Bush did make use of the War on Terror to manage a narrow victory in 2004. But in 2005 foreign policy in general and the war in Iraq in particular emerged not as boons for conservative Republicans but as liabilities as they looked ahead with trepidation to elections in 2006 and 2008.

Although the debacle in Iraq may have doomed the supremacists' animating vision, it did not put an end to the generalized War on Terror—a struggle against a spectral enemy as incapable of being defeated as it is of being seen and as terrifying as the American imagination can render it. The War on Terror originated as a tactical ploy to advance the larger supremacist vision, a strategy for supplanting the prudent multilateralism of international pragmatists by justifying a unilateralist American war in Iraq. But it has taken on a life of its own—so much so that victory over those who struck America in 2001 now primarily requires escaping the maelstrom of the War on Terror itself. A strategy for success in this struggle requires more than understanding who unleashed the storm and why. It requires understanding its self-reinforcing dynamics, how they can be reversed, and how America can sustain an appropriate and effective level of vigilance without unleashing forces that do al-Qaeda's work for it.

Chapter 5

The War on Terror Whirlwind

The notion of a war against al-Qaeda-type terrorists arose as an immediate reaction to 9/11. It then rapidly developed into an abstract and far-reaching War on Terror. The supremacist faction within the Bush administration advanced that slogan to launch a neo-imperial war in Iraq; a war that had nothing to do with terrorism but everything to do with extravagant ideological and political ambitions. When Iraq became a political albatross those ambitions were crushed, but the War on Terror took on a life of its own. It became a kind of permanent national emergency. Its effects surged across the government, overwhelming both legal and budgetary constraints. It has engulfed American society in a whirlwind of activities, none of which can ever be proven successful, but all of which can be criticized as inadequate.

The mechanisms that power this whirlwind are not under the control of any group or collection of individuals. In this sense the origins of the War on Terror, as described in the previous chapter, are quite different from the sources of its continuing and self-reinforcing power. The spiraling reactions that produced this vortex have arisen from diffuse fears of catastrophic terrorism, evoking urgent demands to eliminate or at least abate the threat. This imperative justified the attitude of emergency and defined the situation as a nation mobilizing for war. Opportunities were thereupon created for every group, every company, every sector of society, and every lobbyist to advance its product or preference as crucially important for success in the War on Terror.[1] As voters demanded a greater sense of security against terrorism and as more money was spent on counterterrorism programs, more people, more companies, more lobbyists, and more politicians became identified with the War on Terror as a key element in their own success. This led them not only to accept the categorical importance of the War on Terror but to imagine wider and even more sinister threats, justifying an expanding array of products, policies, and projects for preventing attacks or for coping with their consequences if they occur.

Some reassurance can be gained from the invincible principle of entropy. All forces weaken eventually. All orderliness eventually becomes disorder. Even tornados dissipate. So it will be, eventually, with the whirlwind of the War on Terror. But eventually can be a long time, and the costs and risks of delay are high. The better we understand the War on Terror for the self-organizing trap that it is, the sooner we can proceed to the tasks of recovery, readjustment, and development of measured and sustainable approaches to the real problems we face from al-Qaeda and its clones.

For the War on Terror still does hold America in its grip. Ordinary American citizens along with politicians and bureaucrats are trapped by threats they can neither accurately gauge nor eliminate and by public imperatives that impel them to demand expensive, damaging, and ultimately unsustainable policies. Tragically, Americans cannot help but lose this war, because it is a war with themselves. Escaping from the trap of the War on Terror thus first requires understanding that we are caught in its nets and that the more we strive for "victory" the more entangled we become. With this imperative in mind, we can now try to understand the War on Terror thoroughly enough to think about escaping from it and then coping with the real threats posed to us by "terrorists with global reach."

MECHANISMS OF THE WAR ON TERROR

American democracy was constructed by our founding fathers as a political marketplace. They rejected in fact if not in so many words the idea that the elected representatives of the people could, would, or even should join together in calm deliberation to devise policies most appropriate for achieving the national interest. Such an image of Americans and American politicians, though often honored rhetorically, was viewed by James Madison, Roger Sherman, Alexander Hamilton, and other key Constitution makers and defenders as naive and dangerous. Men would seek elected office to serve their own individual or factional interest. The groups who put them into office would be rewarded. Those who supported losing candidates, failed to enter the fray, or failed to diligently lobby on their own behalf would see their interests suffer. With all citizens aware of their interests, political participation would be lively. Each interest would form its own faction. Each faction would act as a "watchdog" against the others. Temporary coalitions based on unhappy compromises would be the main route to legislation of any kind.[2] The overall result would be to achieve what might be minimally required from government by individual factions at the cost of sacrificing what would have been truly desirable by all. The array of changing policies would reflect, as changing prices do in an economic market, the fluctuating resolution of political forces arising from the diverse and contradictory demands of a fragmented polity and the limited supply of revenue and governmental capacity.

In many ways the enormously complicated system put in place by the founding fathers does behave like an economic market. When some economic activities produce higher returns than others, suppliers losing out in this competition lower prices or change what they produce. These repeated cycles move the system of the marketplace through a fluctuating but fundamentally stable equilibrium that tends, through adjustments in prices, to match available resources to the changing demands of the population. Similarly, in the political marketplace, when a majority pushes its self-interested agenda very successfully, citizens flock to join it, thereby decreasing the benefits available to each member of the majority and raising incentives for other citizens to oppose it. These countermobilizations then attract those excluded from the majority's agenda or those within the majority unsatisfied by what they are receiving as part of it. Again, the system tends, through constant competition, toward a dynamic equilibrium in the distribution of political power.

Under some economic conditions and with regard to some kinds of problems markets fail, however. For example, some tasks and some "public goods," such as street lighting, national security, and a court system, are available to all individuals equally. I do not receive more national security for my tax payment than the citizen who pays much less in taxes than I do. Such tasks will not be performed if left to the market. Since no one can be excluded from the "good," no one has reason to pay for it. "Negative externalities" can also foil market mechanisms. For example, if no individual or company has to pay for dumping garbage in the river or into the air, then even though all may suffer enormously from pollution, economic competition will produce increasing, not decreasing, amounts of it. Nor do markets, whether economic or political, automatically respect collective priorities or values. Increasingly, Americans wonder whether the market mechanism can be relied on for allocating medical care without outraging basic social and ethical norms. Laws ban citizens from buying and selling organs, while massive government intervention through Medicare and Medicaid seeks to compensate for market failure by providing masses of the nonwealthy with some minimal degree of health care.

Another standardly acknowledged source of market failure is poor information. If a population of consumers is not informed enough to know the real benefits of particular products, the market will produce a lower supply of those products—whether books or windmills—than would be optimal. In other words, market failure can result from false beliefs. If consumers falsely believe in the value of a particular product, then supplies called forth by market competition will be much greater than those that would be optimal while other more efficient or rational investments will be starved of resources. This source of market failure is not particularly serious as long as consumers can learn, from the nonperformance of the goods they purchase, of the inefficiency of their purchasing decisions. But false beliefs can become a devastating source of market failure not only if they are pervasive, but if the effectiveness of the products they lead people to buy is difficult or impossible to judge.

At root the ballooning War on Terror can be attributed to a gigantic political market failure. In its final official report the 9/11 Commission seemed to sense the dangerous potential for irrationality associated with subjecting the terrorist threat to the tender mercies of the political marketplace. Among its numerous recommendations were many that urged a wider array and greatly increased expenditures for security-related programs. But the report also warned that efforts to cope with an essentially unlimited array of potential challenges would confront the country with a serious problem of runaway spending. It admonished Congress "not [to] use this money as a pork barrel," even as it acknowledged the difficulty of devising and enforcing "criteria to measure risk and vulnerability." Indeed the commissioners understood how unnatural the American political system would find the demands of the War on Terror. All ten were seasoned politicians with direct and intimate experience with the way that system works. Accordingly, they believed that the decision-making process to allocate War on Terror funding would be a "free-for-all over money," noting that it would be "understandable that representatives will work to protect the interests of their home states or districts."[3]

Sensing, perhaps, the futility of resisting the frenzy of unregulated spending an open-ended War on Terror would unleash, the commission's response to the problem it identified was halfhearted and almost fatalistic. The commissioners exhorted American citizens and politicians to put the "national interest" first, remembering that "this issue [the War on Terror] is too important for politics as usual to prevail." In addition it urged creation of "a panel of security experts" to make key allocation decisions and establish criteria for judging the efficacy of counterterrorism programs.[4] However, no arguments were offered from the experience of the commissioners or the analysis of its staff as to why readers might expect this advice to be accepted and implemented.

Indeed, just as the commission anticipated, major problems of administration and allocation quickly developed for the vast sums of money involved in the counterterrorism effort. In the beginning of the War on Terror funds were practically thrown at the problem, with no guidelines in place and little thought at all about priorities or cost effectiveness. Guiding ideas then emerged based on a fuzzy sense of which locations might be at greatest risk, but whatever strategic thinking guided these allocations was overwhelmed by practices that spread the money to all parts of the country, regardless of risk assessment.

WAR ON TERROR DYNAMICS: CHASING DOLLARS AND GRINDING AXES

In Chapter 2 we considered the vast sums being spent on the War on Terror, but it is wonderfully instructive to drill down beneath the general debate over huge appropriations bills for broad categories of activities by examining one particular agency's experience with homeland security funding. According to a 2005 report of the inspector general of the Small Business Administration (SBA), 85 percent of the businesses that applied for and were granted its low-interest counterterrorism loans failed to establish their eligibility. Seven thousand such loans by private lenders, worth more than $3 billion, were authorized by the SBA. These disbursements were part of a January 2002 congressional program labeled Supplemental Terrorist Activity Relief (STAR) designed to go far beyond disaster assistance to companies directly impacted by the events of 9/11 to assist businesses nationwide that might have been "adversely affected by the [September 11] attacks."[5] Under this program, for example, the SBA underwrote $22 million in loans to Dunkin' Donuts franchises in nine different states.

The STAR program, of course, was implemented very soon after the 2001 attacks as part of the enormous array of spending increases and program creation described in Chapter 3. These expenditures, which continued to increase for at least three more years, reflected the perception of the government and of American citizens that the threat of terrorism called for comprehensive and immediate action with little regard for fiscal constraints. This kind of urgent, even frenzied mobilization was mounted under the rubric of the War on Terror. As is typical in wartime, these activities were not guided by norms of cost effectiveness or affordability. Instead the effort was carried forward with the slogans and emotions of a war—especially defense against impending threats to national security and collective determination to achieve victory over the country's enemies.[6]

By 2005 there were signs that the sheer magnitude of the expenditures involved was beginning to affect the debate over how money to fight terrorism should be spent. While the Bush administration increased its total homeland security request for FY 2006 by 8.6 percent to $49.9 billion (compared to FY 2005),[7] cuts were still made in some areas. For example, in line with a slight decrease in the president's budget request for "State and Local Homeland Security" Congress appropriated $120 million less for "Urban Area Security Initiative" grants for FY 2006 than it did for FY 2005.[8] It soon became apparent, however, that this cut reflected not a substantially new departure toward rationally matching available resources to important objectives but another stage in the continuing and bitter battle over the spoils of the War on Terror.

A major divide in the ongoing fight over funding lies roughly between urban and rural areas. Famously, Wyoming, the vice president's home state, received more money per capita in homeland security funds in 2003 than any other state. Alaska was a close second.[9] Residents of Maine, one of whose senators, Susan Collins, chairs the Homeland Security and Governmental Affairs Committee, also did well. In 2004 Maine received more homeland security funds per capita than Massachusetts, New York, New Jersey, or Connecticut.[10] This funding pattern has triggered regular and sometimes fierce arguments on Capitol Hill over the role that different methods of evaluating risk of terrorist attacks should play in War on Terror funding.

For example, on July 12, 2005, the Senate considered the FY 2006 Homeland Security Appropriations Act. Senators Susan Collins and Joseph Lieberman had drafted language for the bill that determined the allocation of funds using complex formulas and a range of factors that would guarantee base amounts of funding to every state and territory. Speaking on behalf of both Democratic and Republican senators representing states with large urban areas or states in the Southwest thought to have high-value targets for terrorists, and citing a supporting letter from the High-Threat City Joint Working Group on Homeland Security signed by the mayors of twenty-two of the largest cities in the country, Senator Dianne Feinstein (California) spoke on behalf of an amendment to "ensure that covered grants are allocated based on an assessment of threat, vulnerability, and consequence to the maximum extent possible." Senator Collins responded by noting that "the potential of terrorist attacks against rural targets is increasingly recognized as a national security threat" and went on to cite the possibility of terrorist attacks on America's food supply, electricity grids, and power plants. Serving as president pro tem of the Senate, Senator Judd Gregg (New Hampshire) defended the bill as it stood, against amendments from both Collins and Feinstein, by using the tried-and-true method of splitting the difference to achieve a "fair division of the spoils." The theory in the bill, he said, "was to have threat-based allocation" while using formulas that "protected and grandfathered all the States . . . So the actual appropriation in the bill falls about halfway between the two theories put forward here."[11]

The fact is that persuasive arguments against using high-risk targets as the basis for allocating funds rationally are easily made. Early in 2006 former Oklahoma governor Frank Keating warned that a policy of concentrating homeland security funds in high-risk areas would "leave holes in our safety net that invites penetration." Such a policy would boomerang by channeling foreign terrorists to strike in an unprotected "heartland community." Along with other examples of how antiterror funds could be usefully disbursed in rural areas across all fifty states, Keating cited radio communications problems on 9/11 in New

York, in light of which he called "financing for interoperable radio equipment . . . a top priority for communities large and small."[12]

These general arguments for spreading War on Terror funding across the country to rural and urban areas alike are well known. Less well publicized are the exact uses to which many of the "war resources" provided by the federal government have been put. In 2004 North Carolina officials issued an unusually detailed report about homeland security expenditures in that state. According to this report North Carolina used homeland security funds to buy new trucks or SUVs for half its counties; $320,000 was spent in the town of Lincoln for a "command and control center," a weather station for mountainous Cherokee County was installed for $5,800, and $53,800 was spent in the state's smallest county, Tyrrell—population 4,200. Arguing that Charlotte had not received its fair share of the funds, the city's fire chief put it this way: "Everybody has their own interpretation of a threat. Down East, they think it's hog farms. In the Outer Banks, they think it's tourism. But historically, terrorism has been aimed at buildings and symbols, which Charlotte has a lot more of."[13]

The political dynamics that produced this kind of widely distributed pork to worried and appreciative constituents greatly complicated efforts within the government to try to rein in spending or at least rationalize it. After the attacks on the London Underground, DHS Secretary Michael Chertoff received harsh public criticism for his response to calls for more funding to protect subway riders. At that time he stressed how much was already being done to strengthen security for the nation's railways but also said that he and the department were determined to establish and enforce priorities in the use and stewardship of the nation's resources in the War on Terror, priorities that would require it to carefully husband its funding in strict regard to measurements of risk. "DHS must base its work," he said, "on priorities that are driven by risk. Our goal is to maximize our security, but not security 'at any price' . . . Our stewardship will demand many attributes—the willingness to set priorities; disciplined execution of those priorities; sound financial management; and a commitment to measure performance."[14]

Indeed, at the very beginning of 2006 the Department of Homeland Security distributed new guidelines to state and local governments. In keeping with Chertoff's commitment to triage, that is, to formulas for allocating funding based on risk analysis and the opportunities to use funds efficiently to reduce risks, these guidelines meant that fifty medium and large cities would not automatically receive the levels of counterterrorism funding to which they had been accustomed. Risk analyses were being conducted that would result, according to the DHS, in funds being allocated where they would do the most good. That might have been good news for cities such as New York and Los Angeles, but it was bad news for Omaha and St. Louis. As an Omaha official put it, "We still are an urban area. And we still have risks. No one can predict where a terrorist might strike. Look where Timothy McVeigh struck. It was Oklahoma City."[15]

A closer look at the new guidelines shows just how tough it is and will be to discipline antiterror spending. Even as DHS announced the new emphasis on risk-based evaluation of applications for $765 million in Urban Area Security Initiative grants, it also broadened the array of eligible purposes cities could apply to use the monies for. Under the new DHS rules cities need not cite terrorist threats as the reason for applying for counterterrorism funds. Instead, any city seeking these funds is required to specify the relationship of the expenditures they would make to enhancing their capacity to prevent or cope with a list of approved scenarios of terrorist attacks *or* natural disasters. These include influenza outbreaks, hurricanes, and chemical contamination attacks, as well as nuclear explosions and conventional bombings. Although the funds were appropriated under the rubric of the War on Terror, applicants need only show that monies would be used in ways that "could *also* help during a terrorist attack."[16] This dramatic loosening of DHS restrictions on eligibility for its funding, announced as part of an attempt purportedly designed to control spending within the overall War on Terror, is telling evidence of how irresistible are the political forces galvanized by the very existence of the War on Terror.

Space permits review of just a sampling of the imaginative ways Americans have sought to use counterterrorism to advance their own particular interests or pet projects. After September 2001, the Property Casualty Insurers Association of America successfully lobbied for passage of the Terrorism Risk Insurance Act (TRIA), which protected the industry against large claims that might be associated with damage wreaked by terrorist attacks. In 2004 the association's spokesmen praised the National Association of Insurance Commissioners (NAIC) for declaring their support for a two-year extension of the act. Robert Zeman, senior vice president for the association, addressed members of the industry's Terrorism Implementation Working Group: "Our goal, with the assistance of the NAIC, is to make sure that there is a stable insurance market with an appropriate mechanism to address the significant catastrophic loss that can occur as a result of terrorist acts." Zeman's sentiments were echoed by Charles E. Symington, Jr., a senior vice president of the Independent Insurance Agents and Brokers of America: "Without the certainty of a federal backstop, insurers and their policyholders are at risk in the event of terrorist attacks." David Snyder of the American Insurance Association put it simply: "Just as Americans are doing everything we can to help emergency first responders to terrorist acts, TRIA helps the financial first responders."[17]

In March 2002, the National District Attorneys Association passed a resolution condemning the attacks of September 11 as brutal and cowardly and as "clearly intended to intimidate our nation and weaken its resolve." Attached to this resolution was the association's new "antiterrorism policy." The policy emphasized definition of terrorism as criminal activity, thereby highlighting the central role of district attorneys in the War on Terror. "Terrorism is a crime. As prosecutors, we are the ones who are responsible for prosecuting crimes. . . . The battle against terrorism must be a priority for America, and we cannot be distracted from our goal." All prosecuting attorneys were urged to become "integral, productive and informed members of their district's Anti-Terrorism Task Force." The association, however, decried the tendency "to divert money from criminal endeavors to first responders and anti-terrorism efforts" and emphasized that "prosecutors must be explicitly included in funding legislation." In addition to coordinating their activities with state, local, and federal agencies, district attorneys were urged "not [to] wait for an incident to happen" but to immediately "prepare model state legislation or work with [their] state legislature in drafting anti-terrorism legislation" and "to insure that prosecutors are included in any funding legislation."[18]

In 2003 the Association of American Veterinary Medical Colleges issued a special issue of the *Journal of Veterinary Medical Education* under the title: "An Agenda For Action: Veterinary Medicine's Crucial Role in Public Health and Biodefense and the Obligation of Academic Veterinary Medicine to Respond." Citing in particular the possibility that terrorists could introduce hoof-and-mouth disease to decimate American livestock herds, the association called on "the national leadership of America . . . to recognize and nurture the potential of the veterinary profession . . . to meet a national agenda for biosecurity." The association demanded funding increases, especially at the national level, "to increase student enrollments in the veterinary schools . . . and . . . to help the veterinary schools and colleges meet the diverse goals that can be expected of them and . . . to assure meeting the national agenda for a country well-protected against biological threats of both natural and deliberate origin."[19]

In January 2002 Senator Max Baucus (Montana) received a letter with the subject heading "Pharmacy Involvement in Preparedness for and Response to Public Health Emergencies and Terrorism Attacks." The letter was signed by eleven professional and trade associations linked to the pharmaceutical industry, including the American Association of Colleges of Pharmacy, the American Pharmaceutical Association, the National Association of Chain Drug Stores, and the American Society of Health-System Pharmacists. The letter urged "a prominent role for pharmacy in any new legislation that would enhance the ability of the nation to prepare for and respond to an emergency public health situation or terrorist attack." The letter pushed hard for substantial new funding initiatives to train pharmacists as diagnostic first responders and for research in schools and colleges of pharmacy for "research that is directly related to the prevention of and response to terrorism. Examples include ongoing research on antibiotic resistance and the effects of various natural product extracts on bioterrorism agents such as anthrax." Aside from funds for training and research, the government was urged to fund a new and extensive online communication system for pharmacies and their providers and distributors for monitoring the impact of emergency situations or terrorist attacks and disseminating information; to include pharmacy professionals in federal and state terrorism task forces; and in the development and implementation of procedures for stockpiling and distributing drugs in reaction to terrorist attacks. The letter also called for the government to create a kind of pharmacist SWAT team—"a federal pharmacy reserve team to be deployed, when local resources are overwhelmed" regardless of state-by-state regulations.[20]

In April 2002 testimony before the Senate Appropriations Committee, the American Academy of Pediatrics, endorsed by two other pediatric medicine associations, noted that in addition to the pediatricians' traditional priorities, another had been added as a "critical priority— terrorism and emergency preparedness."[21] Their testimony pointed out that "children are not little adults—they require different equipment and supplies, as well as different drugs and drug dosages, if they are to survive a terrorist attack." To integrate pediatricians and child-care facilities into teams of first responders and other public health agencies concerned with terrorism, the academy said it was joining "the broader public health community in recommending at least $940 million for upgrading state and local health capacities in FY 2003."[22]

In the immediate aftermath of 9/11 the board of directors of the American Psychological Association (APA) established a Subcommittee on Psychology's Response to Terrorism. While individual psychologists received considerable funding from intelligence agencies and other branches of government for studies of the "psychology of terrorism,"[23] the APA as a whole sought to join the War on Terror via consulting, outreach, information dissemination, and expertise organization. These contributions were accompanied by and helped justify efforts to advance a long-term institutional goal—increased funding for mental health. The APA thus charged its subcommittee on terrorism with "advocating for legislation to increase mental health resources and access to care." According to an official publication of APA, it "supported the Post Terrorism Mental Health Improvement Act, introduced by Edward M. Kennedy (D-Massachusetts). The bill calls for providing more money to improve states' response capabilities in ensuring that people who need mental health services as a result of terrorist acts get them."[24]

The same dynamic pushing health care providers and activists to clamor for greater funding to fight the War on Terror also affected specific health-related government agencies. Consider the National Institutes of Health as an example. It has been anxious to avoid funding cuts in favor of more urgent War on Terror-related expenditures. It has also been creative in its search for rationales for increased funding to support its crucial contributions to the antiterror struggle. Under "Biodefense Research" NIH's FY 2004 budget announced that the program's "number one priority . . . is supporting research needed for the war against terrorism. To guide this research, NIH last year developed a *Strategic Plan for Biodefense Research*."[25] The total budget request for this program for FY 2004 was $1.6 billion. The program has been a rewarding one for NIH. The FY 2007 budget proposed biodefense funding at $1.9 billion, a 19 percent increase over three years. Of course it is no wonder that NIH raised the profile of biodefense within its portfolio of activities. It was simply responding to the imperatives announced by the Department of Health and Human Services (HHS) as a whole, within which it is located. Just as HHS was fighting for funds with other departments by using the War on Terror, so did NIH use biodefense to do the same within HHS. In his letter introducing the FY 2004 budget request for his department, Secretary of Health and Human Services Tommy Thompson left no doubt as to the crucial role his department] was playing in the War on Terror.

It has been over a year since the tragic events of September 11th occurred, and we continue our vigorous commitment to protecting our Nation. Many of our programs at HHS provide the necessary services that contribute to the war on terrorism and protect us against biologic and other threats. In this area, we are focusing on preparedness at the local level, ensuring the safety of food products, and research and development on vaccines and other therapies to counter potential bioterrorist attacks. As we look to the future, we must continue to expand research, develop anti-bioterrorism strategies and encourage the use of new and emerging technologies. With the President's FY 2004 Budget, the Department of Health and Human Services will uphold its commitment to making our Nation safe.[26]

The War on Terror has also proved to be invaluable for interest groups and politicians with axes to grind. Within one week after the 9/11 attacks, gun control lobbying organizations began campaigns linking their long-standing policy preferences for increased restrictions on access to firearms to the need to protect the country against terrorism. An extensive study sponsored by the Brady Center to Stop Gun Violence quoted Bush's November 2001 speech to the United Nations: "We have a responsibility," said the president, "to deny weapons to terrorists and to actively prevent private citizens from providing them." That was all the anti-gun lobby needed to use the War on Terror for its own purposes. "Terrorists and guns go together," reads the Brady Center study. "The gun is part of the essential tool kit of domestic and foreign terrorists alike. Guns are used to commit terrorist acts, and guns are used by terrorists to resist law enforcement efforts at apprehension and arrest. The oft-seen file footage of Osama Bin Laden, aiming his AK-47 at an unknown target, is now a familiar reminder of the incontrovertible connection between terrorism and guns. . . . For terrorists around the world, the United States is the Great Gun Bazaar."[27]

The War on Terror presented equally potent and equally irresistible opportunities to the National Rifle Association. Quite naturally the NRA claims that the attacks justified their long-standing and diametrically opposed view that the more Americans trained to use and in possession of firearms, the better. In April 2002, NRA executive director Wayne LaPierre was reported to be celebrating "increased momentum since Sept. 11 for laws permitting concealed guns." After the attacks in September 2001, said LaPierre, "people are unsettled and have a fear of the unknown and of a threat that could come from anywhere, they'd rather face that threat with a firearm than without one."[28] In 2003 the gun lobby announced a new program called NRASafe, described by LaPierre as involving all NRA members in a kind of national neighborhood watch program within the War on Terror. "As freedom's keepers, we cannot be a passive observer in this epic confrontation with evil. I believe this great association has a unique role to play in homeland security. God helps he who helps himself, and nobody knows that better than NRA members. We understand that liberty requires eternal vigilance. Not just as a government, but as a people."[29]

Other interest groups found it more difficult to be specific about War on Terror rationales for funding their particular programs. They nonetheless sought to associate themselves with the campaign, often, as in the case of the airlines and restaurant owners, with pleas for federal support based on the particular sensitivity of their industries to the aftermath of 9/11. In the case of the airline industry, this claim was undoubtedly true, however most analysts agree that on September 11, 2001, the airline industry was already undergoing a crisis of profitability. In any event, within a week after the attacks the CEOs of major airlines were asking the federal government for $17.5 billion in cash and loans to save the industry from the effects of the attacks. In testimony before the Senate Committee on Commerce, Science, and Transportation, Leo F. Mullin, chairman and CEO of Delta Airlines, spoke on behalf of the Air Transport Association—the airline lobbying organization. Mullin quickly invoked the War on Terror by quoting then-Transportation Secretary Norman Minetta's exhortation not to "allow the enemy to

win this war by restricting our freedom of mobility." He then asked
Congress to grant the industry a total of $24 billion in direct support
and tax breaks.[30]

Spokesmen for other interest groups expatiated on their constituencies' contributions to the general integrity of the national community,
now under general threat, or strived to protect themselves against government decisions to reduce funding for their programs in the name of
more vividly counterterrorist activities. In November 2001, John J.
Sweeney, president of the AFL-CIO, told the U.S. House of Representatives Committee on Education and the Workforce that shortly after
9/11 his organization had appointed a Special Committee on Economic
Security. Sweeney noted that nearly a thousand union members were
among those who died as a result of "the tragic events of September 11
[that] shocked and horrified the nation and the world." Sweeney called
on Congress to respond to the attacks "with a comprehensive economic
recovery package that boosts the economy while providing support
where needs are greatest." He called for "*real* assistance for laid off
workers, a substantial infusion of direct federal aid to state governments
. . . tax rebates for lower paid workers," and investments in "building,
renovating and modernizing the nation's sadly neglected infrastructure
to boost our national security." He also emphasized that the "attacks
on the World Trade Center and the Pentagon and reports of other
possible or planned attacks serve to underscore our vulnerability and
the urgency of addressing long-ignored critical infrastructure needs." At
minimum, however, the AFL-CIO wanted to make sure that no other
group "take[s] advantage of this painful moment in our national life
and of our collective desire for unity to push through costly, divisive
and ill-advised tax cuts for the well-to-do and that ignore the needs of
working families."[31] Organizations supporting affordable housing made
similar arguments. F. Barton Harvey, chairman and CEO of one such
group, the Enterprise Foundation, warned the Senate's Committee on
Banking, Housing, and Urban Affairs that the "terrible events" of September 11 had "pushed the economy into what could be a prolonged
recession . . . Housing needs," he continued, "likely will worsen further." He advocated substantial increases in housing funding by the
federal government, concluding with another invocation of 9/11: "Now
more than ever, our nation must be strong and united. We believe that

sources of that strength and unity include family, faith, community and a place called home. Now more than ever, home matters."[32]

Inside the government the War on Terror created comparably robust opportunities for protecting or enhancing bureaucratic interests. Every year since 2001 departments and bureaus have strenuously competed with one another to increase or protect budget allocations by stressing their anti-terror contributions. The cost of this pressure on agencies to converge toward missions related to the War on Terror was vividly apparent in the Federal Emergency Management Agency's failed performance in New Orleans after Hurricane Katrina as compared to its effective responses to earlier powerful hurricanes in Florida. Blaming the disastrous federal response to the devastation in New Orleans on the assimilation of FEMA by the Department of Homeland Security, former FEMA Director Michael Brown testified that the War on Terror had made disaster management a "stepchild" within the department. Had there been a report, he said, that "a terrorist had blown up the 17th Street Canal levee, then everybody would have jumped all over that."[33] In other words, aside from issues of sheer administrative incompetence, FEMA's assimilation within the Department of Homeland Security had reduced its preparedness by pushing it away from a focus on natural disasters toward postures more appropriate for a civil defense role in the War on Terror.[34] Even the Department of Homeland Security's approved list of fifteen distinct disaster scenarios—scenarios that limit the kinds of requests for funds each city and state in the country can make—was produced in substantial measure by the push and pull of special bureaucratic interests striving for inclusion of their preferred disasters, those that would make their missions eligible for War on Terror funding. The pattern of inclusion and exclusion of disasters from the list obviously reflects not only a set of real concerns but the desires and successes of some agencies inside the government and some regions of the country to achieve easier eligibility for counterterrorism funding at the expense of others, for example, those who worry about plague (included in the scenario list) not Ebola fever (not included); or those who worry about cyber-attacks (on the list) but not about attacks on liquid natural gas tankers (not on the list).[35] In 2004 I asked one official in close touch with the allocation process to rank the War on Terror on a scale of one to ten. I told him to treat ten as describing the Manhattan Project—when the federal government's focused concern with the German threat to develop an atomic weapon during World War II led it to put scientific experts fully in charge of the project to beat the Germans to the nuclear punch. I told him to treat one as describing an allocation system that was 100 percent "wag the dog"—responsive entirely to political posturing and political pressures. His considered answer was "between 1 and 1.5."

Absent the ability of experts or anyone else to discern and publicly describe actual evidence of the character of and limits to the terrorist threat, there is no real limit to the justifications for spending money that can be generated out of the pervasive public readiness to support counterterrorism measures and the political profit to be made by appearing to be playing a vital role in the War on Terror. Accordingly, enthusiasts of all kinds can use the War on Terror to raise money and mobilize political capital behind long-cherished policy goals, whether noble or ignoble, wise or foolish. Thus have public health activists used the War on Terror. Laurie Garrett, a champion of World Health Organization efforts to mobilize the planet's resources against the threat of pandemics, has characterized avian flu as a disease with global reach that could compromise national security and American military operations in Afghanistan and Iraq.[36] Others have promoted bio-security as a concept anchored in the threat of bioterrorism but including all sources of dangerous diseases, thereby bolstering their efforts to prepare for various kinds of pandemics that might arise.[37] Organizations fighting AIDS in Africa have been torn between arguments that compare casualty rates to show that AIDS is a bigger threat than terrorism[38] and arguments that claim that the devastation AIDS causes in African countries creates breeding grounds and safe havens for terrorists.[39] Americans motivated by either humanitarian or neo-imperial ideals exhort America to make huge economic and military commitments in devastated parts of the world. In pursuit of these objectives they point to the anarchic conditions in Afghanistan that led to a Taliban government ready to protect Osama bin Laden. To prevent more Afghanistans, they say, the War on Terror requires the United States to intervene around the world to prevent or reconstruct "failed states."[40] Others insist that fighting an effective War on Terror will require ending public policies they oppose, such as large-scale tax cuts or ballistic missile defense.[41] In a speech that drew as much on the strange logic of fighting a symptom, "terror," as on the putative target—enemies of the United

States plotting to use catastrophic violence against us—Senator Debbie Stabenow of Michigan urged her fellow senators to "think of the terror a breast cancer patient feels when she is told she needs tamoxifen and cannot afford the $136 a month." Accordingly, Stabenow contended, fighting terrorism means adopting more generous health and drug insurance programs to fight "the terror that too many of our seniors experience when they find themselves in a situation with an illness and they cannot afford the medications they need to be well."[42]

"COVER YOUR ASS" IN THE WAR ON TERROR

Stabenow was probing the rhetorical limits of the War on Terror, but the crisis in American health care associated with extensive litigation and enormous malpractice insurance premiums offers important insights into another source of the multiple vicious cycles that constitute the War on Terror. Doctors in many states face skyrocketing malpractice insurance premiums associated with lawsuits that regularly arise following tragic treatment outcomes. In many cases culpability is obvious, and awards are justly made. But what drives this problem toward the crisis it has become is a structural condition that cripples the market mechanism, based as it is on "fee for service rendered." In obstetrics, for example, small variations in treatment or in the status of a pregnancy—variations that may well lie beneath the observational horizon of the practitioner, can have massive downstream implications. While the state of our knowledge allows doctors to make informed judgments, it is not possible to anticipate when and under what exact circumstances very bad outcomes will occur, that is, when the "service rendered" will be catastrophically less satisfactory than the fee-paying patient had come to expect. After the fact, however, it is often possible to trace exactly the causal chain that led to the outcome, including hypothetical tests and treatments than could have prevented or meliorated it. This imbalance between forensic hindsight and diagnostic foresight makes even the best practitioners enormously vulnerable to lawsuits. One result is that physicians, and in particular obstetricians, are leaving the profession. Another is that doctors are driven toward increasing numbers of ever more expensive and decreasingly helpful tests. In these and other ways this condition of market failure ends up increasing the cost and reducing the supply of health care for everyone.

A very similar kind of failure is occurring in the American political marketplace with respect to terrorism. Americans are convinced their society is threatened with highly potent terrorist pathogens that pose deadly but essentially unpredictable threats. Government officials are being held responsible for protecting voters against those threats. With near-universal belief in the presence of the pathogens and their deadly potential, the only publicly defensible position to take is energetic action. But what kind of action? how much? in which directions? where? at what cost? and for how long? Whatever the real terrorist threat inside the United States may be, the fact is that it cannot be seen. If it cannot be seen, there is no systematic way to tailor our responses to meet the threat. But if an attack does occur, it will be easy after the fact to determine who did not do that which could have prevented it, just as it has been easy to allocate blame toward government officials who can be portrayed as having had access to crucial information about the 9/11 hijackers but who did not use it.

This knowledge, that blame will be easily allocated after the fact with little memory of how nearly impossible it was to predict the attack before the fact, will naturally drive officials at all levels to do what doctors do when they fear lawsuits—choose as conservatively as possible whenever given the opportunity. This means funding more programs targeting increasingly obscure threats at higher levels and for longer periods of time. Given our democratic system, widespread beliefs in the potency of the threat and the possibility of government action to reduce it also means that politicians and bureaucrats will tend to compete with one another to portray the threat as even more important than do their political opponents, thereby driving the system toward an overproduction of decreasingly useful counterterrorism measures, leaving fewer and fewer resources for meeting other needs.

Within the government this particular mechanism is known colloquially as CYA—"cover your ass." In the War on Terror it operates, within regular departments, the intelligence community, the military, and law enforcement agencies throughout the country, to weaken and slow our system's capacity to distinguish useful from wasteful activity. With an enemy imagined as totally ruthless, infinitely cunning, and interested in inflicting as much damage as possible on America, every attack that anyone can imagine occurring eventually becomes a threat that must be considered and countered. Since it is essentially impossible to predict where and when a destructive attack will occur but rather easy to know after the event how it could have been prevented, each decision maker, from voters to bureaucrats to senators and representatives, feels impelled to endorse every measure advanced as possibly helpful in the War on Terror. The compulsion to do so stems in large part from the fear not of terrorism per se but of being blamed after an attack for having vetoed, opposed, or shortchanged precisely the program that might, after the fact, be determined as the measure that could have prevented it, had it only been implemented as proposed. In this way fear of terrorist attacks metastasizes into second- and third-order fears that feed not only on patriotism and profit, but also on fears of being held personally accountable for allowing the unpreventable.

HOW EXPERTS HELP POWER THE WAR ON TERROR

One might imagine that the scientific community, including experts in the social sciences, would be a brake on these vicious cycles. To an extent it is. Experts regularly explain that people (including policymakers) are psychologically predisposed to greatly exaggerating risks of specific negative events, to having enormous difficulty avoiding concentration on very improbable but very particular possible disasters, and to attributing more credibility to pessimistic and worst-case scenarios than to less threatening information.[43] Such explanations, however, generally have little impact on public opinion or on government planners, especially officials exposed to political pressures and in control of budgets. Much more potent are the siren songs of experts who warn of threats yet to be imagined and provide solutions for those threats they might be able to discover if only granted the necessary research funds.

Certainly the media prefers talking heads that sound the tocsin of alarm, and so does the War on Terror. The relationship between the War on Terror and the news media, especially radio talk shows and television news networks, is particularly robust. It is probably not too strong to say that the lifeblood of the War on Terror is the attention of the media to scary questions about disasters that terrorists could visit upon us and to evidence of incompetence or unpreparedness in relation to these imaginable disasters. In short, the War on Terror requires that the media energetically and continuously encourage Americans to ask themselves one all-important question—"Are you and your family really safe?" The news media is happy to oblige. It revels in headlines that maintain the image of a constant state of semi-emergency. For the national media, it is as if, for a local news outlet, a gigantic blizzard or hurricane were permanently identified as "possibly about to strike our city." An added attraction for the media is that terrorism fears make for compelling news stories that are almost as cheap to produce as weather stories. In the two years following 9/11 MSNBC and Fox News saw their viewership soar while their production costs actually declined. Revenues for the three news networks rose so satisfyingly that in 2004 Fox News, CNN, and MSNBC, for the first time, all showed sizable profits.[44]

Apart from the encouragement and remuneration that experts sounding terrorism alarms receive from the media, the relationship of experts and expertise to government funding provides its own powerful impetus for the War on Terror. In May 2002 Dan Mote, president of the University of Maryland, spoke on behalf of the Association of American Universities and the National Association of State Universities and Land Grant Colleges to support increased National Science Foundation (NSF) funding for basic research. The dominant theme in his remarks was that "the events of 9/11 and the subsequent very real concerns with homeland security add even more urgency to the need to fund basic research." Mote pointed out that the supply of international students in graduate and professional science and engineering programs was likely to drop, thereby depleting America's supply of scientific and technical workers. He described the situation as a "crisis whose magnitude has elevated substantially since 9/11," and emphasized that "funding for NSF can make the difference." He went on to describe a dozen different areas where, with proper funding, the NSF "would support grants in critical areas related to the War on Terror."[45] Indeed, according to information available from the NSF, in the four years following 9/11 (2002–5) the foundation awarded $47.7 million in 135 grants for research proposals that mentioned terrorism in their abstracts compared with just $1.5 million awarded to a mere 8 proposals focused on terrorism in the previous four years. Even institutes with quite specialized missions, such as the National Institute for Mental Health, have experienced rapid increases in terrorism-related funding. In 2004 NIMH made thirty-three awards in response to proposals at least partially devoted to terrorism-related research. In 2005 this figure rose to fifty-nine. Related patterns are evident in the activities advertised by the national laboratories. Searches on the Web sites of the Sandia, Argonne, and

Lawrence Livermore National Laboratories suggest greatly increased attention to terrorism and terrorism-related research.[46] The Web site of the Centers for Disease Control and Prevention (CDC) in Atlanta offers information on scores of projects related to the War on Terror, including "the emerging threat of bioterrorism," "the epidemiology of makeshift bombs," development of electronic surveillance systems for detecting biologic outbreaks due to terrorism, development of coding procedures for deaths by terrorism, and a range of activities undertaken by the National Advisory Committee on Children and Terrorism.[47]

In President Bush's FY 2006 budget $132 billion was proposed for scientific research, about the same as 2005 but a 34 percent increase over 2001 levels. Most of this funding is for defense and counterterrorism research. Funds allocated in that general category rose 51 percent over those four years compared with a rise of 16.2 percent for all other categories.[48] Unsurprisingly, along with hundreds or even thousands of new counterterrorism consulting firms, dozens of new institutes dedicated to studying terrorism, counterterrorism, homeland security, bio-security, and so on have sprung up in universities across the country, while previously established centers have seen their funding rise sharply in the post-9/11 environment.

Of course just because a center, a consulting firm, or a research proposal claims expertise about counterterrorism or says it is about terrorism does not mean these claims are true. But that is exactly my point. One characteristic of the War on Terror as a self-powering whirlwind is that many activities, including those that might otherwise have been sustained honestly, on their own merits, must now strive to depict themselves as valuable for the War on Terror, no matter what they really are. In particular, as more researchers portray themselves as experts with new and better ideas about how to anticipate, prevent, or combat terrorism, arguments that more funding is required for terrorism research are strengthened, as are opportunities for counterterrorism consultants trained to use these newly proliferating ideas and techniques.

This dynamic has operated powerfully to shift and spin the research agendas of universities searching for sponsored research funding, individual scientists looking for grant support, and of all kinds of educational institutions on the lookout for courses, degree-granting programs, and new institutes and centers that can attract revenue by representing research and pedagogical products as centrally important to the War on Terror. As one immunologist at the Wistar Institute in Philadelphia put it, "There are ways to do some good basic science in the context of bioterrorism. The market changes and you have to react."[49] According to a *Washington Post* report, hundreds of American colleges and universities have been influenced by the post-9/11 environment to launch courses, majors, and even degree programs designed to "take advantage of a large pool of homeland security money." Steven R. David, identified as directing the homeland security certificate program at Johns Hopkins University, predicted that "homeland security is probably going to be the government's biggest employer in the next decade." Fully 80 percent of community colleges offer courses and/or certificates in homeland security. According to Frank Ciluffo, director of the Homeland Security Policy Institute at George Washington University, "This is our generation's war—it's not going away." But aside from the patriotic calling driving schools toward counterterrorism programs, they also listen to William Kelley, an official in the Department of Homeland Security's Office for Domestic Preparedness. The total funding in grants made available through his office, he said, "is just a staggering amount of money."[50]

One reason the amounts of money are so staggering is because America's best, brightest, and most imaginative researchers and thinkers are enlisted to find new ways to spend it. One high-level Defense Department research meeting I attended just ten weeks after 9/11 was designed to generate new ideas for technologically revolutionary weapons in the just-declared War on Terror. The convener told the group to think of itself as charged to conceive of a new "Manhattan Project," not to make an atom bomb but to find the answer to the problem of the War on Terror. As the discussion proceeded, one participant was reprimanded by the convener, a senior department head, for mentioning the extremely high cost of the idea he had in mind. "I don't want you thinking about costs," said the official. "Remember, we print money in this town."

A typical request for proposal (RFP) relevant to the War on Terror asks social scientists, natural scientists, and engineers to expand their thinking, unleash their imagination, think outside the box, and accept no boundaries, whether fiscal nor conventional, on ideas they might want to propose to fight the War on Terror. The challenge is to think at least as imaginatively as al-Qaeda, which struck such a powerful blow against America with only a few hundred thousand dollars, some fanatics, box cutters, and a spectacularly imaginative plan. American scientists and strategists are therefore exhorted to mobilize all their intellectual talent and creativity to ensure that we will not be outwitted again. According to two leading counterterrorism experts, "American planners must unshackle their thinking and disregard no possibility because it seems unlikely." Describing the horrific consequences of various types of conceivable attacks, they advocate "institutionalizing imaginativeness."[51]

One mechanism for generating new ideas for ways to protect America is first to think creatively about vulnerabilities terrorist enemies might discover and how they might exploit them. This technique is known as "red-teaming"—assigning a team of scientists, intelligence operatives, and even Hollywood screenwriters the task of coming up with scenarios for terrorist attacks that could be accomplished against currently available defenses. The vicious dynamic that arises from most of these red-teaming exercises begins with the discovery of how dauntingly easy it is to wreak havoc, or at least deliver very painful blows, against American civilians. It then continues as a reinforcing impetus for accelerating the War on Terror vortex because every scary and plausible idea for a terrorist attack produces its own requirement for countermeasures. These are almost always more difficult and more expensive than the hypothetical attack. Nor will those countermeasures ever be foolproof, especially against the most imaginative schemes that subsequently constituted red-teams can produce. The result is a spiral of fear, leading to expenditures for red-teaming operations, leading to a wider array of threats, thereby intensifying fears, leading to expensive countermeasures, leading to imaginative red-team terror scenarios that defeat those countermeasures or shift to as-yet-unprotected targets.

For example, during the anthrax scare in October and November 2001, discussions of bioterrorism produced the idea that since anthrax was not communicable from one person to another, a much more frightening possibility would be the weaponization of smallpox. Traces of the germ were said to be in existence. One infected terrorist or victim on one airplane in the United States could, it was said, quickly spread the dread disease to most major cities in the country before it could even be recognized. A popular CBS network television series, *The Agency*, included an episode featuring an attack using a smallpox-infected terrorist.[52] Researchers across the country, including the author, began working on analyses of smallpox and its use as a weapon.[53] In Los Alamos, computer simulations of the entire infrastructural apparatus of the United States were combined with census data and a variety of theories to imagine how red teams there could "be the best terrorists we can be." For a study of possible smallpox attacks the model is run repeatedly, each time producing "more data than the contents of the Library of Congress." While its boosters described the exercise as crucial to protect America, critics decried the cost of each simulation—sometimes tens of millions of dollars.[54] Rising up in the midst of all this activity was a frantic, wasteful, and ultimately cancelled program to vaccinate tens of thousands of "first responders" against smallpox—a campaign that resulted in a small but notable number of fatalities due to bad reactions to the vaccine.

A government program to provide $64 million to colleges and universities to develop antiterrorism programs, although relatively small in scale, had a particularly wide impact because each such program had the potential to produce more funding by generating demands for more counterterrorism technologies.[55] For example, Purdue University's Homeland Security Institute, funded by the National Science Foundation, sponsors an annual essay contest to respond to the 9/11 Commission's criticism of terrorism preparedness as manifesting a "lack of imagination." Entrants in the 2005 competition were encouraged to think about protecting the country from natural as well as terrorism-produced disasters and then "describe and promote a 'new technology' that [they] believe needs to be developed to help with such incidents in the future."[56] Of course new counterterrorism technologies developed in response to these incentives then require the production of more scenarios examining how those technologies could be defeated and improved.

As was widely reported in 2002, the Department of Defense consulted with two dozen Hollywood filmmakers to develop scenarios for possible sequels, as it were, to the 9/11 attacks.[57] The scenario that holds the top position in the array of terrorist threats imagined both inside and outside of government is the detonation of an improvised nuclear device in an urban area after having been smuggled across the border or into a harbor. That was precisely the plot of a Tom Clancy novel made into a 2002 Hollywood movie, *The Sum of All Fears*, featuring the destruction of Baltimore by a nuclear device smuggled inside a shipping container. In June 2005 a government study of precautions taken to prevent such a disaster reported that after four years and $800 million in program investment, "the nation remains extremely vulnerable to [such] a catastrophic attack."[58]

An attack by terrorists with a nuclear or radiological weapon is just one of an immense number of possible kinds of attacks. As noted above, in its red-teaming mode the government developed a list of fifteen "National Planning Scenarios," including twelve terrorist attacks using different weapons against different kinds of targets, and three natural disasters. The terrorist attack scenarios include an urban nuclear weapon attack; the release of sarin gas in an office building; infection of American livestock herds with hoof-and-mouth disease; and introduction of pneumonic plague in public bathrooms.[59] One instructive aspect of the list is how small and arbitrary it is compared to the vast number of possible scenarios and yet how impossibly expensive adequate preparation for even these scenarios would be. Indeed the government's description of the list as "not intended to be exhaustive or predictive" and its explanation of the scenarios' function as a tool for developing a "Universal Task List" as one step toward achieving the "All Hazards National Preparedness Goal" make it perfectly clear how immense is the challenge the government has set for itself and how essentially impossible it will be to ever meet that challenge.[60] Inevitably the logic of the War on Terror drives our country away from rationality, away from any attempt at triage in the face of too many possible threats, and toward a frantic and doomed attempt to make ourselves invulnerable to any conceivable attack. Even before 9/11 a 1998 Presidential Decision Directive concluded that "in the face of this diffuse, nameless, and all-azimuth danger, the government must focus less on specific threats than on identifying and remedying the country's vulnerabilities."[61]

Certainly government efforts have made, and will make, some kinds of terrorist attacks (most notably attacks using passenger airliners) much more difficult to mount and therefore, in principle at least, less likely to occur.[62] But in our enormously complex, open, and densely interdependent society all red-teaming exercises seem to show that suicide terrorists wanting to strike inside the United States will not find it difficult to discover glaring vulnerabilities in any security system. No matter how fast the government runs, and no matter how much money it spends, because its efforts produce images of new and more challenging threats, it can never make enough progress toward "protecting America" to reassure Americans against the fears it is helping to stoke.[63] Among the unchecked threats given wide circulation: a dirty (radiological) bomb smuggled into the country or parked offshore in a cargo container, truck, or train;[64] botulism toxin poured in the nation's milk supply at one or two processing plants;[65] terrorist bombs on subways or trains, in tunnels, or on bridges in major urban areas;[66] or a fast explosive-filled boat ramming into a liquid natural gas freighter in an American harbor.[67]

In a pluralist democracy such as ours, the government does not implement policies because they are necessary but because they satisfy the winners in a continuing and ruthless pursuit of particular interests by individuals and groups. Yet no lobbyist or politician can succeed by justifying particular proposals as deserving of public endorsement simply by emphasizing how much the measure would benefit the lobbyist or politician making the proposal. Coalitions must be built. To do so, and to avoid the bitter and direct opposition that would arise if self-interest were advanced too plainly as justification for particular projects, every proposal for public funding or support must appeal to general principles of community interest. In the extraordinarily diverse landscape of American politics there are normally almost as many (conflicting) principles of community interest as there are particular group interests. Different groups therefore endorse different general principles. Gun enthusiasts and firearm manufacturers use the inviolability of the Second Amendment as their banner. The NRA thus stands for the constitutional rights of all Americans and resistance to potential tyranny, not just for the particular interests in firearms its members share. Meanwhile, gun control groups who do not share NRA members' special interest in firearms appeal to principles of public safety. The National Abortion Rights Action League (NARAL) advances its campaign to protect and expand abortion rights by generalizing its appeal to the principle of individual freedom—the freedom to choose. Right-to-life groups, on the other hand, uphold the principle of the sanctity of human life, de-emphasizing, for their purposes, the principle of individual freedom. The War on Terror thrives by invoking a fear that every interest group can call its own.

OPPORTUNITIES FOR THE OUTLANDISH
IN THE WAR ON TERROR

The fearful belief in a mortal, imminent, and largely nonconfirmable terrorist threat is itself a distinctive mechanism driving the War on Terror as a self-reinforcing whirlwind. Consider the peculiar dynamics of such a widespread belief, especially one so rarely discussed as possibly unjustified. In the political marketplace, in which every participant searches for others who will accept his or her currency of justification, this kind of belief automatically emerges as a dominant currency of political exchange, that is, as a principle of action no one can ignore and that everyone must use to justify their own particular proposals. As I have shown, ambitious persons and interest groups will find themselves impelled to cite their own projects, interests, and policy preferences as serving, in a particularly urgent and necessary way, the imperative to counter the terrorist threat.

An equally powerful dynamic encourages groups and individuals to develop and advocate new schemes for attracting public funding, advancing their unconventional or previously discredited ideas as just the sort of bold steps needed to succeed against the challenge of terrorism that all agree must command the attention and resources of the nation. More insidiously, but almost as inevitably, the more often groups succeed in gaining access to resources based on their putative contribution to the War on Terror the greater will be their commitment to fostering and even deepening public belief in and fear of an abiding terrorist threat, thereby raising demands for more creative thinking to fight terrorism, more counterterrorism services, more new projects, and more energetic efforts to define a broader spectrum of other activities as central to the War on Terror.

In a truly expanding economy "a rising tide lifts all boats"; similarly, an intractable fear nourishes all schemes. In the face of what feels like a limitless terrorist threat, even nutty ideas may be seen as reasonable and can have a major impact on politics, policy-making, and political debate. For example, prior to 9/11 and with no connection to fears of Islamic terrorism, the issue of illegal entrance of Mexicans and others across the Rio Grande had extraordinarily agitated some Americans. Extremist groups like Ranch Rescue and American Patrol had formed in the American southwest to oppose entrance of Mexicans into the United States. Animated by hatred and fear of Hispanics and by beliefs that the Mexican government was plotting to redeem the territory it lost to the United States in the Mexican war, these tiny groups organized paramilitary vigilante activities along the border and vilified the government for not doing anything to enforce immigration laws along the U.S.-Mexican border. Until September 11, 2001, they attracted little attention and no political support from mainstream politicians. But following the al-Qaeda attacks, their activities expanded enormously, as did public attention and support for their cause. Far-right and racist groups like the Council of Conservative Citizens, the neo-Nazi National Alliance, the White Revolution, the National Socialist Movement, Aryan Nations, and the Celtic Knights of the KKK rallied against "illegal brown wretched refuse" and blamed weak immigration policies for the attacks.[68]

Before long, politicians who had toyed with the immigration issue saw the potential offered by 9/11 to advance their ideas and careers. Best known now among these politicians is Congressman Tom Tancredo (R-Colorado) who revived a sagging political career by endorsing vigilante groups like the Minutemen and other citizen organizations trying to stop illegal immigration from the south by conducting their own patrols along the border. On his Web site, Tancredo's embrace of the War on Terror rationale for his long-standing ambitions to close U.S. borders is evident:

Terrorists could exploit the vulnerability of our borders, enter our country illegally, and threaten millions of American lives. A number of OTMs [other than Mexicans] have come from "Countries of Interest" such as Afghanistan, Egypt, Iran, Jordan, Pakistan, Qatar, Saudi Arabia, and Yemen—countries with heavy pockets of radical Islam. Secretary of State Condoleezza Rice earlier this year stated, "Indeed we have from time to time had reports about al-Qaeda trying to use our southern border but also trying to use our northern border." Congress and the president must pass substantive border security measures to prevent another 9/11.[69]

In 1999 Tancredo formed the Immigration Reform Caucus in the House of Representatives, a tiny group of conservatives whose xenophobia-tinged manner isolated them from the conservative mainstream of the Republican Party. There were sixteen members of the caucus on September 11, 2001, but it quickly grew to sixty-two members in 2002 and ninety-two members by the end of 2005. Legislative initiatives by Tancredo and his supporters have included efforts to achieve a moratorium on immigration in a bill labeled the Mass Immigration Reduction Act of 2003, a host of amendments to the Immigration and Nationality Act, and two bills in 2005—the Reducing Immigration to a Genuinely Healthy Total Act (RIGHT Act) and the Real Guest Act. Although none of Tancredo's bills have been passed, his success has been registered by various provisions and allocations within the USA PATRIOT Act and homeland security budgets and by a dramatic shift in the terms of the national debate, that now includes discussion of physical barriers that might be constructed all along the Mexican and Canadian borders.[70]

Most observers credited the pressures represented by Tancredo with President Bush's move toward adopting a posture of "cracking down on the illegal immigrants" in order to "gain control of our borders." This policy shift involved committing $2.3 billion out of a $32 billion homeland security funding bill signed in October 2005 to hire a thousand new border patrol agents.[71] Abandoning its efforts to implement a permanent guest worker program for Mexican illegals, his administration instead retreated to a proposal for a temporary program, now justified not as compassionate or economically wise but for security reasons. As Homeland Security Secretary Michael Chertoff explained to Congress in October 2005, the temporary guest worker program was necessary because although the border had been strengthened with more personnel satellite surveillance and unmanned aerial vehicles, security objectives had still not been met. "We're going to need more than brute enforcement. We're going to need a temporary worker program as well."[72]

By the spring of 2006 the important and complex question of illegal immigrants had moved to the center of the American political agenda. Although it was bound to emerge as an important political issue eventually, the particularly harsh and emotional framing of the question in 2005 and 2006, including proposals to criminalize or deport millions of "illegals" and imprison their employers, was very much due to the impact of the War on Terror. Meanwhile, Tancredo backed away from a Presidential bid of his own, commenting that the illegal immigration issue had developed so robustly that such a move to gain publicity for "immigration reform" was unnecessary. Instead he spoke of plans to run for the Senate in 2008. Tancredo's bright political prospects illustrate how the War on Terror not only transforms the terms of debate in the country over key issues but can also catapult politicians from cranky obscurity to national prominence in a few short years.[73]

DEMOCRACY DOMINATED BY THE WAR ON TERROR

The case of Tom Tancredo and the rapid and intense politicization of immigration policy points to a much more fundamental relationship between the War on Terror and American politics. Few Americans will be surprised or even disturbed by the fact that wars fought by the United States will normally, almost automatically, be spun by the national leadership in ways designed to support the partisan political interests of incumbents and the incumbent party. This idea was pushed to what appeared to be an absurd, if logical, extreme in the 1997 Dustin Hoffman and Robert De Niro film *Wag the Dog*. What was shocking to audiences about the film was the suggestion that a president could announce a war and provide television images corresponding to it without there actually being a war—all in order to distract the country from a pre-election scandal threatening to derail his reelection. In the film, the American public is swept away by a wave of warm patriotic feeling on behalf of a (nonexistent) American soldier. The nonexistent soldier is supposedly missing in action while trying to rescue innocent civilians from a Balkan hellhole. In the storm of publicity and emotion surrounding the drama of his (wholly contrived) exploits, capture, and rescue, the American public ignores the scandal and returns the president to office with an enormous margin of victory.

The War on Terror does not recapitulate the plot of *Wag the Dog*, but it was launched to arouse public support for a political crusade and a foreign policy revolution reaching well beyond the commitment to find and destroy al-Qaeda. Still, as shown by the attacks of 9/11, America was and is faced with real adversaries. In the film, the creators of the advertising campaign not only control the war but use it successfully to achieve their immediate ambitions and then, when it is no longer of use, bring it to a close. What we see with the War on Terror is the success of its architects in achieving the long-coveted invasion of Iraq, but also their failure to make of that invasion a political basis for long-term policies of American empire abroad and conservative ascendancy at home. Even more to the point, the architects of the War on Terror, in sharp contrast to the mastery of their brainchild exercised by the public relations gurus in *Wag the Dog*, rapidly lost control of the "war" they launched. The War on Terror grows and expands unguided by anyone but is powered by the exploitation of it by everyone. In this context it would be astonishing indeed if the protean War on Terror were not also purposefully, systematically, and effectively exploited by politicians.

As early as 1963, political scientist Bernard Cohen remarked that the media affects public opinion more by the topics it prompts the public to worry about than by the specific views it promotes. Writing then about the print media, he commented that "the press may not be successful much of the time in telling people what to think, but it is stunningly successful in telling its readers what to think about."[74] This insight was subsequently developed and substantiated by the research of many political scientists and political psychologists working on topics such as agenda setting, "heresthetics," framing, and priming effects. Collectively this research has made a huge impression on prevailing understandings of relationships among media, public opinion, voting, and election outcomes. Its fundamental finding is that an election victory does not necessarily go to the candidate whose issue positions most voters agree with but rather to the candidate whose positions, *on the issues that are established as salient,* most voters agree with. The key to victory, therefore, is not to persuade the public to adopt the candidate's position or to adopt positions corresponding to those already held by the majority of voters but to use the media to increase the focus on issues favorable to one's candidate.

Unquestionably it is Karl Rove, on behalf of George W. Bush, who has most systematically and successfully applied this body of theory to practical politics. In 2002 a pair of confidential, misplaced, and discovered Power Point presentations prepared by Rove and his then assistant, Kenneth Mehlman (later appointed chairman of the Republican Party), for Republican strategists listed maintaining a "positive issue environment" as the equivalent of the party's prime directive. One issue made salient in 2004 to the enormous benefit of the Bush-Cheney campaign was gay marriage, an issue Rove and his operatives pushed to the forefront in key states by orchestrating the launch of campaigns for constitutional amendments to ban the practice. But nationwide the most important investment made by the campaign in issue salience and the effort that involved more high-level administration officials than any other was to keep the threat of catastrophic terrorism and the War on Terror as close to the top of the national agenda as possible. Rove and other Republican strategists were well aware that even as the president's approval ratings fell in many areas, his reputation for fighting the War on Terror continued to earn him high marks.[75]

Under the president's imprimatur a thirty-seven-page booklet was released by the White House in 2002 to accompany the FY 2003 budget request. Entitled *Securing the Homeland, Strengthening the Nation*, it not only effectively presented George W. Bush as a wartime president but also provided the rhetorical architecture for the War on Terror as the issue of the century. In this respect this booklet set out the overall contours of the public relations strategy that would make the threat of terrorism and the central role of the president's leadership in the War on Terror an effective and uninterrupted source of political support. "The threat of terrorism," wrote the president (with what assistance from Karl Rove and other political advisers we can only speculate),

is an inescapable reality of life in the 21st century. It is a permanent condition to which America and the entire world must adjust.

The need for homeland security, therefore, is not tied to any specific terrorist threat. Instead, the need for homeland security is tied to the underlying vulnerability of American society and the fact that we can never be sure when or where the next terrorist conspiracy against us will emerge. The events of September 11 were a harsh wake-up call to all citizens, revealing to us the danger we face. Not since World War II have our American values and our way of life been so threatened. The country is now at war, and securing the homeland is a national priority.[76]

The pose of an American president leading the country in a struggle, the likes of which had not been seen since Franklin Roosevelt roused the "Greatest Generation" against Hitler, was obviously immensely attractive. And it was not difficult to make this posture credible. In the immediate aftermath of the 9/11 attacks most Americans were naturally worried about whether terrorists were about to deliver even more catastrophic strikes against us. But so far no follow-up terrorist attacks have materialized. The war in Afghanistan came to a swift conclusion and faded from public consciousness. Worst of all, Osama bin Laden eluded capture while the war in Iraq morphed from a sellable "victory over the terrorists" to a Vietnam-style quagmire. For Rove and company it was clear that keeping terrorism and 9/11 as part of the president's positive issue environment would require assiduous efforts to spin and exploit the "realities" of the War on Terror. This Rovian project on behalf of Bush and the Republican Party was and continues to be enormously consequential, perhaps more so than the efforts of any other particular faction. But in its form and basic message it corresponds exactly to the strivings I have described of each lobby and partisan group that has used the threat of terrorism and the War on Terror to promote and protect its own interests.

Frank Luntz is a top Republican pollster and political strategist. For the Bush administration and for the Bush-Cheney 2004 election campaign, no document contained a more precise and consequential statement of how to exploit the fearsome memory of 9/11 in order to maintain a positive issue environment than Luntz's memo entitled "Communicating the Principles of Prevention and Protection in the War on Terror." In July 2004 Luntz spoke frankly about the rhetorical strategy he had recommended to Republicans. Its fundamental tenet was to pound home the theme that "9/11 changed everything." Specifically, the memo recommended that "no speech about homeland security or Iraq should begin without a reference to 9/11."[77]

In his September 2003 *Meet the Press* interview with Tim Russert, Cheney offered a typical example of this rhetorical strategy in action. According to the vice president, "9/11 changed everything. It changed the way we think about threats to the United States. It changed about our recognition of our vulnerabilities. It changed in terms of the kind of national security strategy we need to pursue, in terms of guaranteeing the safety and security of the American people. And I'm not sure everybody has made that transition yet."[78]

From his speech to Republican strategists at the beginning of the 2006 election season it would appear that Karl Rove viewed the 9/11 "Wag" the War on Terror "Dog" as successful enough in 2004 to justify its continued use in 2006. "Republicans have a post-9/11 view of the world. And Democrats have a pre-9/11 view of the world. That doesn't make them unpatriotic, not at all. But it does make them wrong—deeply and profoundly and consistently wrong."[79]

The single most obvious measure taken by Republican political strategists in 2004 to exploit the 9/11 attacks and the image of Bush rallying New York City firefighters at the site of the disaster was to hold the

Republican National Convention in New York City. It is a common-place to note how often, and in how many different contexts, the president invoked 9/11 during the campaign and in the televised debates with Senator John Kerry. Such invocations and calls to arms in the War on Terror were regular features of George W. Bush's stump speech. Likewise, in his acceptance speech for the nomination the words "terror," "terrorists," and "terrorism" appeared nineteen times, along with six mentions of 9/11.[80]

Aside from maintaining the prominence of 9/11 in the public's imagination, Rove's team conducted an extraordinarily energetic effort to shape the media's general treatment of the War on Terror as a salient, if not the most salient issue in the campaign. Karl Rove and other top administration political operatives showed themselves at their most aggressive and imaginative in their engagement with the shaping of media narratives touching on Bush's image as a wartime president and as commander-in-chief of American forces in the War on Terror. Of course every administration provides talking points to its supporters, and the Bush administration is no different, feeding material regularly to conservative pundits and political talk-show hosts.[81] Thanks to the special prosecutor's investigation of the outing of Valerie Plame as a clandestine CIA operative, however, we also know how tight have been their relationships with some high-profile figures in the mainstream media, such as Bob Woodward and Judy Miller. From that same investigation we know how active the White House has been in efforts to spin stories perceived to be politically important, or to retaliate against those working against the spin.

The whole Valerie Plame investigation tends to vindicate David Letterman's interpretation of a rather bizarre but revealing episode in the spring of 2004. On his March 29, 2004, late-night comedy show, Letterman showed a videotape featuring a bored and yawning young boy standing on a stage almost directly behind Bush as the president was making an emphatic speech about the War on Terror and other topics. The tape was deemed funny enough that CNN broadcast it twice the next day, followed by an announcement that the White House had informed the network that the Letterman show had used trick photography to insert a yawning boy behind the president. Letterman responded with an absolute denial of tampering with the tape. For its part, CNN then changed its story, saying first that although the yawning boy was at the rally, he was not positioned where he appeared to be in the tape. A bit later CNN changed its story again, saying that although two CNN announcers had reported the call from the White House, in fact no such call had ever been received. While CNN then apologized for what it said was an error of miscommunication, Letterman insisted that he knew, from reliable sources, that the White House had indeed made the phone call just as CNN originally reported.

It is in light of other similar episodes of aggressive involvement by Rove's Office of Strategic Initiatives in the shaping of the issue environment that we need to consider the development of a very public conversation about the likelihood of terrorist attacks disrupting the 2004 election and the possibility or even advisability of postponing the election. Serious public consideration of such a radical break with American traditions and constitutional processes coupled with well-timed announcements about "increased chatter" heard by intelligence agencies about possibly imminent terrorist attacks and sudden increases in the color-coded threat level reinforced terrorism and the War on Terror as defining issues during the presidential campaign year.

General Tommy Franks, who commanded U.S. forces in the Afghanistan war against al-Qaeda and the Taliban and also led the invasion of Iraq, has been an outspoken supporter of President Bush. In November 2003, Franks was quoted as suggesting that a terrorist attack involving a weapon of mass destruction could lead to the unraveling of the Constitution and the assumption of power by the military.[82] At the end of 2003 the news network CNBC hosted a meeting of two hundred executives from inside and outside the government. It was reported that in this group 75 percent believed that a terrorist attack even bigger than 9/11 would occur in the United States by the end of 2004, designed to impact the election process.[83] In his end-of-the-year predictions for 2004, neoconservative columnist William Safire included "a major terror attack in the United States" as the election's "October surprise."[84]

Speculation about a major terrorist attack affecting the elections escalated after the March 11, 2004, bombings in Madrid that appeared to have a major impact on the subsequent election in that country.[85] Citing the incidents in Spain, FBI Director Robert Mueller emphasized the importance of preparing for a similar attack in the period leading up to the U.S. presidential election. Conservative columnist David Brooks anticipated that a major attack just before the election would lead

Americans to rally behind their president.[86] Suggestions that the elections would have to be called off if the terrorists struck were made by conservative talk-show hosts such as Sean Hannity on the Fox television network and Rush Limbaugh in his syndicated talk-radio show. In an Associated Press story titled "Officials Worry of Pre-Election Attack," *USA Today* quoted a political psychologist as to the "staggering" implications of the attack in Madrid: "This is the first time that a terrorist act has influenced a democratic election. This is a gigantic, loud wakeup call. There's no one they'd like to have out of office more than George W. Bush." The newspaper reported that "the administration has made no attempt to hide its concern about another attack" and published remarks by National Security Adviser Condoleezza Rice about "our worst nightmare," a WMD terrorist attack on the homeland. Said Rice, "We live in an age of terror, in which ruthless enemies seek to destroy not only our nation and not only to destroy all free nations but to destroy freedom as a way of life."[87]

The topic reappeared on July 8 when the secretary of the Department of Homeland Security warned on July 8, that al-Qaeda was planning a large terrorist attack on the United States "in an effort to disrupt the democratic process."[88] For weeks the airwaves and newspapers were filled with accounts of memos circulating among officials at the U.S. Election Assistance Commission, the Departments of Justice and Homeland Security, the FBI, and the intelligence committees of the House and Senate. In addition to waves of public commentary there was a plethora of reporting about high-level, closed-door briefings, discussions, and contingency plans regarding the legal and administrative mechanisms for postponing the elections.[89]

Although Osama bin Laden did release a videotape at the tail end of the election that may well have affected the outcome, no terrorist attacks occurred in 2004 in the United States. Nor were any terrorists arrested who were actually planning an attack. On the other hand, there were plenty of warnings from the administration that a terrorist attack, a big one, was about to occur—a series of warnings that ended after the election but that from January through August helped keep terrorism and the War on Terror in the public's consciousness.

Election year 2004 had begun with Black Hawk helicopters hovering over Times Square. Well-publicized measures to defend against anticipated terrorist attacks on New Year's Eve and New Year's Day in New

York included snipers on rooftops, bomb-sniffing dogs, and deployment of counterterror units equipped with chemical, biological, and radiological detection gear. Extraordinary measures were taken as well in Las Vegas and at the Rose Bowl in Pasadena. The Department of Homeland Security announced a temporary suspension of oil shipments from Valdez, Alaska. In the week prior half a dozen flights between Paris and Los Angeles were canceled. Flights between London and Washington were canceled on January 1 and 2. These actions were all based on a decision announced on December 11, 2003, by DHS Secretary Tom Ridge to raise the alert level to code "orange" (high risk).

The U.S. intelligence community has received a substantial increase in the volume of threat-related intelligence reports. These credible sources suggest the possibility of attacks against the homeland around the holiday season and beyond.

The strategic indicators, including al-Qaida's continued desire to carry out attacks against our homeland, are perhaps greater now than at any point since September 11th, 2001.

The information we have indicates that extremists abroad are anticipating near-term attacks that they believe will either rival, or exceed, the attacks that occurred in New York and the Pentagon and the fields of Pennsylvania nearly two years ago.

Ridge attributed the decision to recent intelligence information and urged every family in America "to go over [their] . . . emergency plans," telling them, "if you haven't developed one by now, please do so." He promised that "the government will stand at the ready, 24 hours a day, seven days a week, to stop terrorism during the holiday season and beyond."[90]

In January the primary season got under way. By May it was clear that Senator John Kerry would be the Democratic Party's presidential nominee. Meanwhile Bush's approval ratings were suffering. The prisoner abuse scandal at Abu Ghraib dominated the headlines. Polls in mid-May showed that public approval for the president's handling of the war in Iraq had dropped from 44 percent to 35 percent in one month and that in a two-way race Kerry would beat Bush 46 percent to 45 percent. On May 26, the president's press secretary announced that Attorney General John Ashcroft and FBI Director Robert Mueller would later that day hold a news conference to discuss heightened anxieties about an attack terrorists were thought to be planning "over the next few months, during this summer or fall time period." Scott Mc-Clellan, the president's press secretary, urged "all Americans to be on a heightened state of awareness and vigilance as we enter this serious threat period." When one reporter asked him, "how important is the election campaign in this?" McClellan did not respond directly. Instead he argued that efforts to defend the country within the homeland were not just law enforcement activities; they needed to be understood as part of a war. And, he said, "The President's number one priority is the war on terrorism."[91]

Ashcroft's announcement was indeed a stunner. With Mueller at his side, Ashcroft told the nation that "credible intelligence from multiple sources indicates that al-Qaeda plans to attempt an attack in the next few months. This disturbing intelligence indicates al Qaeda's specific intention to hit the United States hard." He said that the government estimated that al-Qaeda was "almost ready to attack the United States." Warning that al-Qaeda was "seeking recruits who can portray themselves as Europeans," he asked for "unprecedented levels of cooperation" from all levels of law enforcement and from the public. When Mueller stepped to the podium, he identified "Fourth of July celebrations, the Democratic and Republican conventions, and the November presidential election" as possible terrorist targets. He added spice to his warning by displaying pictures of seven individuals who were believed to have the intention and training to attack America—individuals who, he suggested, might already be in the United States. All Americans were asked to help in the effort to track them down. When asked about the timing of the announcement, Ashcroft acknowledged that no "specific information about the origin of a specific terrorist plan" had been received and that the government had been on the lookout for these particular individuals for some time. However, said Ashcroft, "we believe that the public, like all of us, needs a reminder."[92]

On July 29, John Kerry officially received the Democratic Party nomination for president. A crucial strategic element in any presidential campaign, especially by a challenger, is the "bounce" that positive coverage and excitement surrounding the party's national convention gives to the candidate. Kerry did get a bounce in the polls as a result of the convention, but just as he and his running mate, Senator John Edwards of North Carolina, set out for their first campaign swing, media coverage shifted to terrorism. The shift was not in response to a terrorist attack but to the Department of Homeland Security's announcement of a fresh terror alert within seventy-two hours of the end of the Democratic Convention.

On August 1, black-uniformed paramilitary police with assault rifles were stationed in the Wall Street district in New York and in Newark, New Jersey. As noted above, just three weeks earlier Ridge had announced a heightened terror alert. After briefing media outlets, including television news anchors, Ridge appeared in an unusual Sunday news conference to declare that for the first time DHS was designating particular locations as in danger of experiencing a large-scale terrorist attack. The government possessed, he said, "new and unusually specific information about where al-Qaeda would like to attack. And as a result, today, the United States Government is raising the threat level to Code Orange for the financial services sector in New York City, Northern New Jersey and Washington, DC."[93] Ridge described the intelligence involved as "rarely seen" and "alarming in both the amount and specificity of the information," and he promised public updates "as the situation unfolds." Ridge took advantage of the occasion to remind the public of the danger of terrorists using weapons of mass destruction during the summer election season. The Democratic Convention had proceeded successfully, he said, in part because "thousands of radiological pagers have been given to law enforcement around the country, and more are on their way. At work are more HAZMAT technicians, undercover agents, and emergency response teams, and more K-9 units capable of detecting explosives and weapons of mass destruction. Advanced air monitoring technologies that can check for biological pathogens are operating in key locations." By praising President Bush for policies that enabled the alert and the measures he was announcing, Ridge delivered the key political message in unusually explicit terms. "We must understand," he said, "that the kind of information available to us today is the result of the President's leadership in the war against terror."

In separate appearances both President Bush and Vice President Cheney characterized the alert as highlighting the continuing al-Qaeda threat. In a news conference the president said, "the alert shows there's an enemy which hates what we stand for. . . . It's serious business . . . I mean, we wouldn't be, you know, contacting authorities at the local level unless something was real."[94] Senator Kerry was circumspect about the episode, even though it had thrown a wrench into his campaign.

Many Democrats and commentators, however, questioned the motives behind this and other alerts, and their timing. On CNN former Vermont governor Howard Dean responded to the August 1 alert. Dean had lost the race for the presidential nomination but was soon to become chairman of the Democratic Party. He said he was concerned "that every time something happens that's not good for President Bush, he plays this trump card, which is terrorism. . . . It's just impossible to know how much of this is real and how much of this is politics, and I suspect there's some of both in it. . . . The question is, do I believe this is being fabricated? No, of course I don't believe that. But I do think that there is politics in this, and the question is, how much is politics and how much is a real threat?" Although Dean drew back from accusing the administration of fabricating the terrorist threat, he did accuse President Bush directly of "playing politics" with the threat and the alerts. For this, Republicans accused Dean of something close to treason. Kerry distanced himself from the remarks. Democratic Senator Joseph Lieberman questioned Dean's sanity. "No one in their right mind would think the president or the secretary of homeland security would raise an alert and scare people for political reasons."[95] White House press secretary Scott McClellan called suggestions that the alert was based on old information "wrong and plain irresponsible."[96]

Of course there were no terrorist attacks. Indeed information soon emerged that tended to strongly confirm the suspicions of Dean and others. On August 3, the *Washington Post* reported that the "new" information Ridge was referring to when he made his dramatic announcement two days earlier actually was old, and that it pertained to surveillance activities that occurred before September 2001. One senior law enforcement official was quoted as saying "there is nothing right now that we're hearing that is new. . . . Why did we go to this level? . . . I still don't know that." Virtually the entire basis of the alert were files found on a laptop computer discovered in Pakistan, but none of the files were dated past September 11, 2001.[97]

Late in October 2004, the *New York Times* published a detailed assessment of the basis for the terrorist alerts that had been issued during the presidential campaign and for the repeated warnings by government officials that al-Qaeda was likely to act to disrupt the American election process. In what the *Times* described as an "extensive" investigation based on two dozen interviews with officials "regularly briefed on terrorism developments," it found no evidence of a concrete threat. Regarding the threat of a terrorist attack to disrupt the election, the article quoted "one senior American counterintelligence official" as commenting, "'On a scale of one to a hundred, I'd give it about a two.'" European and Middle Eastern officials involved at senior levels in counterterrorism were described as "perplexed and uneasy about American officials' warnings," having seen no evidence of an impending attack in their own intelligence reports.[98] Well after the election a Congressional Research Service investigation into the string of terror alerts from 2002 to 2004 concluded that they were unreliable, confusing, and marred by a lack of coordination across agencies. In their urgency and severity the warnings issued were found often to have been based on unreliable sources and on judgments that did not reflect the considered opinion of relevant government experts.[99] Soon after the release of this report Tom Ridge defended himself, seeking to "debunk the myth" that he had been responsible for repeated orange alerts. Ridge, who had recently been replaced as secretary of homeland security by Michael Chertoff, told reporters that "More often than not we were the least inclined to raise [the threat level]. Sometimes we disagreed with the intelligence assessment. Sometimes we thought even if the intelligence was good, you don't necessarily put the country on [alert]. . . . There were times when some people were really aggressive about raising it, and we said, 'For what?'"[100]

THE RIDDLE OF ABSENT ATTACKS

Nothing is more mysterious in the War on Terror than that in more than four years the enemy has failed to fire a shot, at least not in or against the American homeland. How is this to be explained? Polls suggest the American public thinks the answer to this riddle is simply "luck." Top U.S. officials regularly proclaim the absence of attacks as attributable to, and only attributable to, their vigorous and effective prosecution of the War on Terror. Is this explanation credible? It might be, if some evidence that concrete terrorist plans to attack particular targets had been discovered or if actions to implement such plans had been thwarted. But as we saw in Chapter 3, unless one counts a mentally disturbed truck driver's idea to bring down the Brooklyn Bridge with a blowtorch, serious terrorist plots against American targets have been neither discovered (despite a no-holds-barred effort to do so) nor thwarted. Still, these claims might be found minimally persuasive if there had actually been attacks in the United States after September 2001. Such attacks could have permitted many Americans critical of the government to believe that they would not have occurred had the War on Terror been waged properly, while supporters of the administration could have argued that worse attacks and more of them would have taken place had it not been for the War on Terror.

Occasionally spokespeople for the War on Terror claim that the absence of attacks since September 2001 is due to the effectiveness and vigor of its prosecution.[101] In fact, the utter absence of acts of terrorism in the United States since 9/11, whether catastrophic (in the 9/11 mold) or minor (such as explosives placed in a shopping mall), has been a real puzzler for the War on Terror. The riddle is particularly difficult in view of how easy it would be to conduct at least small-scale terrorism operations against American targets. After all, consider how many terrorist attacks have occurred inside of Israel despite the hardening of Israeli society with redundant blankets of security measures well beyond anything even yet imagined in this country.

There are certain kinds of terrorist attacks, especially those based on the hijacking of airliners, that have almost certainly been rendered less likely by the extensive security measures implemented in our airplanes and airports. But the real answer to the riddle lies in shifting our expectations about its meaning. What should puzzle us more than the absence of attacks is the pervasiveness and certainty of expectations that they will occur despite the absence of evidence that terrorists are doggedly trying to launch them. The belief that we are fighting a war implies the presence of an enemy. If the enemy then seems not to be present, that is inevitably puzzling. My point is not that terrorist attacks inside the United States will not or cannot occur. We live on this planet with billions of other people. We are the strongest country in the world and have been for a long time. Our power, great as it is, has helped many. Inevitably it has hurt and humiliated many others and involved us, wittingly or unwittingly, as a factor in political struggles around the world. Therefore it is inevitable that politically ambitious individuals and groups, including groups with ideas as kooky as those we can find on the fringes of our own political system, will see political opportunities in striking at us violently. So there will be terrorist attacks, as there will be airplane crashes and rampages by disgruntled former employees.

But we will not stop flying and we will not stop firing workers for incompetence. To do either would be utterly irrational, but no more irrational than a War on Terror that has become, much more than any shadowy group of terrorists, the enemy we must learn to fight.

Fighting a phony but colossal War on Terror is an inefficient, self-defeating approach to the problem that does worlds of damage to the country and its ability, in the long run, to cope with real threats, both terrorist and otherwise. In previous chapters I showed that the War on Terror did not originate as a rational response to a problem requiring a war to solve it. In this chapter I have shown how it has taken on a life of its own, why it has grown so extravagantly, and that its continuation is not subject to the self-correcting forces which normally operate in American politics. Since the War on Terror is fed by individuals and groups serving their own interests in its name, attentive readers may wonder what makes me any different. After all, not only have I served as a consultant for different parts of the government engaged in the War on Terror, but the opportunity to publish this book appeared only because of it. So yes, I may be part of the problem. My work can become part of the solution, however, to the extent that it fosters critical assessments of the War on Terror itself rather than of the effectiveness of its prosecution. My hope is that my analysis can point toward ways of escaping from the vortex of fear and extravagant waste that has powered it. Accordingly, in the next chapter I analyze the nature of the real terrorist threat as a crucial step toward coping with it and defeating the War on Terror.

Chapter 6

Freeing America from the War on Terror

A fundamental principle of military affairs is "know your enemy." The War on Terror is the enemy of the American people, overshadowing threats posed by terrorists. We now know the dynamics and specific mechanisms of the War on Terror, making a successful struggle against it possible. But although knowing the enemy is necessary for victory, it is not sufficient. Indeed, the power of the War on Terror as an enemy of the American people is manifest not only in its robust expansion but also in its ability to suppress criticism of itself.

The War on Terror's defense mechanisms have operated spectacularly well against politicians. Consider the experience of John Kerry in October 2004. In an interview with *New York Times* reporter Matt Bai, Kerry was asked when and how Americans would be able "to feel safe again." Kerry responded with unusual candor about the actual proportions of the terrorist threat and a realistic assessment of the character of the problem and how to cope with it, saying, "We have to get back to the place we were, where terrorists are not the focus of our lives, but they're a nuisance. . . . As a former law-enforcement person, I know we're never going to end prostitution. We're never going to end illegal gambling. But we're going to reduce it, organized crime, to a level where it isn't on the rise. It isn't threatening people's lives every day, and fundamentally, it's something that you continue to fight, but it's not threatening the fabric of your life."[1]

Kerry's categorization of the terrorist threat as a chronic law enforcement problem is one of the only thoughtful comments that any candidate made about combating terrorism during the entire campaign. It was certainly not the sustained message of the Kerry campaign. In fact it was contrary to almost everything else about the War on Terror the senator said during the campaign. His standard speeches and formal position papers were laden with harsh criticism of President Bush's conduct of the War on Terror while presenting himself as more capable of performing the role of "wartime president." "The War on Terror is not a clash of civilizations," he said on February 27, 2004. "It is a clash of civilization against chaos; of the best hopes of humanity against the dogmatic fears of progress and the future. . . . I do not fault George Bush for doing too much in the War on Terror, I believe he's done too little. . . . George Bush has no comprehensive strategy for victory in the War on Terror—only an ad hoc strategy to keep our enemies at bay. If I am Commander-in-Chief, I would wage that war by putting in place a strategy to win it."[2]

In language that would be repeated throughout the campaign (apart from that one *New York Times* interview), Kerry went on to promise ramped-up efforts across the board in the War on Terror, including vigorous multilateral diplomacy, 200,000 more first responders, military strikes against terrorist operatives, more effective prosecution of the war in Iraq, new programs to protect America against possible chemical and biological weapon attacks, new safeguards for nuclear facilities, and new technology to detect nuclear weapons entering American ports.

It is difficult to believe that at the climax of the presidential campaign in October 2004, the Democratic challenger perceived a political payoff in describing the War on Terror in terms so radically different terms from those the voting public had been conditioned to understand. The only explanation of such a frank and politically dangerous framing of the issue is that it was a lapse, an accidental relaxation in an otherwise determined effort to conceal his genuine assessment of the entire War on Terror. If Kerry had any doubts about why he had been so apparently determined to conceal that assessment, they were removed by the firestorm of criticism his "nuisance" remark triggered.[3]

Republicans launched an advertising blitz focused on this one passage in the published interview. Sticking faithfully to the Rove/Luntz strategy of depicting 9/11 as a watershed in American history and politics, Bush campaign chairman Marc Racicot described Kerry as having "equated it to prostitution and gambling, a nuisance activity. You know, quite frankly, I just don't think he has the right view of the world. It's a pre-9/11 view of the world." Republican Party chairman Ed Gillespie used the same language: "Terrorism is not a law enforcement matter, as John Kerry repeatedly says. Terrorist activities are not like gambling. Terrorist activities are not like prostitution. And this demonstrates a disconcerting pre-September 11 mindset that will not make our country safer. And that is what we see relative to winning the war on terror and relative to Iraq."[4] President Bush himself took aim at the quote, saying, "I couldn't disagree more. Our goal is not to reduce terror to some acceptable level of nuisance. Our goal is to defeat terror by staying on the offensive, destroying terrorist networks and spreading freedom and liberty around the world."[5]

Meanwhile, Democrats countered, somewhat feebly and inaccurately, that the Republicans were taking Kerry's words out of context. In any case, they added, a Republican former national security adviser, Brent Scowcroft, had used the word "nuisance" to describe the terrorist threat two years earlier.[6] However, Democrats rapidly abandoned any attempt to explain, elaborate, or defend Kerry's depiction of the War on Terror as overblown. Instead, Democratic Party spokesmen shifted to the standard Kerry line that he would fight the War on Terror more vigorously and more successfully than Bush had. Some of the language adopted was unusually savage. Said Kerry campaign adviser Debra Deshong, "John Kerry believes that we can win the war on terror, unlike President Bush, who last August said we can't win the war on terror." Unlike Bush, she said, Kerry believed the United States could "eradicate terrorists from this world. . . . He knows that we need to go after these terrorists where they are, find them, and kill them." Phil Singer, Kerry campaign spokesman, and Governor Bill Richardson of New Mexico, chairman of the Democratic National Convention in July 2004, both rejected the Republican attacks that Kerry saw terrorism as merely a "nuisance," insisting that "John Kerry has always said that terrorism is the No. 1 threat to the U.S." In the third and final televised debate with President Bush, John Kerry took pains to realign his image, if not his actual views, as ready to wage a full-scale and even expanded War on Terror. Promising to remain "deadly focused on the real war on terror" and to "double the number of Special Forces so that we can fight a more effective war on terror," Kerry claimed that he would "do a better job of waging a smarter, more effective war on terror and guarantee that we will go after the terrorists. I will hunt them down, and we'll kill them, we'll capture them. We'll do whatever is necessary to be safe."[7]

Thus has the War on Terror come to enjoy a kind of immunity from criticism or rational assessment by politicians. In this illustration we can see how it not only deflected public analysis of itself but even transformed its critics into its vassals, more anxious than ever to declare their fealty to the war, its necessity, and its expansion. If this is true of politicians, is it true of experts? Can they publicly analyze the actual dynamics of the War on Terror? For the most part the answer is that experts either cannot or prefer not to criticize the War on Terror or its assumptions. Whatever criticisms they do offer usually take the form of doubts that it is being waged with all necessary vigor and seriousness.

Consider the very sensible book published in 2005 by two established experts on Islamism and counterterrorism, Daniel Benjamin and Steven Simon. Benjamin directed counterterrorism activity in the Clinton White House from 1994 to 1999 and served as a foreign correspondent for *Time* magazine and the *Wall Street Journal.* Steven Simon is a veteran of the National Security Council staff and the Department of State, with degrees from Columbia, Harvard, and Princeton. Their first book, *The Age of Sacred Terror: Radical Islam's War Against America*, described jihadist threats to America and was put under contract prior to the September 11 attacks.[8] The title of their second book is most instructive: *The Next Attack: The Failure of the War on Terror and a Strategy for Getting It Right.*[9] It conveys the impression of an imminent attack on the United States on the order of 9/11. The book's opening words are "We are losing." By appealing to the American reading public's expectations, beliefs, and fears the authors and publisher do everything they can to conform to the assumptions of the War on Terror. One blurb on the book jacket penned by Richard A. Clarke tells potential readers that the book's message is "*it's not over yet.* This is an important contribution to a nation that is still all too vulnerable to another 9/11-like tragedy at the hands of the jihadists."

Revealingly, the rhetoric of *The Next Attack*, its title, its opening words, and the way it was promoted disguise and even suppress its actual message. Despite the sky-is-falling rhetoric and severe criticism of the Bush administration for confusion and ineptitude in waging the struggle against terrorism, Benjamin and Simon report finding no evidence of an imminent threat of terrorism in the United States.[10] Nor do they call for increased budgets or deployments in the War on Terror. Instead they identify cultural trends in the United States that polarize relations between America and the Muslim world as the deep problem to be solved.[11] Stressing that large and disgruntled Muslim minorities in Western Europe are fertile ground for the development of al-Qaeda clones or "self-starters," they warn that in the long run the United States should ensure that its own Muslim citizens do not lose their sense of satisfaction with life in America or feel alienated or excluded by a War on Terror that unfairly targets them. They save their sharpest criticism for the biggest single piece of the War on Terror, namely, the "invasion and occupation of Iraq [that] . . . has led to the growth of violent anti-Americanism, which is propelling us toward a future of more terrorist attacks in more places with increasing lethality."[12] Although they consider military operations against active terrorists abroad to be sometimes necessary, their most important piece of advice is for the United States to stop defining the terrorist threat as a military problem, to tone down its rhetoric, and to cope with jihadist fanatics by building strong relationships with Islamic communities based on mutual respect and understanding. In other words, the book's substantive message is the danger that rhetorical, cultural, and military aspects of the War on Terror pose to our country. Yet because of the discursive, political, and economic imperatives associated with the War on Terror, the book is packaged so as to appear as a clarion call by a pair of counterterrorism experts that the War on Terror is not being waged well enough or urgently enough to ward off new 9/11-type attacks.[13]

It is important for Americans to realize that the period following the 9/11 attacks is not the first time the United States has been gripped by a consuming fear leading to irrational, self-reinforcing responses.[14] In 1949 the Soviet Union stunned America by exploding an atomic bomb. This terrifying achievement by the Soviets was due in part to espionage activities of communist agents in the United States. An anticommunist hysteria then erupted in the United States that was driven as much by fear as by ideology. Reaching its peak in the early 1950s, the witchhunt led by Senator Joseph McCarthy convinced Americans to believe that communist sleeper cells and active Soviet agents had penetrated every nook and cranny of the country. The backgrounds of ordinary people were scrutinized for contacts, incidental or not, that could indicate their participation in plots of the Red menace or their sympathy for it. In the process, thousands of lives were ruined or terribly damaged. In the end, no "conspiracy on a scale so immense as to dwarf any previous such venture in the history of man"[15] was found; no sleeper cells of brilliant but pathological communists were uncovered. The peak of the hysteria lasted half a decade, but for many years afterward a political culture of anticommunism and fear of worldwide Soviet expansionism distorted both American politics and American foreign and military policy.

What is most striking about the comparison between American responses to Soviet atomic power and to the jihadist threat after 9/11 is how much greater the danger from the Soviet Union was. Although the United States posed an even more overwhelming threat to the Soviet Union, Moscow quickly achieved the ability to inflict horrible damage on the United States, eventually achieving the capacity to destroy us entirely. This power was in the hands of people who officially and, in the minds of most Americans, were diabolically determined to "bury" us (as Khrushchev put it).

Nevertheless, despite pervasive fear and terrifying images the American people and their leadership managed to adjust to the continuous possibility of nuclear incineration. This relatively calm, sustained steadfastness was a political achievement of the first order. It was mainly accomplished by reliance on rationality—a "rational" posture of mutual assured destruction (imagining both nuclear superpowers as each rationally deterred from striking the other for fear of thereby triggering its own destruction) and by a rationally designed grand strategy of containment.

At the outset of this book I alluded to the seminal article by George F. Kennan, published under the pseudonym "X" in July 1947, as a model for the kind of sober, realistic analysis without which the War on Terror will continue to dominate America and damage American interests.[16] The article was based on the famous "long telegram" sent by Kennan from his diplomatic post in Moscow in 1946. It was a detailed, sensitive, and prescient assessment of the strengths, weaknesses, motivations, and propensities of the Soviet state and its communist leadership. Kennan's recommendation of the containment policy was based on a careful assessment of the enemy. He judged a Soviet-communist enemy too untrustworthy for an alliance, too strong to be eliminated by force, but not strong enough to defeat us in a "long twilight" of economic, political, cultural, ideological, and military rivalry.

Kennan had been studying the Soviet Union and its leadership for decades. He regarded the Kremlin leadership as representing a "mystical, Messianic movement" fundamentally committed to the defeat of the United States and the overthrow of the democratic capitalist way of life.[17] Kennan identified the strategic weakness in Soviet communism to be its failure to come to grips with how the power it had achieved could be used to produce an egalitarian society without loosening its grip on power. But loosening the Party's grip meant that some elements in Soviet society would be able to operate without Party direction and independent of Stalin's control. This the Party leadership would not tolerate. Though it wiped out virtually all traces of opposition at home, it could and did invoke the threat of foreign capitalists and imperialists to justify continued totalitarian rule domestically. In Kennan's analysis what motivated Soviet foreign policy was, despite their rhetoric, not a "do-or-die program to overthrow our society."[18] Rather, he saw the Soviets as under a domestic political imperative to maintain a constant but unresolved struggle with the West. This "duel of infinite duration" would be accompanied by promises of inevitable victory, forever postponed.[19] In this way the Party could sustain its ruthless insistence on absolute and rigidly enforced power at home.

From this fundamental assessment Kennan argued that the West could eventually defeat the Soviet Union and unravel the communist bloc without a world war. The key element in his containment strategy was to calmly but palpably and repeatedly expose the myth of the Kremlin's claim to infallibility. While the Communist Party's infinite tactical flexibility and its complete command of the mass media within Russia's borders could protect the image of infallibility from any unpleasant eventuality, a constant series of political, economic, or military defeats abroad, wherever the Soviet Union sought to expand its power, would expose the fundamental weakness of the system. The strains such constant external frustration would place on the politically incapacitated economy of the Soviet Union would eventually lead to cracks within the façade of Party unity and ultimately to a collapse of the Soviet system. Kennan's strategic recommendation therefore was "a policy of firm containment, designed to confront the Russians with unalterable counter-force at every point where they show signs of encroaching upon the interests of a peaceful and stable world."[20]

Kennan's article laid the basis for two generations of American foreign policy, helped prevent a third world war, and contributed mightily to the collapse and disappearance of Soviet communism. For our purposes, what is absolutely crucial to note is how Kennan's analysis was based on intimate knowledge of the enemy and careful consideration of links between its domestic political imperatives and the nature of its foreign policy. Fully 90 percent of the article was devoted to a detailed analysis of the psychological, political, cultural, and ideological motivations and predicaments of the Kremlin leadership. He arrived at his conclusions by following a meticulous, clinical approach to evidence and clearly grasping the logical implications of his observations for American foreign policy. He also preached what he practiced. Above all, he warned against hysteria or impulsive overreaction. The policy he recommended, he said, "has nothing to do with outward histrionics: with threats or blustering or superfluous gestures of outward 'toughness.' . . . it is a *sine qua non* . . . that the government . . . should remain at all times cool and collected."[21]

Without a comparably serious understanding of the motivations and predicaments of al-Qaeda and other jihadist groups, we are doomed to suffer self-inflicted wounds more devastating than anything we do to our foes. Yet a clear-eyed, politically sophisticated understanding of why al-Qaeda attacked us in 2001 has never played an important role in the determination of American counterterrorism policies. Accordingly we have been deprived of the single most important element in any successful strategy—knowledge of the enemy and what that knowledge can be understood to imply about the enemy's plans as well as his strengths and weaknesses. If we can develop a keen appreciation of the actual calculations and motives of the terrorists who struck us on 9/11 and threaten us still, we will have acquired the wherewithal to break the grip of the War on Terror and by so doing focus our attention and power on the real security problems that face us, including the particular dangers posed by jihadists.

The War on Terror relies heavily on a simplistic but very particular image of the enemy. President Bush commonly portrays jihadist terrorist groups like al-Qaeda as "evil," as "killers," or as "Islamo-Fascists." He presents their objectives and strategy simply and dramatically to the American people, claiming their goal is "establishment, by terrorism and subversion and insurgency, of a totalitarian empire that denies all political and religious freedom. . . . these extremists want to end American and Western influence in the broader Middle East, because we stand for democracy and peace, and stand in the way of their ambitions. Their tactic to meet this goal has been consistent for a quarter-century: They hit us, and expect us to run."[22] John Kerry put it similarly. Our struggle with Islamic terrorists, he said, is not a struggle between civilizations but "a clash of civilization against chaos."[23]

The enemy we imagine, and that is imagined for us by our leaders and by the War on Terror more generally, is invisible but immensely dangerous; pathological but disciplined; extremely patient but driven by incalculable hatreds. It is, moreover, an enemy with no moral qualms in pursuit of its objective. The respected co-chair of the 9/11 Commission, former Indiana congressman Lee Hamilton, summed up everything he knew, thought he needed to know, and thought we needed to know, about the motivation and purposes of the terrorist enemy. "We know what terrorists want to do: they want to kill as many Americans as possible."[24] Director of National Intelligence John Negroponte offered fundamentally the same characterization, of an enemy whose reason for being is, for all intents and purposes, simply to hurt America as much as possible for as long as it was able to do so: "Attacking the US Homeland, US interests overseas, and US allies—in that order—are al-Qa'ida's top operational priorities. The group will attempt high-impact attacks for as long as its central command structure is functioning and affiliated groups are capable of furthering its interests, because even modest operational capabilities can yield a deadly and damaging attack."[25]

This simplistic view of the enemy dominates conversations even in closed government deliberations. The *locus classicus* of the Bush administration's beliefs about the War on Terror is the "National Security Strategy of the United States," a thirty-five-page white paper issued by the White House in September 2002. In florid rhetoric it depicts the United States as having entered a new era of epochal conflict, challenged again to "rid the world of evil": "The United States of America is fighting a war against terrorists of global reach. The enemy is not a single political regime or person or religion or ideology. The enemy is terrorism—premeditated, politically motivated violence perpetrated against innocents."[26] The substantive nature, aims, and strategy of the enemy are not explained. The document simply advances a number of bald and supposedly self-evident claims. The terrorist enemy seeks to use weapons of mass destruction against the United States to cause "mass civilian casualties." The enemy cannot be deterred. It represents "chaos" and opposes civilization.[27] Essentially the same wholly abstract and absolute image of the enemy is used by the authors of the leaked "National Scenarios" exercise described in Chapter 5. The terrorist enemy in those documents is referred to simply as the "universal adversary"—a kind of satanic force whose particular human form is treated as utterly irrelevant for any exercise hoping to gain insight into its purposes or techniques.[28]

However appropriate many of these extreme descriptions may be of al-Qaeda and of jihadist fantasies more generally, they point much more clearly to what the jihadists want us to think about them, or what we most fear about them, than to what actually motivates and constrains their behavior. Constantly repeated by our leaders, such images of the enemy can convince Americans to be afraid and to mobilize their energies to fight but cannot guide effective use of American resources to identify and combat whatever actual threats exist. For in these formulations the enemy has no agenda but to attack, no short- or medium-term goals to accomplish on the road to its apocalyptic ambitions, no internal political or organizational requirements that shape its decisions, and no splits or disagreements that might provide clues about preferred tactics or openings for aggressive exploitation of weakness. Instead the enemy is simply a brute force, out to hurt us terribly.

Even when dressed up in academic language, War on Terror analyses of the "enemy" end up as simple as the assumptions of the War on Terror itself. In the book *Knowing the Enemy: Jihadist Ideology and the War on Terror* Mary R. Habeck emphasizes that al-Qaeda's objective is to destroy America and democracy. "The United States is recognized by the jihadis as the center of liberalism and democracy, a center that is willing to spread its ideas and challenge other ways of organizing society, and thus must be destroyed along with democracy itself."[29] Muhammad Atta and the other hijackers, she says, were motivated by the prospect of "killing as many Americans as they could."[30] While allowing that al-Qaeda may in part have desired to trigger an "unconsidered response" so as to "energize" the Muslim world against the West, she hails President Bush for launching the War on Terror and goes on to praise the success of the war in Iraq as a means of taking the war to the terrorists and building democracy.[31]

These are primitive ideas, devoid of any nuance or particularity that might offer clues about the enemy's behavior. They offer an image of the struggle as a kind of gigantic arm-wrestling contest, with each side mobilizing all its will and strength in a direct effort to defeat the other. That kind of *mano a mano* fight is just what we would most prefer. No force in the world can match American military or economic power if the contest directly pits armies against armies or economies against economies. Naturally, therefore, we would prefer to fight the sort of enemy that fights that sort of war. But nations do not choose their enemies, and enemies do not choose their strategies to suit the battles their adversaries would prefer to fight. The terrible truth about the War on Terror is that it has become the most powerful weapon in the hands of our jihadi enemies, more dangerous than their training, ideology, skills, access to money and weapons, and willingness to die.

By abandoning, in the midst of this War on Terror, any careful, discriminating analysis of the enemy, we cripple our ability to fight that enemy effectively. We also become vulnerable to spectacularly effective forms of psychological and political manipulation. The War on Terror sustains itself along with the objectives of al-Qaeda by hampering efforts to truly know the enemy. It produces the ridicule of those (such as John Kerry in October 2004) who use other than the official catechism when speaking of the threat of terrorism. It is also imposes a radically simplified image of the challenge facing us that distorts both public and private debate (as illustrated by the words quoted above of Lee Hamilton or the Department of Homeland Security's notion of the "universal adversary"). At the level of general information we see how self-censorship by the media, albeit under pressure by the government, tends to prevent publication or broadcast of the full texts of interviews or statements by al-Qaeda leaders, substituting instead unheard images of Ayman al-Zawahiri or Osama bin Laden with voice-overs of trivially short quotations from their sometimes elaborate messages.[32]

To escape the trap of the War on Terror we must ask the same questions about al-Qaeda and its ilk that we would ask about any other opponent. What are their short- and long-term objectives and their capabilities? Where do we figure in their lineup of antagonists? What role does attacking us play for them? What are the constraints under which they operate culturally, politically, psychologically, and logistically? How do they analyze our strengths and weaknesses? In light of those perceptions on their part, what interest do they have in what kind of political violence, delivered how, and to what effect?

On the strategic level there is one basic difference between us and our enemies. While we are trying to arm-wrestle, al-Qaeda and its clones are using judo.[33] The primary principle of judo is to use your adversary's strength against him. That is what al-Qaeda did on 9/11. A small group of terrorists with box cutters hijacked American airliners filled with jet fuel and used them to destroy the World Trade Center and attack the Pentagon. They deftly transformed America's sophisticated transportation system into a devastating weapon of attack against us. Then, thanks to the War on Terror, al-Qaeda effectively hijacked the American political system itself, unleashing enormous but fundamentally irrational and even counterproductive responses to the challenge of "terrorism with global reach."

As we have seen, al-Qaeda's attack in 2001 gave the whip hand in foreign and national security policy to the supremacist cabal, leading directly to an invasion of Iraq and a generalized War on Terror. The war in Iraq served al-Qaeda's purposes by bringing what it called a "crusader army" into the heart of the Muslim world, leading to tens of thousands of Muslim casualties, producing bitter feelings of humiliation and anger, and creating a new training ground for jihadis as well as a vastly enlarged recruitment pool. Though polls in the Muslim world still show very little support for al-Qaeda's long-run goal of a caliphate sovereign over all Muslim lands, the American reaction to 9/11 did convince large numbers of Muslims to sympathize with al-Qaeda in its battle with the United States and persuaded majorities of Muslims to adopt key elements of the jihadi worldview. In a sophisticated October 2005 poll of 3,900 respondents in six Arab countries, only 6 percent registered support for al-Qaeda's aim of a renewed caliphate over all Muslim lands; 39 percent, however, said they sympathized with al-Qaeda's desire to "confront the United States." More than 70 percent endorsed the view that American objectives in the Middle East were to dominate the region, protect Israel's interests, and weaken Muslims. Only 5 percent of respondents said they believed the United States was motivated by the desire to spread democracy.[34] A separate set of surveys has been conducted in three large Muslim countries whose governments support the United States in the War on Terror (Turkey, Indonesia, and Pakistan). In these "pro-U.S." countries "favorable opinion" toward America dropped from an average of 50 percent in 1999/2000 to 28 percent in 2005.[35]

It is true enough that the War on Terror and particularly the war in Iraq reflect an American response so clumsy and powerful as to provide the jihadis with a massively useful anti-American backlash.[36] But there is an even more important sense in which America's response to 9/11 has served al-Qaeda interests. Well beyond the war in Iraq and its effects, the generalized War on Terror served al-Qaeda objectives by drawing virtually every interest group and sector of American society into a maelstrom of worry, witchhunt, and waste.[37] As a result, although many terrorists and al-Qaeda leaders have been killed or imprisoned, the balance sheet of the War on Terror is overwhelmingly in favor of the Muslim fanatics. Aside from thousands of American lives lost or bodies maimed and hundreds of billions or even trillions of dollars in expenditures or commitments, the War on Terror preoccupies our people, distracts them and our political system from real problems and real solutions, and embroils us in unwinnable, demoralizing conflicts. It mobilizes vast amounts of American energy and resources and then effectively aims most of that power against Americans themselves. In a fundamental sense it leads to a deep confusion in America about what we as Americans can do in the world and what kind of satisfying and secure role we can play apart from an unattainable fantasy of global domination. Most specifically, and most importantly to our enemies, the War on Terror destroys the standing and reputation of the United States in the Muslim world, thereby turning our efforts in the name of freedom and the victims of 9/11 into more power and more opportunities for Islamic radicals.

Fortunately, we have the resources, ideals, and potential allies necessary to prevail over the long haul against enemies of human freedom and progress. We also have most of the knowledge we need to fashion and implement a prudent, effective, and sustainable counterterrorism policy. Our military and intelligence services are learning important lessons and slowly absorbing new principles and doctrines. Among the new buzzwords of doctrine and theory are "effects-based operations," pointing to the inadequacy of the sheer ability to hit and destroy targets as a measure of national security effectiveness; "asymmetric conflict," arising from the seamless relations between politics and military affairs and the crucial role of sustainable political purpose and tactical imagination in protracted conflicts; and "stabilization and reconstruction" operations as inherently critical for missions accomplished by transforming zones of hostility into zones of peace rather than by achieving victory through "shock and awe." By adopting the principles of judo ourselves—remaining centered on our own requirements, meticulous in our evaluation of threats, and disciplined in our analysis of our adversary—we can both free ourselves from the enemy's trap and protect ourselves to the extent humanly possible in this intrinsically uncertain and unpredictable world.

We must begin by looking clearly at the adversary. On the rare occasions when politicians or War on Terror spokespeople or analysts offer evidence for their portrayal of al-Qaeda's goal to inflict "maximum pain" on Americans, they most regularly cite a specific quotation from a Kuwaiti named Sulaiman Abu-Ghaith, who served as al-Qaeda's spokesman in Afghanistan in 2001. Little is known about him, although Iranian authorities announced that he was among several hundred members of al-Qaeda detained in Iran after the war in Afghanistan. In a statement posted on an al-Qaeda Web site in June 2002, Abu-Ghaith justified the principle of massive attacks on the United States by calculating the number of Muslims who had been unjustly killed as a result of American and Israeli actions. Based on this calculation Abu-Ghaith declared that al-Qaeda had "the right to kill 4 million Americans—2 million of them children—and to exile twice as many and wound and cripple hundreds of thousands."[38]

Let us assume that al-Qaeda leaders and many or even most of their supporters accept this justification for the mass killing of Americans, and the use of weapons of mass destruction to do so. Such an assumption is worth making, just as it would have been worth assuming that Adolf Hitler meant exactly what he said about the Jews in *Mein Kampf*. It provides an unassailable justification for considering al-Qaeda our enemy, if we considered any additional justification necessary after 9/11, and it certainly justifies serious attention to how we can reduce al-Qaeda's capacity to accomplish their aims or to attract support for doing so. But just as it would have been silly to devise a war plan for the defeat of Nazi Germany based only on reading and believing *Mein Kampf*, so it is silly, and worse, to treat a propaganda tract by a second-tier al-Qaeda leader as sufficient to instruct us as to the proper strategic response to al-Qaeda. To do so would not only deprive us of the detailed knowledge of the enemy we need to combat him successfully but greatly contribute to al-Qaeda's reputation in the Muslim world and to its ability to attract material and ideological support. In other words, by parroting the most vicious statements attributable to al-Qaeda, we fall directly into the trap of treating the enemy as on a par with the greatest challenges we have ever faced, indeed as just the kind of threat Osama bin Laden wants to be treated as—one posing an unprecedented and terrifying challenge to the confidence of Americans and the destiny of the United States as a global superpower and the dominant political force in the Middle East.

There are signs Washington is beginning to realize something is amiss in our general approach. Perhaps uncomfortable with the fundamental illogic of a war declared against an emotion (terror), the Department of Defense in 2006 appeared ready to abandon the terms "War on Terror" or "War on Terrorism" for "the long war"—a moniker that would more effectively establish the generational and worldwide scale of America's struggle against Islamic militants.[39] What we need, however, is not a new name for the war we are trapped within but a fundamentally new approach to the problem—an approach based on the same kind of detailed and levelheaded analysis of al-Qaeda that Kennan provided of the Soviet Union sixty years ago. The genesis of al-Qaeda has been described in many sources. It was a product of a complex combination of the talents, ambitions, and resources of Osama bin Laden, a far-flung recruitment pool of tens of thousands of Muslim veterans of the U.S.-backed "jihad" against the Soviet Union in Afghanistan, and an array of failed but still active groups of Egyptian Muslim fundamentalists searching for strategies and resources to overthrow the Egyptian regime that had not collapsed after the assassination of Anwar Sadat in 1981. These groups operated unsuccessfully within the semi-authoritarian systems that dominated the Arab and Muslim world but were able to tap wellsprings of broad Muslim discontent with those regimes, deep resentment due to regional issues such as those in Palestine, Bosnia, Lebanon, Chechyna, and Kashmir, and a pervasive malaise associated with the failure of Muslim and Arab countries to progress politically or compete successfully in the world market.

The transnational subculture within which al-Qaeda emerged was distinct from the broader, well-established Islamist movement—organized pervasively in the Sunni Muslim world by the Egyptian-based

Muslim Brotherhood. The Muslim Brothers adopted a very long view of the struggle to return Islam to greatness. Their strategy was and has been to work slowly, steadily, and, to the extent possible, legally, to transform Muslim societies, penetrate all sectors of power, and eventually, perhaps over generations, assume political power. Implicit in this strategy has been an acceptance of other Muslims, and even Muslim governments, as wayward, but still Islamic, as misguided but as targets for persuasion and as fully qualified potential allies. What distinguished Salafi (this name stems from the Arabic for "ancestors," and specifically the companions of the Prophet) or jihadi Islamic fundamentalist groups from this broader Islamist movement has been their rejection of other Muslims, including the Muslim Brothers, who adapt to local conditions and compromise with secularists and "unbelievers" or who do not share the Salafis' rigid, puritanical, and scripturalist ideological stance. By adopting the principle, right, and even duty of *takfeer* (the practice of declaring that a person claiming to be a Muslim is an unbeliever), these extremist groups justified categorization of Muslims and Muslim governments, including those who consider themselves Islamic believers or as representing the interests of Islam, as the equivalent of infidels who, under a wide variety of circumstances, could be attacked and killed.

Understanding this distinction between the much broader Islamist movement and the much smaller but more extreme Salafist movement and its violent jihadi offshoot is crucial to understanding just how marginal Osama bin Laden and his group were when they appeared. Although the terms "Salafi" and "jihadi" are used differently by various analysts, what is important is to understand that Salafis reject centuries of Muslim jurisprudence. Instead they attempt to reproduce or mimic patterns of belief and behavior of seventh-century Muslims by drawing on the Koran or well-established traditions of the beliefs and behavior of Muhammad and his Companions. "Jihadis" are Salafis who accept an imperative to treat non-Salafis as unbelievers or apostates and undertake jihad, including armed struggle, against all unbelievers hindering Islam, including those regimes and individuals who may nominally be Muslim.[40]

In the late 1990s jihadis represented a tiny group within the smaller Salafist community. Although this group quickly became known as al-Qaeda, the formal name of their organization was the World Islamic Front for Jihad Against Crusaders and Jews. Bin Laden and Ayman al-

Zawahiri were the first of five names listed at the bottom of the group's manifesto issued in February 1998. Apart from the obscurity of the organization, its name registered how radical a break bin Laden and al-Zawahiri were making, not only from the mainstream Islamist movement and from the smaller Salafi community but from the tiny but violent jihadi movement itself. By calling for attacks on the United States directly, what bin Laden and al-Zawahiri were doing was opposing the entire basis of twenty years of violent efforts by Islamists to overthrow the Egyptian and other *takfeer* regimes. They were, as Fawaz Gerges documents and emphasizes in his outstanding study, substituting the "far enemy" for the near.[41]

In the case of al-Zawahiri, raising the banner of striking directly at "the head of the snake" (meaning the United States) was a dramatic reversal.[42] In Egypt he had consistently counseled patience in the organization of support in the military in order to avoid premature attempts to take power. His advice was ignored. He was imprisoned and went into exile. Even from his remote headquarters in Afghanistan, while in league with bin Laden before the launching of the World Islamic Front, al-Zawahiri focused all his efforts on organizing attacks in Egypt and other Muslim countries composing the "near enemy." As Gerges shows, it was after the complete failure of this wave of attacks to shake the political foundations of these regimes, and in particular that of President Husni Mubarak's regime in Egypt, that the jihadi movement found itself in desperate straits. Starved of funds, splintered into various rival factions at war with one another and with mainstream Islamist movements, the jihadis seemed to be at the end of the road.[43] If corrupt regimes in the Muslim world were to be replaced, perhaps the only way was to follow the long-term, semilegal, and fundamentally nonviolent tactics of the Muslim Brothers.

This was the context of organizational and ideological crisis that framed bin Laden's distinctive strategy and made his command of substantial financial resources so important. Bin Laden believed that striking American targets, especially in spectacular ways, was the key to saving the jihadi movement. In a December 1998 interview bin Laden described the struggle as he saw it, and wanted all Muslims to see it, substituting the far enemy for the near:

There are two parties to the conflict: World Christianity, which is allied with Jews and Zionism, led by the United States, Britain, and Israel. The second party is the Islamic world. In such a conflict, it is unacceptable to see the first party mount attacks, desecrate my land and holy shrines, and plunder the Muslims' oil. When Muslims put up resistance against this party, they are branded as terrorists. This is stupidity. It is an insult to people's intelligence. We believe that it is our religious duty to resist this occupation with all the power we have and to punish it using the same means it is pursuing against us.[44]

A major problem, however, was the difficulty of reaching American targets. The attacks of 9/11 and their exploitation by the supremacist cabal to invade Iraq and launch a global War on Terror solved that problem by inserting hundreds of thousands of American targets into the middle of the Arab-Islamic world. Horror stories of the Abu-Ghraib and Guantanamo prisons, along with looting, anarchy, economic distress, uncounted thousands of collateral damage casualties in Iraq, the general hegemonist demeanor of the United States toward the Muslim world, continued close and highly visible relations between America and Israel, and U.S. support for authoritarian or corrupt regimes like those in Pakistan, Uzbekistan, and Egypt solved the larger problem of convincing hundreds of millions of Muslims that the "American/Christian/Zionist threat" to Islam was by far the most important challenge facing Muslims today. In other words, in excellent judo fashion, 9/11 was used to harness American power to solve bin Laden's problems. By making Americans look like Mongols and crusaders he succeeded in making the ravings of a modern-day Ibn Taymiyya seem compelling.[45]

What is crucial for devising an effective and sustainable policy to defeat the jihadis is to note that the objective in striking America was and is *not* simply to kill as many Americans as possible. Nor was the objective to establish a world Islamic state, liberate Palestine, drive the West out of the Middle East, overthrow corrupt regimes in Muslim countries, or inspire masses of Muslims to return to orthodox versions of their faith. The objective was and is to prevent the jihadi movement from disappearing completely as a result of its internal divisions and its consistent and dismal record of failure to take power and exercise it effectively in the lands of Islam. The diabolical brilliance of bin Laden and al-Qaeda was to make up for the essential powerlessness of his organization by harnessing the immensity of the power of the United States. In brutal terms this meant hitting the United States in such a painful and humiliating way as to trigger a vast and thoroughly exploitable response.

To suit al-Qaeda's needs, the attack on the United States had to be styled in a way that would highlight jihadi heroism, self-sacrifice, and technical proficiency while presenting bin Laden's Muslim audience with a spectacularly symbolic and satisfying drama. There is no gainsaying that he designed and implemented a plan to do just that—laying low the tallest towers of American pride in its world financial center and striking a direct blow against the American government and military. These key requirements of al-Qaeda's help to explain the otherwise baffling fact that despite the ease of poisoning food and water, of planting nail bombs in shopping malls, or of spraying a busy street with machine-gun fire, such "low status" attacks on random rather than on symbolically important targets have not occurred. What al-Qaeda wanted was not only a "heroic" and dramatically potent attack but one big enough to goad America into sending its armies directly into the Middle East, thereby staging the "crusader" war on the Muslim world the jihadis had predicted and needed to survive and prosper. As a result of such a war, al-Qaeda calculated, the fragmented and dispirited Salafist movement, as well as perhaps the entire Muslim world, would quickly learn to find crucial elements of the jihadi message not only plausible but palpably true. Commenting on U.S. reaction to 9/11, Gerges points out that the "way to go was not to declare a worldwide war against a nonconventional, paramilitary foe with a tiny or no social base of support and try to settle scores with old regional dictators. That is exactly what bin Laden and his senior associates had hoped the United States would do—lash out militarily against the ummah."[46]

To support this analysis, Gerges quotes from Seif al-Adl, one of bin Laden's top three or four surviving lieutenants, as gloating in 2005 that "the Americans took the bait and fell into our trap."[47] Just after 9/11, but before the United States invaded Iraq, Quintan Wiktorowicz warned of this trap. Stressing the isolation and weakness of the jihadi Salafis in the Muslim world as a whole and the tendencies at the time among Salafis themselves to reject violent jihad, he recommended doing everything possible to avoid providing evidence that might help bin Laden defeat his rivals. "Highly visible American military action," wrote Wiktorowicz, "may inadvertently provide empirical credibility for jihadi framings and tip the balance of power with the Salafi movement away from the reformist counter-discourse. If this were indeed the case, it would radicalize the transnational Salafi movement and undermine the U.S. policy goal of eradicating terrorism by creating a new legion of jihadi supporters that expands the terrorist network and its base of support."[48]

Al-Qaeda's sophistication must not be underestimated. It is capable of framing its strategy in terms quite familiar to western military doctrine. The leading Saudi theorist of al-Qaeda, Abu Jandal al-Azdi (Fares Ahmad al-Shuwayl al-Zahrani) published an article in March 2004 entitled "The Al-Qaeda Organization and the Asymmetric War." A key part of the analysis in this article describes how al-Qaeda "took and will take advantage of the American psychology and nature to be easily provoked. Hence, the United States reacts in a manner of a cowboy's revenge, instead of taking time to study the problem before retaliation." According to Reuven Paz, al-Azdi even quoted the concept of "asymmetry" in warfare as used by General Henry Shilton of the U.S. Joint Chiefs of Staff to describe al-Qaeda's thinking. When, in retaliation for al-Qaeda attacks on the American embassies in Kenya and Tanzania, the United States destroyed a pharmaceutical factory in Sudan, al-Azdi commented that "al-Qaeda managed . . . to make the huge American machinery serve it as a company for public relations. As well as following the September 11 attacks, it managed to make the United States look like it was waging a global war against Islam, and hence it managed to recruit the Islamic world against America."[49]

In his 2004 "October surprise" videotape bin Laden himself (no doubt intentionally) helped tilt the election to Bush over Kerry. In a largely ignored, but astonishingly vivid and precise analysis, bin Laden explained how al-Qaeda was exploiting America's political gullibility, economic power, and corporate interests for its own purposes and how unintentionally cooperative the Bush administration had been. It is easy, said bin Laden,

for us to provoke and bait this administration. All that we have to do is to send two mujahidin [jihadists] to the furthest point east to raise a piece of cloth on which is written al-Qaida, in order to make the generals race there to cause America to suffer human, economic, and political losses without their achieving for it anything of note other than some benefits for their private companies . . .

So we are continuing this policy in bleeding America to the point of bankruptcy. . . . That being said . . . when one scrutinises the results, one cannot say that al-Qaida is the sole factor in achieving those spectacular gains.

Rather, the policy of the White House that demands the opening of war fronts to keep busy their various corporations—whether they be working in the field of arms or oil or reconstruction—has helped al-Qaida to achieve these enormous results.

And so it has appeared to some analysts and diplomats that the White House and us are playing as one team towards the economic goals of the United States, even if the intentions differ. . . . for example, al-Qaida spent $500,000 on the event [the 9/11 attacks], while America, in the incident and its aftermath, lost—according to the lowest estimate—more than $500 billion.

Meaning that every dollar of al-Qaida defeated a million dollars by the permission of Allah, besides the loss of a huge number of jobs.[50]

In the spring of 2006 the tactic bin Laden described was being used by Iranian radicals, led by their fanatical President Mahmoud Ahmadinejad. Their bravado about Iranian uranium enrichment appears designed to polarize Iranian relations with the west to their faction's internal political advantage. As if on cue, War on Terror pundits in Washington, including members of the cabal that orchestrated the American-led invasion of Iraq, have begun promoting the idea of the preventive bombing of Iran, followed up if necessary by an invasion.[51] According to information leaked by officials within the Pentagon opposed to such ideas, even the preemptive use of nuclear weapons against Iran is under consideration.[52]

Many observers have wondered what role President Bush's plummeting approval ratings and the desperation of a Republican Party seemingly headed for defeat in the fall 2006 elections might play in authorizing such an attack. In line with the analysis presented here such calculations, along with supercharged policy arguments regarding Iranian nuclear capacities, reflect nothing so much as the frightening capacity the mechanisms of the War on Terror may have to produce the enemies the war needs to sustain itself. Indeed, as even the advocates of such a policy acknowledge, the regime in Tehran and its Hezbollah allies based in Lebanon would respond to American attacks with a worldwide campaign of terrorism against U.S. targets. These attacks would dwarf anything al-Qaeda has been or could be capable of mounting, thereby contributing a list of 9/11-type outrages long enough to help sustain the War on Terror for many years to come.

This book began with a paraphrase of the first sentence of Karl Marx's *Communist Manifesto*. It could do worse than end with a question famously posed by Vladimir Lenin: What is to be done?

The first and most difficult step to take is to open up debate over the logic and appropriateness of the War on Terror that American opinion leaders and the public at large have been trapped into serving. As a self-powered system the War on Terror permits them criticism of the way it is conducted but not questions about whether it should be fought at all. In this way the War on Terror transforms almost all criticism into its own cannon fodder. By publicly debating the existence and justification of the War on Terror itself we can begin to expose the psychological and political nets that entangle us within it and begin to cut them away.

This will not be easy. Those who begin the discussion, especially politicians, are likely to pay a heavy price. Their message can easily be misunderstood or distorted as a refusal to take the problem of terrorism seriously, to learn the lessons of our lack of preparedness on September 11, or to recognize al-Qaeda as the force for evil it is in the world. Many will find their political, economic, and even personal interests so well served by the discourse, fears, and escalating expenditures of the War on Terror that, consciously or not, they will resist evidence of its counterproductive effects and destructive dynamics. Inexorably, however, as the War on Terror continues to expand, breaking every barrier in our constitutional system and budgetary system, it will overextend itself so grossly that even many Americans who benefit from it will be emboldened to think critically and speak publicly about it.

Having seen the problem, how can we solve it? How can we break the vicious circles that transform our mobilization to combat terrorists into the raw material they need to succeed? Almost all experts agree that despite the 9/11 attacks in New York and Washington, such European countries as France, Britain, Spain, Italy, and Germany, with their large and sharply discontented Muslim minorities, face a substantially more serious terrorist threat than does the United States.[53] Yet, in Europe the problem is dealt with productively and much less disruptively as a law enforcement issue, not as a war that elevates the terrorists into a world historic force. Instead of glorifying terrorist groups as enemies of civilization on the order of the Axis powers, we should follow Europe's example by treating terrorists as the dangerous but politically insignificant criminals they would be without our help. For to the extent that al-Qaeda and its clones are motivated by the overreactions they can trigger from us, mounting a "war" against them plays directly into their hands.

To appreciate the impact our War on Terror has on the visibility and influence of al-Qaeda in the Muslim world, consider the following thought experiment. First let us note that anti-Muslim white supremacists in Idaho are as marginal in America and as far away from the accepted boundaries of political competition in the United States as al-Qaeda was from the accepted boundaries of political life in the Muslim world in the late 1990s.[54] Now imagine that black Africans were overwhelmingly Muslim. Imagine that Africa was united as the most powerful country in the world; more powerful than the United States. What might be the result if Christian white supremacists carried out a devastating terrorist attack against targets in Nairobi or Johannesburg? If United Africa reacted the way the United States reacted to 9/11, it would launch a global War on Terror targeting the Aryan Nations, the Ku Klux Klan, the neo-Nazis and other such groups in America. To much of the world, however, including most Americans, this war would seem to be aimed more generally at white Christians. Now imagine that in the name of that war United Africa invaded and occupied Idaho and other portions of the United States where they believed "Christian terrorists" or terrorist sympathizers were operating. The fringe racist groups would take part enthusiastically in the insurgency, helping to transform their image in most American minds from frightening and dangerous kooks to martyrs and heroic champions in a struggle with racial and religious enemies. White racist terrorism would have provoked an immense but clumsy response from Africa, transforming the terrorist fanatics into sympathetic figures and catapulting them to places of prominence and honor with startling rapidity.

When America labels tiny bands of Muslim fanatics as posing the kind of existential threat to the United States and the western way of life associated with Nazi Germany or the Soviet Union, we enhance their stature enormously in the minds of all Muslims, whether they agree with al-Qaeda or not. Al-Qaeda terrorists are criminals in every western country, and in almost every other country, and should be treated accordingly. Yet one effect of the War on Terror has been to make the accusation that someone believes that terrorism is a law enforcement problem a conversation stopper. To say as much is to provide prima facie proof of naiveté, to identify oneself as a holdover from the Clinton administration or as suffering from a "pre-9/11 mindset." But we must understand this discursive fact, that is, public intolerance for the notion that terrorism is a law enforcement problem, as a weapon used by the War on Terror against us. Marc Sageman has made the substantive point forthrightly. He emphasizes how effective small-scale, pinpoint operations against terrorist hubs and cells can be and how preferable they are to campaigns elevated to the status of a war. The key is to carry them out as part of a sustained, low-profile, international campaign against violent law breakers: "These [operations] should be treated as straightforward law enforcement matters. This will reduce terrorism to simple criminality and not allow terrorists to promote their agenda of jihad, which might further inspire alienated young men to take up the cause. Winning the media war to label terrorists as criminals rather than brave mujahedin is especially important to eliminate the appeal of self-sacrifice for a cause and discourage potential terrorists from engaging in such behaviors."[55]

Sageman mentions but does not emphasize another crucial advantage of treating terrorism fundamentally as a law enforcement problem.[56] The most important asset America has in preventing terrorism inside the homeland is the loyalty of millions of American Arab and Muslim citizens. They have an unparalleled ability to discern, identify, and help apprehend Arab or Islamic extremists who might be involved in terrorism. But the War on Terror, as a "war," quickly became a confrontation between a distrustful government and communities of Muslim and Arab citizens treated as possibly aiding and abetting the enemy and as, in effect, "detainable until proven innocent." Thus, by suspending normal procedures of legal due process, the War on Terror discouraged precisely those Americans most able to help identify terrorists from trusting the FBI, speaking freely with investigators, or even becoming available as informers and infiltrators.

Obviously, terrorism cannot be treated only as a law enforcement issue. When terrorist groups such as al-Qaeda find command sanctuaries and build training facilities in countries such as Afghanistan, military power will be required to engage them directly and destroy their capabilities. But today's terrorists do not rely mainly on state sponsors or even the shelter of states. They form transnational, global networks, seek refuge in anarchic regions, or nest inside well-organized societies, whether democratic and industrialized or authoritarian and backward. As such they confront the United States and its allies in the law-governed world with a challenge that is directly comparable to the challenge of organized crime and that must be dealt with in just the same way—not with superheated but clumsy wars, but with the well-funded, sustained, disciplined, professional, aggressive, internationally cooperative, but understated efforts employed to pursue, prosecute, and punish criminals.

Of course one implication of defining terrorism as a challenge to law enforcement rather than as an enemy to be vanquished militarily is that terrorism will not be entirely eradicated. We will always have crime, and we will always have terrorism, that is, violence used against civilians for political purposes. The question is whether we can build and maintain societies that are satisfying enough for enough people, and resilient enough, to sustain good lives for law-abiding citizens despite the possibility and occasional reality of crimes of violence, whether politically motivated or not.

The challenge of building resilient societies is not only, or even mainly, a law enforcement problem. It is a problem of opening opportunities for peaceable people of all cultural backgrounds to lead free and satisfying lives. International polls show that France is by far the most highly regarded western country in the eyes of Muslims all across the globe. Yet the eruption of violent riots and protests by Muslims throughout France in November 2005 shows how taut and difficult are relations in Europe between titular majorities of Christian Europeans and rapidly growing communities of Muslim immigrants and long-time Muslim citizens. On a global level the same underlying explosiveness in the relationship between Muslims on the one hand and Christians and Jews on the other was evident when weeks of deadly rioting erupted across the Muslim world following publication in Europe, New Zealand, and Australia of a cartoon depicting the Prophet Muhammad wearing a turban shaped like a bomb. Significantly, violence did not erupt among Muslims in the United States. Why? One reason is that despite obvious problems, American Muslims are substantially better integrated into society and politics than are Muslims in European countries. Compared to European Muslims, Arabs and Muslims in America feel more equal, more accepted, and better able to take advantage of opportunities for advancement open to all citizens. The same stimulus toward violent action had less effect among American Muslims, who are generally more satisfied with their position in society, than among Muslims in other parts of the world.

The general policy implications for reducing Islamic-oriented terrorism are clear and have even been indirectly noted by the State Department. In response to a question about the violent results of worldwide Muslim anger against publication of the cartoon, State Department press secretary Sean McCormack stressed that "what we have called for is tolerance and understanding, not incitement to violence. And we call upon all governments to *lower the temperature*, to urge calm and to urge dialogue and not misunderstanding."[57]

Indeed it does makes sense to encourage tolerance, understanding, and dialogue; to "lower the temperature" as a way to make conditions in the Muslim world less combustible and less hospitable for violent elements. This same logic applies equally well with respect to substantive policies of the United States that lead Muslims to believe the worst about our country and to see us as agents of domination, humiliation, and injustice. Neither law enforcement efforts nor wars can reduce the fanaticism that produces Muslim terrorists unless we lower the temperature in the Muslim world that creates more jihadis for everyone killed or imprisoned. To think otherwise is to believe that water in a pot could be prevented from boiling not by lowering the temperature beneath the pot but by identifying and removing the individual molecules just as they appear ready to burst into steam.

The good news about reducing the temperature in the Muslim world is that official American policies need not change; they need only be implemented. The United States stands for democracy, justice, and peaceful relations among the states and peoples of the Middle East. We are also committed to implementing all United Nations Security Council resolutions. The importance of implementing American policies is the good news. It is also the bad news, because of the domestic political difficulty of pressing any Israeli government to do anything—even something it may wish to do. Indeed, what has inflamed Muslim resentment against America is not simply the plight of the Palestinians but the perception that America not only tolerates but enables Israeli policies of occupation, dispossession, and de facto annexation of Arab/Islamic lands.[58] To be sure, the United States has officially moved far toward the international consensus on the solution of the problem—a real Palestinian state in the West Bank and Gaza living in peace with a prosperous and secure State of Israel. However, the United States has also chosen to allow dozens of Middle East diplomatic minuets to stagger into oblivion rather than bring its influence to bear in a way that would constrain both Israelis and Palestinians to accept each other's minimum requirements.

Let us be clear about this argument. Our enemies are clever and they know more about us than we do about them. They know that political pressures in the United States constrain American governments to take positions on Israel-related issues that can cripple any American effort to build effective alliances in the Muslim world or redeem its image among average Muslims. They know that when Americans talk to Arabs and Muslims they almost always try to change the topic when Israel comes up. So naturally al-Qaeda will always try to make Israel the topic that is front and center. If we use our influence in concert with European allies and moderate Arab countries, however, we can deprive al-Qaeda of this public-relations trump card by quickly orchestrating a solution acceptable to the vast majority of Palestinians and Israelis.[59] By implementing our own policy on this issue we can significantly "lower the temperature" that inflames the minds of ordinary Muslims helping to provide a constant stream of recruits for the jihadis.

Again, it is not that al-Qaeda and the jihadis care particularly about the Palestinians. They do not.[60] They were not motivated by the Palestinian cause when they struck on September 11, and they will not cease their activities no matter what happens in Palestine. What they do care about is exploiting our political weaknesses to multiply their political opportunities. Accordingly, in virtually all of bin Laden's interviews and *fatwas* and in the writings and interviews of al-Zawahiri, vastly disproportionate attention is directed to the "Crusader-Zionist alliance,"[61] the Palestine question, Israeli abuse of Palestinians, and Jewish and Zionist influence in America.[62] In a 2000 al-Qaeda recruitment video Palestine and Israel are mentioned or visually featured twenty-one times, compared to ten visual or verbal references to Saudi Arabia, the Hijaz, or Mecca and Medina.[63] Al-Qaeda harps on the Palestinian problem partly because of widespread anti-Semitism among Muslims, but even more because America is so conveniently and so tightly tied in Muslim minds to Israeli governments and to anti-Palestinian policies. Al-Qaeda knows its audience: the masses of Muslims whose hearts they want to inflame and whose minds they want to capture. Regardless of whether al-Qaeda genuinely cares about Palestine per se, its leadership knows their audience *does* and tends to deeply resent the double standard they see in Washington when it comes to anything related to the Jewish state.[64]

However, no matter how effectively America joins with its allies to bring the power of the law to bear on the criminals who use violence against innocent civilians; and no matter how wise our foreign policy may become or how greatly we may alleviate the hostility in Muslim countries toward the United States, we will never eradicate terrorism. Terrorists attacked the World Trade Center, the federal building in Oklahoma City, and abortion clinics in various locales before September 2001, and they will attack other targets in America after September 2001. That is a difficult idea for Americans to accept, that they must live in a world in which vicious terrorist attacks on our soil can and probably will happen. True, as John Mueller has pointed out in his broader argument about relative unimportance of the risk that terrorist activity poses to Americans, "outside of 2001, fewer people have died in America from international terrorism than have drowned in toilets."[65] Indeed Americans tolerate without panic on the order of 5,000 workplace accident deaths annually, 17,000 homicides, and 50,000 auto accident fatalities. These victims are as permanently and as tragically dead as those who die from acts of terrorism. But it seems to be a psychological fact that when the threat of death appears to be associated with the intent to do harm rather than as a product of chance or of avoidable circumstances, it is more feared and more likely to impact the way we live our lives.[66] It is in part that psychological irrationality in humans that terrorists leverage into the outsized political impact they hope to achieve.

Therefore, the more rational we can be, the less exploitable or vulnerable we will be to terrorist manipulation and attack. In that regard we need to change the fundamental way we approach the problem. Inevitably, our society will be vulnerable to destructive things that individuals or small groups could do. Trying to eliminate all such vulnerabilities would be as impossible as trying to eliminate all individuals who might have such intentions, and much more expensive as well. For example, if the odds of dying as a result of a terrorist attack on an airplane, on a bridge, in a tall building, or in a tunnel were judged to be lower than dying as a result of a lightning strike or shark attack, we should be prepared to accept that kind of fact of our collective life rather than spend endless amounts of money and sacrifice even more civil liberties or privacy rights in a frantic attempt to push those odds to absolute zero. This is the logic we apply, quite naturally and relatively effectively, toward pollution and toxins in our environment. It would be possible, perhaps, but absurdly expensive to transform the East River in New York City into a pristine stream from which untreated water could be safely drunk. It might not even be possible to remove all toxins known to cause cancer from our food and water, but we know it would be absurdly expensive to try to do so. So what do we do? We establish levels of acceptable risk. For example, the Environmental Protection Agency's approach to the risk of benzene pollution has been to set "an upper limit of acceptability of 1 in 10,000 lifetime cancer risk for highly exposed individuals" along with "a target of protecting the greatest number of persons possible to an individual lifetime risk level no higher than approximately 1 in 1,000,000."[67] In other words, the EPA and the public are aware that some people in fact will die as the result of even these low levels of benzene exposure, but we accept those levels, believing that the cost of trying to reduce those odds even more would prevent us from using our resources much more productively.

The same logic applies to security concerns. We need to accept that politically motivated violence will be a chronic problem, just like crime and pollution. Just as every large company and government agency has to conduct environmental impact studies and take into consideration the effects of its policies on pollution levels, so do large companies and government agencies now need to take security against terrorist attacks into consideration when designing new projects and in the normal course of their work. Taking into account problems and risks of pollution or security vulnerabilities does not mean allowing such considerations to dominate our thinking or rule out activities that are of interest and value to our society. Rather it means that reasonable and cost-effective measures to reduce those risks will become standard expectations along with detailed formulas and standards that will evolve over time as technologies, values, and specific challenges change.

In this connection, note that we treat contamination that might arise from nuclear power plant accidents or waste disposal differently than we approach problems of PCBs in drinking water, arsenic in wells, or sulfur dioxide in the air. Nuclear plant meltdowns can be sudden and catastrophic. Therefore we regulate the building and operation of nuclear power plants in exquisite detail, going far to ensure their safety even as the costs involved discourage their construction. The analogy with terrorism is that the public and the government are correct to view the potential of a terrorist attack using an improvised nuclear device with particular seriousness. Indeed it is one of the implications of what we have learned that the War on Terror is so out of control and so resistant to criteria of rationality and cost effectiveness, that we will almost certainly not direct our counterterrorism resources with the necessary focus and effectiveness on nuclear or other unlikely but extremely high impact threats.

Good work on the threat of nuclear terrorism is being done.[68] One key to dealing with the nuclear threat is recognizing that building a crude device and bringing it into the United States or near its shores is not the most difficult challenge facing potential nuclear terrorists. Their most difficult problem is accumulating enough of the properly enriched nuclear material for a bomb and then establishing confidence that it will work without testing it. With these bottlenecks in mind, our military, intelligence, and law enforcement agencies, in cooperation with those of our allies participating in the nuclear nonproliferation regime, can conduct aggressive, effective, but necessarily secret operations of the general type described by James Risen with respect to the marketing of faulty plans for building a bomb.[69]

Finally, let us stare straight into the face of the possibility that our country could be hit by a nuclear terrorist attack. Although even al-Qaeda has tended to shy away from actual threats to use nuclear weapons, for both ideological and political reasons it is conceivable that such an organization could attempt such an attack.[70] Experts agree that an attack designed to contaminate an urban area with deadly levels of radioactivity would be far easier for terrorists to mount than the explosion of even a crude atomic bomb. Such an attack, however, delivering death and disfigurement over generations to thousands of random individuals, lacks the sort of heroic or dramatic profile that jihadi terrorists require. A spectacular nuclear explosion would be more consistent with their objectives and their modus operandi. The national planning scenario for a nuclear attack by terrorists on Washington, D.C., projects the scale of devastation to be orders of magnitude greater than any other type of terrorist action, including a radiological bomb. The scenario predicts tens of thousands or even hundreds of thousands of fatalities, many more injuries, including tens of thousands of blinded victims, destruction or severe damage to buildings within 3,500 feet of the blast site, contamination of up to 3,000 square miles depending on wind conditions, a substantial increase in the cancer rate, and a recovery period of years with a cost of many billions of dollars and the strong possibility of a national economic downturn.

The prospect is truly horrific, and we must do what we can to minimize the likelihood of it happening. But even with respect to this kind of catastrophe we must be prepared to think clearly. The energy and recruits our blundering War on Terror has provided al-Qaeda and its clones, along with the continuing waste of our resources, confidence, and international reputation, shows that wounds inflicted by the impulsive use of our own enormous power can be the most damaging result of terrorist actions against us. The number of Americans killed and maimed in Iraq has already far surpassed the awful casualty toll on 9/11. Accordingly, even if the worst occurs and, despite our best concentrated, focused efforts to prevent it, we are struck by terrorists wielding a crude but devastating nuclear device, we must remember that we can and will recover from such a blow. Whether we would be able to recover from the effects of the destruction we would be tempted to immediately inflict on others is a much more difficult question. Only a society based on confident resilience, not debilitating hysteria, and leaders acting out of courage and discipline rather than impulse and bravado could survive such an ordeal without lashing out so massively as to render the planet unsafe for Americans for generations. Since 9/11 Americans have not been well served by their leaders. It is therefore up to all Americans to build the society we need and choose the leaders we deserve, not only to escape the War on Terror trap but to protect ourselves from the real threats we face.

NOTES

PREFACE

1. X, "The Sources of Soviet Conduct," *Foreign Affairs* 25, no. 4 (July 1947): 566–82. This article, anonymously published, was based on George F. Kennan's "long telegram" sent back to Washington while on diplomatic assignment in Moscow in 1946.

CHAPTER 1

1. Department of Justice, "The September 11 Detainees: A Review of the Treatment of Aliens Held on Immigration Charges in Connection with the Investigation of the September 11 Attacks," Office of the Inspector General, June 2003, http://www.usdoj.gov/oig/special/0306/chapter2.htm.

2. Ibid.; http://www.usdoj.gov/oig/special/0306/chapter2.htm; http://grassley.senate.gov/index.cfm?FuseAction = PressReleases.View&PressRelease _id = 78.

3. Lowell Bergman, Eric Lichtblau, Scott Shane, and Don Van Natta, Jr., "Spy Agency Data After Sept. 11 Led F.B.I. to Dead Ends," *New York Times*, January 17, 2006.

4. http://www.fbi.gov/aboutus/faqs/faqsone.htm; Washingtonpost.com, "One Year Later Inside the FBI: Internet Tip Line," interview with David Rushing, supervisory special agent, September 12, 2002, http://discuss.wash ingtonpost.com/wp-srv/zforum/02/fbi_rushing091202.htm.

CHAPTER 2

1. "President Discusses War on Terror at National Endowment for Democracy," The White House Office of the Press Secretary, October 6, 2005, http://www.whitehouse.gov/news/releases/2005/10/20051006–3.html.

2. http://www.whitehouse.gov/news/, October 29, 2005. The same pattern is apparent in the speeches given to these organizations by high-ranking Defense Department officials. See http://www.defenselink.mil.

3. Heritage Foundation Web site, http://www.heritage.org/Press/Events/index.cfm, October 30, 2005.

4. The information in this paragraph was collected via searches within the

official Department of Defense Web site, http://www.defenselink.mil, accessed October 30, 2005.

5. Statement by the director of national intelligence, John D. Negroponte, to the Senate Select Committee on Intelligence, February 2, 2006, http://intelligence.senate.gov/0602hrg/060202/witness.htm.

6. Technically this was not a State of the Union address, since a newly inaugurated president does not have the responsibility of giving such a speech, but it was a speech to a joint session of Congress at the time of the year when such a speech is given and may be treated as such for all intents and purposes.

7. These speeches were coded so that any form of the word related to the topic was counted. So mentions of education include words such as "educate" or "educating," and include references to "drug education" and education of women in third-world countries. Mentions of terrorism include "terror" or "terrorist," mentions of taxes include "tax," "taxpayer," or "taxation."

8. Brian Jenkins, "Four Years After 9/11, War on Terror Slogs On," *San Diego Union-Tribune,* September 11, 2005, http://www.rand.org/commentary/091105SDUT.html.

9. Joshua S. Goldstein, *The Real Price of War: How You Pay for the War on Terror* (New York: New York University Press, 2004), p. 6.

10. Ibid., pp. 127–28.

11. Ibid., pp. 178–201.

12. Results of the Foreign Policy Association's National Opinion Survey: For 2003, see http://www.fpa.org/usr_doc/nobr_2003_results_.pdf; for 2004, see http://www.fpa.org/info-url_nocat2402/info-url_nocat_show.htm ?doc_id = 242123.

13. There is a significant terminological issue here. It can be argued that the official name of the war the country is putatively fighting is the "War on Terrorism." This is certainly a more apt description than "War on Terror" since the latter suggests an effort to defeat an emotion that is probably a natural and inevitable aspect of human nature, while the former could reasonably be considered an ideology of "terror," which as a political program or practice could be seen, albeit somewhat figuratively, as the enemy in a war. The Defense Department and Central Intelligence Agency do indeed feature "War on Terrorism" as the overall label for the effort, at least on the home pages of their respective Web sites. Apparently because it is more difficult to quickly and easily pronounce "terrorism" as opposed to "terror," the term "War on Terror" has become much more prevalent than "War on Terrorism" and even appears just as often as "War on Terrorism" in the speeches, publications, and Web pages of the Defense Department and the CIA. As commander in chief in this war, President Bush almost invariably uses the "War on Terror" moniker.

14. Daniel Yankelovich, "Poll Positions: What Americans Really Think about U.S. Foreign Policy," *Foreign Affairs* 84, no. 5 (September/October 2005): 2–17 (quotes on pp. 4, 15).

15. Pew Research Center for the People & the Press Survey Reports, Press Release, "More Say Iraq War Hurts Fight Against Terrorism, Support for Keeping Troops in Iraq Stabilizes," July 21, 2005, http://people-press.org/reports/print.php3?PageID = 981.

16. Lexis-Nexis, accessed November 4, 2005, http://www.lexisnexis.com/.

17. http://www.cbsnews.com/stories/2005/07/15/opinion/polls/main70 9488.shtml.

18. CBS News Poll, July 13–14, 2005, http://www.pollingreport.com/ter ror3.htm.

19. The vast majority of the money spent on the War on Terror is allocated by the federal government. In 2002 local- and state-funded expenditures on homeland security were estimated at $1.3 billion. Bart Hobijn, "What Will Homeland Security Cost?" Federal Reserve Bank of New York, May 17, 2002, p. 6; http://www.diw.de/deutsch/produkte/veranstaltungen/ws_consequen ces/docs/diw _ws_consequences200206_hobijn.pdf.

20. Office of Management and Budget, "Department of Homeland Security," http://www.whitehouse.gov/omb/budget/fy2007/dhs.html.

21. Department of Homeland Security, "Fact Sheet: Department of Homeland Security Appropriations Act of 2005," http://www.dhs.gov/dhspublic/display?theme = 43&content = 4065&print = true.

22. Department of Homeland Security, "Fact Sheet: U.S. Department of Homeland Security FY 2006 Budget Request Includes Seven Percent Increase," http://www.dhs.gov/dhspublic/display?theme = 43&content = 4337 &print = true.

23. "Winning the War on Terror," message accompanying FY 2005 budget request to Congress, http://www.nd.edu/~dbetson/Econ441/FY05Budget/winning.pdf (supplemental, p. 22).

24. http://www.whitehouse.gov/omb/budget/fy2006/protecting.html.

25. Amy Goldstein, "2007 Budget Favors Defense: Medicare Takes Biggest Hit in $2.7 Trillion Plan," *Washington Post*, February 5, 2006. Calculations are difficult because of complex categories. For the White House's breakdown of the categories that can justify describing larger increases in the FY 2007 budget, see Office of Management and Budget, "Homeland Security," http://www.whitehouse.gov/omb/budget/fy2007/dhs.html.

26. *Wall Street Journal*, September 30, 2005.

27. Ibid.

28. Tom Regan, "Iraq War Costs Could Top $2 Trillion," *Christian Science Monitor*, January 9, 2006.

29. Amy Belasco, "The Cost of Iraq, Afghanistan and Enhanced Base Security Since 9/11," Congressional Research Service, October 7, 2005, http://www.opencrs.com/rpts/RL33110_20051007.pdf.

30. Congressional Budget Office, "Federal Funding for Homeland Security," April 30, 2004; http://www.cbo.gov/showdoc.cfm?index = 5414&sequence = 0.

31. Regarding discretionary spending, see http://www.heritage.org/research/features/BudgetChartBook/charts_S/s11.cfm.

32. The federal government's Department of Education spends approximately $71.5 billion per year; see http://www.ed.gov/about/overview/budget/index.html?src = gu.

33. For a close analysis of the distance between 24's fictionalized world and the actual world of counterterrorism in America, see Spencer Ackerman, "How Real Is '24'?" http://www.salon.com/ent/feature/2005/05/16/24/index.html.

34. http://www.tv.com/tracking/viewer.html&ref_id = 28827&tid = 80733&ref_type = 101. The show was advertised with the come-on "What do you really know about your neighbors?"

35. http://www.9–11pdp.org/press/2005–12–05_summary.pdf. For the entire report, see http://www.9–11pdp.org/press/2005–10–20_report.pdf.

36. Remarks by Chairman Thomas H. Kean and Vice Chair Lee H. Hamilton, Final Report of the 9/11 Public Discourse Project, December 5, 2005, http://www.9–11pdp.org/press/2005–12–05_statement.pdf.

37. http://www.msnbc.msn.com/id/10323273, December 4, 2005. For an editorial hectoring the government for not scoring higher on the criteria applied by Kean and Hamilton, see "Failing on Homeland Security," *New York Times*, December 6, 2005.

CHAPTER 3

1. Department of Defense, "Secretary Rumsfeld and Gen. Myers News Transcript," August 5, 2003, http://www.defenselink.mil/transcripts/2003/tr20030805-secdef0525.html.

2. See Timur Kuran and Cass R. Sunstein, "Availability Cascades and Risk Regulation," *Stanford Law Review* 51, no. 4 (April 1999): 683–768; and Barry Glassner, *The Culture of Fear* (New York: Basic Books, 1999).

3. Luke Mitchell, "A Run on Terror: The Rising Cost of Fear Itself," *Harper's*, March 2004.

4. Adam Liptak, "In Terror Cases, Administration Sets Own Rules," *New York Times*, November 27, 2005.

5. Barton Gellman, "The FBI's Secret Scrutiny," *Washington Post*, November 6, 2005.

6. Ibid. This quote is from the text of the letter itself.

7. These practices were known by *New York Times* reporters for a year before their description in articles published by the paper in December 2005. See Eric Lichtblau and David E. Sanger, "Administration Cites War Vote in Spying Case," *New York Times*, December 20, 2005; and Eric Lichtblau and James Risen, "Spy Agency Mined Vast Data Trove, Officials Report," *New York Times*, December 24, 2005.

8. Federal Bureau of Investigation, "The FBI's Counter-terrorism Program Since September 2001: Report to the National Commission on Terrorist Attacks upon the United States," http://www.fas.org/irp/congress/2004_hr/mueller_statement.pdf.

9. http://www.fbi.gov/congress/congress04/pistole080304.htm.

10. In 2003 the FBI announced plans to reduce the number of its agents working on drug-related crimes by 29 percent. Mark Eddy, "War on Drugs: Legislation in the 108th Congress and Related Developments," Congressional Research Service, Domestic Social Policy Division, updated May 1, 2003, http://www.boozman.house.gov/UploadedFiles/Warpercent20On percent20 Drugs percent20Legislation percent20in percent20the percent20108thpercent 20Congress percent20and percent20Related percent20Developments.pdf.

11. http://www.fbi.gov/congress/congress04/pistole080304.htm.

12. http://www.fbi.gov/congress/congress04/mueller041404.htm.

13. http://www.usdoj.gov/ag/testimony/2005/022805fy06aghousetestim onyfinal.ht m.

14. http://cfrterrorism.org/security/liberties_print.html. This figure refers only to the years 2001–4. For a 2003 documentary dealing with the issue of the detention of 5,000 "persons of interest," see *Persons of Interest* (Icarus Films), http://www.frif.com/new2004/poi.html.

15. *Philadelphia Inquirer*, November 16, 2005.

16. Mitchell, "A Run on Terror."

17. Raphael Perl, "Terrorism and National Security: Issues and Trends," Congressional Research Service Issue Brief for Congress, September 8, 2005. For an evaluation of the results and rationale of the new formula for compiling terrorism data, see Josh Meyer, "Reports of Terror Attacks Jump—Iraq Incidents Added for First Time," *San Francisco Chronicle*, April 29, 2006.

18. "Nuclear Threat Greatest Danger, Ashcroft Says," January 28, 2005, Associated Press, http://www.billingsgazette.com/newdex.php?display = red news/2005/01/28/build/nation/40-nuclear-threat.inc.

19. Dan Eggen and Julie Tate, "U.S. Campaign Produces Few Convictions on Terrorism Charges," *Washington Post*, June 12, 2005. Studies by Syracuse University and New York University of the record of federal prosecutions of terrorism offenses after 9/11 came to conclusions virtually identical to those arrived at by the *Washington Post* reporters. See "Criminal Terrorism Enforce

ment Since the 9/11/01 Attacks," A TRAC Special Report, Syracuse University, December 8, 2003, http://trac.syr.edu/tracreports/terrorism/report 031208.html, and Karen J. Greenberg, "The Courts and the War on Terror," The Center on Law and Security, New York University, April 2005, http://www.law.nyu.edu/centers/lawsecurity/publications/documents/TerroristTrialReportCardinsert.pdf. A *Frontline* broadcast on PBS, "Chasing the Sleeper Cell," agreed with these analyses (http://www.pbs.org/wgbh/pages/frontline/shows/sleeper). In light of the Justice Department's inability to defend its claim about 395 terrorism prosecutions, it is perhaps unnecessary but still interesting to note the even more extravagant claim included in the department's 2005 report to Congress that "since the September 11th attacks, the U.S. Attorneys have prosecuted and obtained convictions in over 1,000 terrorism-related cases, including both international and domestic terrorism, terrorist financing, and other anti-terrorism cases." No explanation was offered for the meaning of these categories or the sources of the data. Department of Justice, Report to the Office of Management and Budget for the Fiscal Year 2005, p. 210, www.whitehouse.gov/omb/budget/fy2005/justice.html. Nor was any explanation available for its reduced claim, registered in the following year, that 661, not "over 1,000," convictions had been achieved in counterterrorism cases. http://www.whitehouse.gov/omb/budget/fy2005/justice.html.

20. Eggen and Tate, "U.S. Campaign Produces Few Convictions."

21. http://www.sho.com/site/sleepercell/home.do. Jeffry Anderson took the metaphor to a new level in a mass-market novel called *Sleeper Cell*, about Muslim terrorists who unleash nano-robots into the cells of Americans to trigger a holocaust that would kill "every American man, woman, and child."

22. For a detailed chronology of events in this case, see http://www.pbs.org/wgbh/pages/frontline/shows/sleeper/inside/cron.html.

23. Peter Slevin, "Detroit 'Sleeper Cell' Prosecutor Faces Probe," *Washington Post*, November 20, 2005.

24. Ronald J. Hansen, "Terror Prosecutor Indicted," *Detroit News*, March 30, 2006.

25. Interview with Harry Smith, *CBS Early Show*, February 10, 2006.

26. John Ashcroft, "Attorney General Ashcroft Speaks About the Patriot Act," Boise, Idaho, August 25, 2003, http://www.lifeandliberty.gov/subs/speeches/patriotactroadspeech_boise_082503.htm.

27. Three who cooperated with the government were sentenced to prison terms of seven to ten years and one member of the group was killed by Pakistani forces in Afghanistan. Two others were sentenced to eighteen years imprisonment and one to three years in a work camp.

28. Maureen O'Hagan, "A Terrorism Case That Went Awry," *Seattle Times*,

November 22, 2004, http://seattletimes.nwsource.com/html/localnews/2002 097570_sami22m.html.

29. It is not clear that Faris is mentally competent. On the negligible possibility that Faris was actually likely to inflict or capable of inflicting any damage on the Brooklyn Bridge, see Daniel Benjamin and Steven Simon, *The Next Attack: The Failure of the War on Terror and a Strategy for Getting It Right* (New York: Times Books, 2005), p. 117.

30. *Washington Post*, July 14, 2005, http://www.archives2005.ghazali.net/html/dr__tamimi_sentenced.html. In February 2006 al-Tamimi's appeal to the Fourth Circuit Court of Appeals was pending.

31. http://www.usdoj.gov/ag/speeches/2005/ag_speech_050831.html.

32. http://nyjtimes.com/Stories/2005/CA-TerrorPlotsFoiled-FBI-Intel.htm.

33. CNN report, August 2, 2005, http://www.cnn.com/2005/LAW/07/28/sheikh.sentence.

34. Robert Spencer, "Terrorist Professor," *FrontPage*, August 26, 2005, http://www.campus-watch.org/article/id/2165. For the indictment against al-Arian and the others, see http://news.findlaw.com/hdocs/docs/alarian/usalariano203ind.pdf.

35. *New York Times*, April 7, 2005.

36. *New York Times*, June 4, 2005. The parents of these girls had applied for asylum status many years earlier, with their cases still in abeyance. The diary entries, school essay, and "diagram" that attracted FBI attention were eventually judged innocuous and irrelevant. Adama Bah from Guinea was released on condition that she say nothing about the circumstances of her confinement or about her interrogation. Tashnuba Hayder was released only on condition that she immediately depart the United States for Bangladesh, where she did speak about her ordeal.

37. McGregor W. Scott, "Lodi Man Indicted for Providing Material Support to Terrorists," Office of the United States Attorney, Eastern District of California, September 22, 2005, http://www.usdoj.gov/usao/cae/PRESS/pdf_2005/09–22–05hayat.pdf. See also Dan Eggen and Evelyn Nieves, "Father, Son Tied to Al Qaeda Camp Are Held," *Washington Post*, http://www.washingtonpost.com/wp-dyn/content/article/2005/06/08/AR2005060800455_2.html.

38. Abdus Sattar Ghazali, "$250,000 Paid to Infiltrate Pakistani Community," Dawn of the Internet, February 20, 2006, http://www.dawn.com/2006/02/20/top9.htm; Alexander Cockburn, "Courtroom Bumps for the War on Terror," *The Free Press*, April 14, 2006, http://www.freepress.org/columns/display/2/2006/1353.

39. Cockburn, "Courtroom Bumps."

40. Statement by John D. Negroponte, director of national intelligence,

to the Senate Select Committee on Intelligence, February 2, 2006, http://intelligence.senate.gov/0602hrg/060202/witness.htm.

41. David Cole, "Are We Safer," *New York Review of Books* 53, no. 4 (March 9, 2006). The thrust of this article is to call not for an end to the War on Terror but for its more effective prosecution.

42. "Secret FBI Report Questions Al Qaeda Capabilities," March 9, 2005. http://abcnews.go.com/WNT/Investigation/story?id = 566425&page = 1.

43. Presidential remarks to the National Endowment for Democracy, October 6, 2005, http://www.ned.org/events/oct0605-Bush.html.

44. Peter Baker and Susan B. Glaser, "Bush Says 10 Plots by Al Qaeda Were Foiled," *Washington Post*, October 7, 2005.

45. Sara Kehaulani Goo, "List of Foiled Plots Puzzling to Some: White House Document Mixes Half-Baked Plans with Serious Terrorist Threats," *Washington Post*, October 23, 2005.

46. In a revealing slip of the tongue, suggesting his hope to use this particular story to good political advantage, the president mistakenly referred to the alleged target as the *"Liberty* Tower." In 2002 the name of the building was the Library Tower; it is now the U.S. Bank Tower. Tabassum Zakaria, "Bush Details Qaeda Plot to Hit LA," Reuters, February 9, 2006, http://news.yahoo.com/s/nm/20060209/ts_nm/bush_plot_dc.

47. "Bush Gives New Details on Terror Plot," CBS News, February 9, 2006, http://www.cbsnews.com/stories/2006/02/09/terror/main1300711.shtml

48. "Bush Details Foiled 2002 al-Qaeda Attack on L.A.," February 9, 2006, CNN.com, http://www.cnn.com/2006/POLITICS/02/09/bush.terror/index.html. Based on information regarding one of the alleged plotters imprisoned in Malaysia, the *New York Times* posted an Associated Press article on its Web site the following day indicating that the "plot" to attack the tower in Los Angeles was aborted by the decision of one member of the nascent team to leave the jihadi movement. The article also raised questions about whether counterterrorist operations actually "thwarted" the attack by suggesting that Khalid Sheikh Mohammed, the mastermind of the 9/11 attacks and the source of the information about the "second wave" attack on Los Angeles, may have in any case actually have forgotten about the idea altogether. "Officials: Terrorist Pulled Out of Plot," February 10, 2006, http://www.nytimes.com/aponline/international/AP-Terror-Plots.html?_r = 1&pagewanted = print&oref = slogin.

49. Helen Thomas, "Homegrown Terrorists," Background Briefing, Radio National, July 25, 2004; http://www.abc.net.au/rn/talks/bbing/stories/s1163768.htm.

50. Office of the U.S. Attorney, East Texas District, "Prison Sentence for Possessing Chemical Weapons," News Release, May 4, 2004, http://www.usdoj.gov/usao/txe/news/krar_bruey_rivers.pdf.

CHAPTER 4

1. See especially Thomas R. Hietala, *Manifest Design: Anxious Aggrandizement in Late Jacksonian America* (Ithaca, N.Y.: Cornell University Press, 1985).

2. The *Oxford English Dictionary* defines a cabal as a "small body of persons engaged in secret or private machination or intrigue; a junto, clique, coterie, party, faction." Secretary of State Powell's chief of staff from 2002 to 2005, Lawrence B. Wilkerson, used the term "cabal" to describe the supremacist faction led by Vice President Cheney and Secretary of Defense Rumsfeld against which he, Powell, and other pragmatists fought a losing battle. Lawrence B. Wilkerson, "The White House Cabal," *Los Angeles Times*, October 25, 2005. See also Joshua Muravchik, "The Neoconservative Cabal," *Commentary* 116, no. 2 (September 2003): 26–33. My own first use of the term to describe the neoconservative core of the group driving the country toward war in Iraq was in a *Middle East Policy* forum on Capitol Hill on October 1, 2002. See http://www.campus-watch.org/article/id/442 and http://www.mepc.org/public_asp/forums_chcs/31.asp.

3. Other prominent neoconservatives associated with the *Weekly Standard* include executive editor Fred Barnes along with Charles Krauthammer, Reuel Marc Gerecht, and David Frum, all listed by the magazine as contributing editors.

4. William Kristol and Robert Kagan, "Toward a Neo-Reaganite Foreign Policy," *Foreign Affairs* 75, no. 4 (July/August 1996): 18–32.

5. http://www.newamericancentury.org/statementofprinciples.htm.

6. http://www.newamericancentury.org/iraqclintonletter.htm. For sympathetic treatments of the meaning of "neoconservative," see Mark Gerson, *The Neoconservative Vision: From the Cold War to the Culture Wars* (Lanham, Md.: Madison Books, 1996); Muravchik, "Neoconservative Cabal." For a very different view, see Anne Norton, *Leo Strauss and the Politics of American Empire* (New Haven, Conn.: Yale University Press, 2004). For the backgrounds of some key neoconservative activists, see George Packer, *The Assassins' Gate: America in Iraq* (New York: Farrar, Straus and Giroux, 2005), pp. 15–32. For Armitage's "defection" to the Powell camp that tried to block the PNAC agenda, he was widely regarded within the cabal as a political traitor.

7. http://www.jinsa.org/articles/articles.html/function/view/categoryid/149/documentid/381/history/3,2359,2166,1306,149,381.

8. May be accessed at http://www.jinsa.org/articles/articles.html/function/view/categoryid/159/documentid/454/history/3,2359,2166,1306,159,454. For further information about JINSA and its links with other similarly minded organizations, see Jason Vest, "The Men from JINSA and CSP," *Nation*, September 2, 2002, http://www.thenation.com/doc/20020902/vest.

9. http://www.israeleconomy.org/strat1.htm.

10. Naomi Klein, "Baghdad Year Zero: Pillaging Iraq in Pursuit of a Neocon Utopia," *Harper's* 309, no. 1852 (September 2004): 43–53.

11. On Cheney's dominant role in national security and foreign policy, see James Mann, *The Rise of the Vulcans: The History of Bush's War Cabinet* (London: Penguin, 2004), pp. 275, 296–97.

12. For an instructive, even if "official" history of the national security adviser post and its relationship to the president, the secretary of state, and other top foreign policy principals, see Office of the Historian, Department of State, "History of the National Security Council, 1947–1997," August 1997, http://www.whitehouse.gov/nsc/history.html.

13. James Fallows, "Blind into Baghdad," *Atlantic Monthly*, January/February 2004, p. 72. See also David L. Phillips, *Losing Iraq: Inside the Postwar Reconstruction Fiasco* (Boulder, Colo.: Westview Press, 2005), pp. 64–65.

14. Indeed Secretary of Defense Rumsfeld was furious at the raids because authorization for them originated from the uniformed military, coordinated directly with the president, and not from his office. Bob Woodward, *Plan of Attack* (New York: Simon & Schuster, 2004), pp. 14–15.

15. See Phillips, *Losing Iraq*, 56–57; Mann, *The Rise of the Vulcans*. For a depiction of Scowcroft's prudent realism as the underlying viewpoint of the pragmatic internationalists and its contrast with Paul Wolfowitz's ambitious idealism, see Jeffrey Goldberg, "Breaking Ranks: What Turned Brent Scowcroft Against the Bush Administration," *New Yorker*, October 31, 2005, pp. 54–65. For the distinction between "pragmatic internationalists" and what they refer to as "assertive nationalists," see Ivo H. Daalder and James M. Lindsay, *America Unbound: The Bush Revolution in Foreign Policy* (Hoboken, N.J.: John Wiley & Sons, 2005), p. 55.

16. Deborah Schoeneman, "Armani's Exchange . . . Condi's Slip . . . Forget the Alamo," *New York*, April 26, 2004, http://www.newyorkmetro.com/nymetro/news/people/columns/intelligencer/n_10245.

17. Seymour M. Hersh, *Chain of Command: The Road from 9/11 to Abu Ghraib* (New York: Harper, 2004), p. 167.

18. Condoleezza Rice, "Campaign 2000: Promoting the National Interest," *Foreign Affairs* 79, no. 1 (January/February 2000): 45–62.

19. Richard A. Clarke, *Against All Enemies: Inside America's War on Terror* (New York: Free Press, 2004), pp. 227–28; Phillips, *Losing Iraq*, p. 19.

20. Daniel Pipes and Laurie Mylroie, "It's Time for a U.S. 'Tilt': Back Iraq," *New Republic*, April 27, 1987.

21. Clarke, *Against All Enemies*, pp. 231–32.

22. Ibid., p. 232.

23. For ways Wolfowitz and other supremacists used Mylroie's thesis to

point America's response toward Iraq immediately after 9/11, see also Daniel Benjamin and Steven Simon, *The Next Attack: The Failure of the War on Terror and a Strategy for Getting It Right* (New York: Times Books, 2005), pp. 143–56.

24. Daalder and Lindsay, *America Unbound*, pp. 61–69.

25. In 1995 the Clinton administration had authorized a Chalabi-centered insurrection in Iraq that fizzled disastrously, embarrassing the CIA, exposing its agents in Iraq, and resulting in the execution of 136 opposition leaders within Iraq.

26. Woodward, *Plan of Attack*, pp. 21–23; Hersh, *Chain of Command*, pp. 168–69.

27. Packer, *The Assassins' Gate*, p. 38.

28. Walter Pincus, "For Some, Syria Looms as Next Goal," *Washington Post*, April 8, 2003; Jim Lobe, "Calls to Attack Syria Come from a Familiar Choir of Hawks," *Foreign Policy in Focus*, April 16, 2003, http://www.fpif.org/fpiftxt/852. For remarks on the eve of the Iraq War by Richard Perle and John Bolton regarding the need for U.S. action to achieve regime change in Libya, Iran, North Korea, and other countries in addition to Iraq, see Amir Taheri, "Perles of Wisdom: An Interview with Richard Perle," March 7, 2003, National Review Online, http://www.nationalreview.com/comment/comment-taheri030703.asp; and Aluf Benn, "Sharon Says U.S. Should Also Disarm Iran, Libya and Syria," *Haaretz*, February 18, 2001, http://www.haaretzdaily.com/hasen/pages/ShArt.jhtml?itemNo = 263941. For evidence of planning by Rumsfeld and Wolfowitz to achieve forcible regime change in Iran, see James Risen, *State of War: The Secret History of the CIA and the Bush Administration* (New York: Free Press, 2006), pp. 216–17. When in May 2003 Jay Garner was replaced by Paul Bremer as America's plenipotentiary in Iraq, he had a brief meeting with Bush and Cheney while both were still in the flush of the "victory" in Iraq. George Packer describes the end of the meeting as follows: " 'You want to do Iran for the next one?' the president joshed as the meeting came to an end. 'No, sir, me and the boys are holding out for Cuba.' Bush laughed and promised Garner and the boys Cuba." Packer, *The Assassins' Gate*, pp. 145–46.

29. Ian S. Lustick, "Storm Warnings for a Supply-Side War," *Nation*, March 24, 2003, http://www.thenation.com/doc/20030324/lustick.

30. Clarke, *Against All Enemies*, p. 239.

31. Daalder and Lindsay, *America Unbound*, p. 86.

32. In a June 2003 meeting with Palestinian leaders, including Palestinian President Mahmud Abbas (Abu Mazen) and Nabil Sha'ath, Bush explained his decision to invade Afghanistan and Iraq and linked it to his commitment to Palestinians and Israelis. "I'm driven with a mission from God. God would tell me, 'George, go and fight those terrorists in Afghanistan.' And I did, and then God would tell me, 'George, go and end the tyranny in Iraq . . .' And I

did. And now, again, I feel God's words coming to me, 'Go get the Palestinians their state and get the Israelis their security, and get peace in the Middle East.' And by God I'm gonna do it." British Broadcasting Corporation, Press Office, "God Told Me to Invade Iraq, Bush Tells Palestinian Ministers," October 6, 2005, http://www.bbc.co.uk/pressoffice/pressreleases/stories/2005/10_octo ber/06/bush.shtml.

33. Woodward, *Plan of Attack*, pp. 24–25. "UBL" is an acronym for Usama bin Laden. A military source within the Pentagon told James Fallows that within two days of the attack "his group was asked to draw up scenarios for an assault on Iraq, not just Afghanistan." Fallows, "Blind into Baghdad," p. 56.

34. Fallows, "Blind into Baghdad," pp. 54–56.

35. Clarke, *Against all Enemies*, pp. 30–31.

36. Ibid., p. 32.

37. David Plotz, "Osama, Saddam, and the Bombs," *Slate*, September 28, 2001, http://www.slate.com/id/116232/#ContinueArticle.

38. Hersh, *Chain of Command*, p. 169, quoting from Perle's speech to the Foreign Policy Relations Institute in Philadelphia in November 2001.

39. Paul R. Pillar, "Intelligence, Policy, and the War in Iraq," *Foreign Affairs* 85, no. 2 (March/April 2006): 20.

40. Nicholas Lemann, "The War on What? The White House and the Debate About Whom to Fight Next," *New Yorker*, September 16, 2002. See also Mann, *The Rise of the Vulcans*, p. 318.

41. Gerry J. Gilmore, "U.S. 'Will Hunt Down and Punish' Terrorists, Bush Says," Armed Forces Information Service, Sept. 11, 2001, http://www.defense link.mil/news/Sep2001/n09112001_200109112.html.

42. George W. Bush, "Address to a Joint Session of Congress and the American People," September 20, 2001, http://www.whitehouse.gov/news/releas es/2001/09/20010920–8.html.

43. George W. Bush, "State of the Union Address," January 29, 2002, White House, Office of the Press Secretary, http://www.whitehouse.gov/news/re leases/2002/01/20020129–11.html.

44. George W. Bush, "President Bush Delivers Graduation Speech at West Point," June 1, 2002, White House, Office of the Press Secretary, http:// www.whitehouse.gov/news/releases/2002/06/20020601–3.html.

45. Larry Diamond, *Squandered Victory: The American Occupation and the Bungled Effort to Bring Democracy to Iraq* (New York: Times Books, 2005), pp. 27–31.

46. For details, see Phillips, *Losing Iraq*, pp. 59–65, 121–29; Fallows, "Blind into Baghdad"; Hersh, *Chain of Command*, pp. 177–79; Daalder and Lindsay, *America Unbound*, pp. 61–69, 166–71; and Packer, *Assassins' Gate*, pp. 128–48.

47. Clarke, *Against All Enemies*, pp. 239–43.

48. Woodward, *Plan of Attack*, p. 137.

49. In his now-famous ninety-minute interview with Sam Tannenhaus of *Vanity Fair* on May 10, 2003, Wolfowitz listed various reasons for having invaded Iraq. The Iraqi weapons of mass destruction threat was just one of them, and so, he suggested, if these weapons were not found it would not eliminate the rationale for the war. Nevertheless, in terms of the war's public justification, he explained that "for reasons that have a lot to do with U.S. government bureaucracy we settled on the one issue that everyone could agree on, which was weapons of mass destruction." The interview appeared in *Vanity Fair*, July 2003. An extensive discussion of the quotation, and its context, with Tannenhaus can be found at http://edition.cnn.com/transcripts/0305/30/se.08.html.

50. On the decisive role of the Office of Special Plans in implementing the Cheney-Rumsfeld-Wolfowitz-Feith strategy of stifling all independent intelligence judgments about Saddam's involvement with al-Qaeda, his actual WMD capacity, and the difficulties of postwar reconstruction, see Kenneth M. Pollack, "Spies, Lies, and Weapons: What Went Wrong," *Atlantic Monthly* (January/February 2004): 88–90; and Packer, *The Assassins' Gate*, pp. 104–8. For authoritative insider reports describing the successful cabal campaign to cook American intelligence findings according to the supremacist recipe, see Pillar, "Intelligence, Policy, and the War in Iraq," pp. 15–27; and Karen Kwiatowski's whistle-blowing portrait of the Office of Special Plans. Kwiatowski provides a wealth of specific information on the contributions, attitudes, and intentions of William Luti, deputy undersecretary of defense for Near Eastern and South Asian affairs, Undersecretary of Defense Douglas Feith, and Director of the Office of Special Plans Abram Shulsky. Lieutenant-Colonel Kwiatowski published her account in a three-part series of articles in the *American Conservative*, December 1, 2003; December 15, 2003; and January 19, 2004, titled, respectively, "In Rumsfeld's Shop," "Conscientious Objector," and "Open Door Policy."

51. Nicholas Lemann, "The Controller: Karl Rove Is Working to Get George Bush Reelected, But He Has Bigger Plans," "Profiles," *New Yorker*, May 12, 2003.

52. Clarke, *Against All Enemies*, pp. 241–42. Clarke is quoting Randy Beers. "Wag the Dog" is a reference to the movie by that name dramatizing the politically effective use of a nonexistent but media-hyped war. See below, Chapter 5, for a discussion of this movie and its relationship to political strategies implemented during the 2002 and 2004 elections.

53. http://web.archive.org/web/20030211230634/http://www.liberationiraq.org. See also Jim Lobe, "Committee for the Liberation of Iraq Sets Up Shop," November 2002; *Foreign Policy in Focus*, http://presentdanger.irc-online.org/pdf/reports/PRlibiraq.pdf.

54. In a very concrete sense a War on Terror casts the enemy not as an organization or set of adversaries but as a tactic or as fear itself. The equivalent might be not a "war on influenza" but a "war against fever."

CHAPTER 5

1. For closely related arguments that general perceptions of pervasive threats and vulnerabilities associated with terrorism produce perverse incentives and opportunities to profit from exaggerating the threats, see Frank Furedi, "The Politics of Fear," 2004, http://www.frankfuredi.com/articles/politicsFear-20041028.shtml; Lawrence Freedman, "The Politics of Warning: Terrorism and Risk Communication," *Intelligence and National Security* 20, no. 3 (September 2005): 379–418; and Benjamin H. Friedman, "The Hidden Cost of Homeland Defense," *Audit of the Conventional Wisdom*, MIT Center for International Studies, 05–12 (November 2005).

2. For classic statements of the Constitution's logic in these regards, see Alexander Hamilton, John Jay, and James Madison, *The Federalist Papers*, especially papers 15 and 51.

3. *The 9/11 Commission Report Including Executive Summary: Final Report of the National Commission on Terrorist Attacks upon the United States* (Baton Rouge, La.: Claitor's Publishing Division, 2004), p. 396.

4. Ibid.

5. According to the report, neither the congressional action itself nor bureaucrats implementing the legislation were able to define "adversely affected." Lenders whose loans were subsidized by the SBA were allowed to make relevant judgments themselves, without submitting their evidence to the government. Office of the Inspector General, U.S. Small Business Administration, "Audit of SBA's Administration of the Supplemental Terrorist Activity Relief Loan Program," Report Number 6-09, December 23, 2005, http://www.sba.gov/ig/6-09.pdf, pp. 2–3.

6. One other common theme in wartime, the need for sacrifice by all citizens, has been notably absent from the official War on Terror discourse, perhaps helping to inoculate the War on Terror against popular criticism.

7. James Jay Carafano, "The FY 2006 Budget Request for Homeland Security: A Congressional Guide for Making America Safer," Heritage Foundation, March 18, 2005, http://www.heritage.org/Research/HomelandDefense/bg1835.cfm.

8. Shawn Reese, "FY2006 Appropriations for State and Local Homeland Security," Congressional Research Service, Government and Finance Division, June 16, 2005, http://www.fas.org/sgp/crs/homesec/RS22050.pdf; and Eric Lipton, "New Rules Set for Giving Out Antiterror Aid," *New York Times*, January 3, 2006.

9. CBS News, "Small States, Big Anti-Terror Fund," June 27, 2003; Lipton, "New Rules."

10. For a state-by-state breakdown for 2004 homeland security expenditures, see a report by the National Conference of State Legislatures: http://www .ncsl.org/programs/pubs/slmag/2004/04SLDec_StateStats.pdf.

11. U.S. Senate, Department of Homeland Security Appropriations Act, 109th Cong., 1st sess., 2006, S. Rept. S8093-S9106. On September 21, 2002, the International Association of Fire Investigators released a "Congressional Fire Service Institute Legislative Update" describing efforts by Congressman Mike Ross of Arizona to boost War on Terror spending for rural firefighters and volunteer fire departments. For an example of an equally self-serving argument on behalf of War on Terror spending via allocations that would deliver the overwhelming majority of the funds to large urban centers, see a *New York Times* editorial, "An Insecure Nation: Real Security, or Politics as Usual?" May 1, 2005.

12. Frank Keating, "Bad Things Happen in Small Places," *New York Times*, January 11, 2006.

13. Scott Dodd, "Wasteful or Worth the Price? Local Carolinas Officials Spend Terror Funds on Pickups and Plasma Screens," *Charlotte Observer*, September 12, 2004.

14. Prepared remarks by Secretary Michael Chertoff, "U.S. Department of Homeland Security Second Stage Review," Department of Homeland Security, July 13, 2005, http://www.dhs.gov/dhspublic/interapp/speech/speech_ 0255.xml.

15. Lipton, "New Rules."

16. Lara Jakes Jordan, "Homeland Security to Expand Aid Not Linked to Terror Fight," Associated Press, January 3, 2006 (emphasis added).

17. IBA West, quoted passages from "Insurer Coalition Commends NAIC Adoption of TRIA Extension," http://www.ibawest.com/cgi-bin/beta.asp? SecID = 677&ID = 6662. For more on efforts by the insurance industry along these lines, see a 2004 letter to key representatives from the Coalition to Insure Against Terrorism (CIAT) at http://www.aba.com/NR/rdonlyres/ 6F8B26C2–14D1–4D14–906A-16ED2A97A29C/35736/BakerKelly.pdf; as well as reactions to TRIA's extension, with some modifications, for another two years beginning in 2006, including statements by the National Association of Mutual Insurance Companies, "NAMIC Congratulates President, Congress for Extending TRIA," December 22, 2005, http://www.namic.org/news releases05/051222nr1.asp; and the Insurance Information Institute, "Terrorism Risk and Insurance," January 2006, http://www.iii.org/media/hottopics/in surance/terrorism/.

18. Resolution and policy adopted by the National District Attorneys Asso-

ciation, March 23, 2002, Costa Mesa, California, http://www.ndaa-apri.org/publications/ndaa/ndaa_antiterrorism_resolution_emay_june_2002.html.

19. *Journal of Veterinary Medical Education* 30, no. 2 (2003), http://www.utpjournals.com/jvme-feature-article.html.

20. For the text of this letter, see the Web site of the Academy of Managed Care Pharmacy at http://www.amcp.org/data/legislative/analysis/21202.pdf.

21. U.S. Senate, Committee on Appropriations, Subcommittee on Labor, Health and Human Services, and Education statement, on behalf of the American Academy of Pediatrics, Senate, 107th Cong., 2nd sess., April 15, 2002, p. 1.

22. Ibid., pp. 5–6.

23. See, for example, Randy Borum, *Psychology of Terrorism* (Tampa: University of South Florida, 2004), http://www.ncjrs.org/pdffiles1/nij/grants/208552.pdf.

24. Sara Martin, "Thwarting Terrorism," *Monitor on Psychology* 33, no. 1 (January 2002), http://www.apa.org/monitor/jan02/terrorism.html.

25. U.S. Department of Health and Human Services, "FY2004 Budget in Brief," http://www.hhs.gov/budget/04budget/fy2004bib.pdf; "2007 Budget Even with FY 2006," *NIH Record*, 58, no. 4, http://www.nih.gov/nihrecord/02_24_2006/story02.htm

26. U.S. Department of Health and Human Services, "FY2004 Budget in Brief," http://www.hhs.gov/budget/04budget/fy2004bib.pdf.

27. Loren Berger and Dennis Henigan, "Guns and Terror: How Terrorists Exploit Our Weak Gun Laws," Brady Center to Prevent Gun Violence, 2001, http://www.bradycenter.org/xshare/pdf/reports/gunsandterror.pdf.

28. Steve Friess, "NRA Counts on 9/11 Momentum at Convention," *USA Today*, April 25, 2002. For an insightful study of how the larger movement of gun rights activists have changed their narrative to capitalize on the War on Terror, see Christy Allen, "The Second Amendment IS Homeland Security: American Gun Rights Activism Post September 11, 2001," http://www.essex.ac.uk/sociology/postgraduates/6_allen.pdf.

29. Allen, "Second Amendment," p. 9.

30. U.S. Senate, Committee on Commerce, Science, and Transportation, testimony of Leo F. Mullin, chairman and CEO, Delta Airlines, 107th Cong., 2nd sess., September 20, 2001, http://www.house.gov/transportation/full chearings/09–19–01/mullin.html. See also David Armstrong, "Airline Crisis: Bush Offers $5 Billion as Part of Aid Package to Help Airlines Avoid Financial Disaster," *San Francisco Chronicle*, September 20, 2001. Regarding demands under this rubric by the more general travel and tourism industry, see, for example, U.S. House, Subcommittee on Commerce, Trade, and Consumer Protection, 107th Cong., 2nd sess., testimony of Michael Sternberg, CEO of Sam & Harry's, on behalf of the National Restaurant Association, May 23, 2002, http://www.restaurant.org/tourism/tourism_bestpractices.cfm. Sternberg was urging

passage of the American Travel Promotion Act to provide $100 million to advertise travel and tourism.

31. U.S. House, Committee on Education and the Workforce, testimony of John J. Sweeney, November 14, 2001, 107th Cong., 1st sess., http://www.aflcio.org/mediacenter/prsptm/tm11142001.cfm?RenderForPrint = 1.

32. U.S. Senate, Committee on Banking, Housing, and Urban Affairs, testimony of F. Barton Harvey, chairman and CEO, The Enterprise Foundation, 107th Cong., 2nd sess., November 29, 2001, http://www.enterprisefoundation.org/resources/policyinfo/federal/federalpublic policy/testimony/Testimony_HUD2003budget.htm.

33. Lara Jakes Jordan, "Ex-FEMA Chief Shifts Katrina Blame to DHS," Associated Press, February 10, 2006, http://abcnews.go.com/Politics/HurricaneKatrina/wireStory?id = 1604472&CMP = OTC-RSSFeeds0312.

34. Andrew Lakoff, "From Disaster to Catastrophe: The Limits of Preparedness," Social Science Research Council Web site, September 30, 2005, http://understandingkatrina.ssrc.org/Lakoff.

35. These scenarios are the official basis for funding guidelines for national, state, and local preparedness operations, meaning that no funds could be allocated *unless* those funds are justified as related to tasks or capabilities required to cope with one of these *particular* disaster scenarios rather than to any other kind of catastrophe any state or locality might find more worrisome or plausible. For a list of the fifteen scenarios, see "National Preparedness," a Power Point presentation prepared by the State of Iowa's Department of Homeland Security and Emergency Management, http://www.iowahomelandsecurity.org/asp/resource_room/Dec_13_Exercise.ppt. See also Eric Lipton, "U.S. Report Lists Possibilities for Terrorist Attacks and Likely Toll," *New York Times*, March 16, 2005, and *Times* (London), March 17, 2005.

36. Laurie Garrett, "The Next Pandemic?" *Foreign Affairs* 84, no. 4 (July/August 2005): 17–23.

37. See, for example, the professional journal (inaugurated in 2003) *Biosecurity and Bioterrorism: Biodefense Strategy, Practice, and Science,* http://www.biosecurityjournal.com/; a new manager-level course at MIT entitled "Combating Bioterrorism/Pandemics: Implementing Policies for Biosecurity," http://web.mit.edu/mitpep/pi/courses/combating_bioterrorism.html; and a Federation of American Scientists program entitled "Biosecurity Education for Biologists," http://www.fas.org/main/content.jsp?formAction = 297&contentId = 150. See also materials available at the Web site of the newly formed Center for Biosecurity at the University of Pittsburgh Medical Center, http://www.upmc-biosecurity.org/bb/archive/bb051111.html. The center describes its mission as follows: "to affect policy and practice in ways that lessen the illness,

death, and civil disruption that would follow large-scale epidemics, whether they occur naturally or result from the use of a biological weapon."

38. Salih Booker, director of Africa Action, quoted by Agence France-Presse, June 2, 2004, http://www.globalexchange.org/campaigns/wbimf/2950.html.

39. President Bush himself made the link for viewing the struggle against poverty and AIDS in Africa as part of the War on Terror. "America is committed to the success of Africa because we recognize a moral duty to bring hope where there is despair, and relief where there's suffering. America is committed to the success of Africa because we understand failed states spread instability and terror that threatens us all. America is committed to the success of Africa because the peoples of Africa have every right to live in freedom and dignity, and to share in the progress of our times." President George W. Bush, remarks at a meeting of the Corporate Council on Africa's U.S.-Africa Business Summit, June 26, 2003, http://www.data.org/archives/000122.php.

40. Sebastian Mallaby, "The Reluctant Imperialist: Terrorism, Failed States, and the Case for American Empire," *Foreign Affairs* 81, no. 2 (March/April 2002): 2–7; Robert I. Rotberg, "Failed States in a World of Terror," *Foreign Affairs* 81, no. 4 (July/August 2002): 127–40; Stuart E. Eizenstat, John Edward Porter, and Jeremy M. Weinstein, "Rebuilding Weak States," *Foreign Affairs* 84, no. 1 (January/February 2005): 134–46; "Giving Back: A Conversation with Ruth Messinger," *Reform Judaism*, Winter 2005, http://reformjudaismmag.org/Articles/index.cfm?id = 1091; Stewart Patrick, "A Strategy to Prevent Failed States," *Miami Herald*, July 17, 2005, http://www.cgdev.org/content/opinion/detail/3116.

41. Daniel Benjamin and Steven Simon, *The Age of Sacred Terror: Radical Islam's War Against America* (New York: Random House, 2002), pp. 406–7.

42. U.S. Senate, Terrorism Risk Insurance Act of 2002, 107th Cong., 2nd sess., June 18, 2002, S5663; http://frwebgate.access.gpo.gov/cgi-bin/getpage.cgi?dbname = 2002_record&page = S5663&position = all.

43. Paul Rozin and Edward B. Royzman, "Negativity Bias, Negativity Dominance, and Contagion," *Personality and Social Psychology Review* 5, no. 4 (2001): 296–320; Paul Slovic, "Trust, Emotion, Sex, Politics and Science: Surveying the Risk-Assessment Battlefield," http://oregonstate.edu/dept/IIFET/2000/papers/slovic.pdf; W. Kip Viscusi, "Alarmist Decisions with Divergent Risk Information," *Economic Journal* 107, no. 445 (November 1997): 1657–70.

44. Information posted on the site of Journalism.org, "The State of the News Media," http://www.stateofthenewsmedia.org/2005/chartland.asp?id = 226&ct = line&dir = &sort = &col1_box = 1&col2_box = 1&col3_box = 1; and http://www.stateofthenewsmedia.org/2005/printable_cabletv_economics.asp.

45. U.S. House, Science Committee, Subcommittee on Research, testimony

of C. D. Mote, Jr., president, University of Maryland, College Park, 107th Cong., 2nd sess., May 9, 2002, http://www.aau.edu/research/Test5.9.02.html.

46. For an overview of the galvanizing effect of the War on Terror and associated funding priorities on the work of the national laboratories, see Deborah Shapley, "Homeland Bill Ignites Race Among National Labs," *Government Executive*, July 24, 2002, http://www.govexec.com/dailyfed/0702/072402cdam1.htm; and James Kitfield, "National Labs Seek Edge in Homeland Security Technology," *Government Executive*, January 10, 2003, http://www.govexec.com/dailyfed/0103/011003nj1.htm.

47. See, for example, http://www.cdc.gov/search.do?action = search&queryText = terror&x = 7&y = 7.

48. Tom Avril, "Defense Gets Larger Slice of Research Aid," *Philadelphia Inquirer*, November 5, 2005.

49. Ibid.

50. Susan Kinzie and Sari Horwitz, "Colleges' Hottest New Major: Terror," *Washington Post*, April 30, 2005.

51. Benjamin and Simon, *Age of Sacred Terror*, pp. 400–401.

52. The episode, entitled "The Plague Year," aired on CBS March 7, 2002, and was described as follows: "The CIA tracks an Algerian suicide bomber as he enters the U.S., but the agents do not realize he is infected with smallpox until he is taken into custody. When they learn his mission is to infect the Agency first, the agents race to ensure the virus is contained before more people are infected." http://www.tv.com/agency/show/2126/episode_guide.html.

53. Benjamin M. Eidelson and Ian S. Lustick, "VIR-POX: An Agent-Based Analysis of Smallpox Preparedness and Response Policy," *Journal of Artificial Societies and Social Simulation* 7, no. 3 (2004), http://jasss.soc.surrey.ac.uk/7/3/6.html.

54. Ariana Eunjung Cha, "Computers Simulate Terrorism's Extremes," *Washington Post*, July 4, 2005.

55. http://www.purdue.edu/eas/news/newsletter/2–14–05.pdf.

56. "Essay Contest for the Purdue Homeland Security Institute," document provided by Bethany Naylor in a personal communication, Purdue Homeland Security Institute. See also http://www.purduehomelandsecurity.org/.

57. BBC News, "Hollywood: The Pentagon's New Advisor," March 2002, http://news.bbc.co.uk/1/hi/programmes/panorama/1891196.stm.

58. Eric Lipton, "U.S. Borders Vulnerable, Officials Say," *New York Times*, June 22, 2005.

59. Eric Lipton, "Scenarios of Possible Terror Strikes Read like Doomsday Plan," *New York Times*, March 16, 2005.

60. Department of Homeland Security, "Fact Sheet: Homeland Security:

Strengthening National Preparedness: Capabilities-Based Planning," http://www.ojp.usdoj.gov/odp/docs/CBP_041305.pdf.

61. Benjamin and Simon, *The Age of Sacred Terror*, pp. 402, 477.

62. See Richard Falkenrath's (short) list of War on Terror accomplishments to make America safer: Richard A. Falkenrath, "Grading the War on Terrorism: Asking the Right Questions," *Foreign Affairs* 85, no. 1 (January/February 2006): 124.

63. Note that this explanation for fear in the virtual absence of credible threat would be strengthened by, but does not require, designs by political leaders to keep the public apprehensive about its security.

64. Stephen E. Flynn and Lawrence M. Wein, "Think Inside the Box," *New York Times*, November 29, 2005.

65. Lawrence M. Wein, "Got Toxic Milk?" *New York Times*, May 30, 2005.

66. "Trouble on the Tracks," *New York Times*, October 17, 2005. For more *New York Times* editorials and articles in this vein, see its archive under the heading "Insecure Nation" at http://www.nytimes.com/insecurenation.

67. Ben Raines and Bill Finch, "Study Talks of Possible LNG Disaster as Result of Accident," *Mobile Register*, December 7, 2003, http://www.wildcalifornia.org/cgi-files/0/pdfs/1076793906_Humboldt_Bay_LNG_Mob_Reg_Study_Possible_Disaster.pdf; Mac Daniel, "Fire Officials Voice Concerns on LNG Threat," *Boston Globe*, February 27, 2004; Institute for the Analysis of Global Security, "LNG—Not in My Backyard," in *Energy Security*, January 21, 2004, http://www.iags.org/n0121041.htm. For an instructive collection of essays outlining a litany of threats and vulnerabilities, see Russell Howard, James Forest, and Joanne Moore, eds., *Homeland Security and Terrorism* (New York: McGraw-Hill, 2006). The authors focus on aviation, public transportation, border security, cyber threats, critical infrastructure, shipping containers, water supply, and biosecurity in agriculture and the food industry. Each author advocates more spending and more serious attention to terrorist threats in his or her domain of interest.

68. Anti-Defamation League, *Border Disputes: Armed Vigilantes in Arizona*, 2003, p. 2, http://www.adl.org/extremism/arizona/arizonaborder.pdf.

69. http://tancredo.house.gov/reformnow/bordersecuritycrisis.shtml.

70. In December 2005 the House of Representatives passed an immigration bill including provisions for a physical barrier to be built all along the Mexican border and ordered the Department of Homeland Security to study the feasibility of erecting barriers on the border with Canada. When the bill was passed, the Speaker of the House, Dennis Hastert, referred to the "age of terrorism" as justifying the new measures.

71. Gary Martin, "Tancredo Says Plan Is 'Poor Public Policy' and Runs

Contrary to Public Opinion," October 19, 2005, http://www.alipac.us/article-823.html.

72. Jim Abrams, "Bush Says Guest-Worker Plan a Necessity," *Boston Globe*, October 19, 2005, http://www.boston.com/news/nation/washington/articles/2005/10/19/bush_says_guest_worker_plan_a_necessity.

73. Anne C. Mulkern, "Tancredo Backs Away from Presidential Bid," *Denver Post*, April 14, 2006, http://www.denverpostbloghouse.com/washington/?p = 655#more-655. See also Jonathan Tilove, "Reform Caucus a Barometer of the Republican Schism on Immigration," Newhouse News Service, 2002, http://www.newhousenews.com/archive/story1a052302.html; Carrying Capacity Network Action Alert, "Pushing for an Immigration Moratorium Now," November 2002, http://www.carryingcapacity.org/alerts/alert1105.html; and Peter Andreas, *A Tale of Two Borders: The U.S.-Mexico and U.S.-Canada Lines After 9–11*, Working Paper 77, The Center for Comparative Immigration Studies, University of California, San Diego, May 2003.

74. Bernard C. Cohen, *The Press and Foreign Policy* (Westport, Conn.: Greenwood Press, 1963), p. 13, as quoted by Heinz Brandenburg, "Communicating Issue Salience: A Comparative Study into Campaign Effects on Media Agenda Formation," paper prepared for presentation at the EPOP 2004 Annual Conference, Oxford, United Kingdom, September 10–12, p. 4.

75. After the 2004 election, Bush's approval ratings fell dramatically, in all domains. By June 2005 polls indicated that "how the President is handling U.S. campaign against terrorism" was the *only* issue with respect to which more respondents expressed approval than disapproval. *Washington Post*/ABC News Poll, June 2005, http://www.washingtonpost.com/wp-dyn/content/article/2005/06/07/AR200506070029 6.html. According to political analyst William Schneider, Rove told the Republican National Committee in January 2006 that "the Republicans won on the terrorism issue in 2002, they won again on it in 2004, and they have every intention on running yet again on the terrorism issue, making it their issue in 2006." Schneider went on to advise Democrats to make fighting the War on Terror their issue if they were to have a chance at victory in the November elections. Schneider was interviewed by Lou Dobbs on CNN, January 23, 2006, http://www.alipac.us/article1004.html.

76. President George W. Bush, *Securing the Homeland, Strengthening the Nation*, The White House, February 1, 2002, http://www.whitehouse.gov/homeland/homeland_security_book.pdf, p. 2.

77. David Brancaccio, interview with Frank Luntz, *NOW*, Public Broadcasting Service, July 2, 2004. Transcript accessible at http://www.pbs.org/now/transcript/transcript327_full.html#luntz.

78. *Meet the Press*, NBC, September 7, 2003, transcript of interview at http://msnbc.msn.com/id/3080244.

79. E. J. Dionne, Jr., "Rove's Early Warning," *Washington Post*, January 24, 2006.

80. This may be compared with six and two references, respectively, in Senator Kerry's acceptance speech at the Democratic Party convention.

81. In an interview with Jon Stewart, Richard Clarke described the intensive White House campaign of "character assassination" against him. "There are dozens of people in the White House . . . writing talking points, calling up conservative columnists, calling up talk radio hosts, telling them what to say. It's interesting, all the talk radio people all across the country, saying exactly the same thing, exactly the same words." http://www.comedycentral.com/sitewide/media_player/play.jhtml?itemId = 12500.

82. Tommy Franks, interview with John O. Edwards, *Cigar Aficionado*, December 2003, as reported by newsmax.com, http://www.newsmax.com/archives/articles/2003/11/20/185048.shtml. Franks made an impassioned speech on behalf of the president at the Republican National Convention, September 2, 2004, emphasizing the War on Terror as the main issue facing the country and endorsing Bush "because his vision to take the fight to the terrorists is the best way to protect our country." http://www.command-post.org/2004/2_archives/014961.html.

83. David Rothkopf, "Terrorist Logic: Disrupt the 2004 Election," *Washington Post*, November 23, 2003, http://www.washingtonpost.com/ac2/wp-dyn/A5269–2003Nov21.

84. William Safire, "Office Pool, 2004," *New York Times*, December 31, 2003.

85. For a collection of examples of public commentary on the possibility of terrorism interfering with the American elections in 2004, see Maureen Farrell, "Will the 2004 Election Be Called Off? Why Three Out of Four Experts Predict a Terrorist Attack by November," BuzzFlash, April 6, 2004, http://www.buzzflash.com/farrell/04/04/far04011.html.

86. David Brooks, "Al-Qaeda's Wish List," *New York Times*, March 16, 2004.

87. *USA Today*, March 15, 2004.

88. CNN.com, "Officials: Bin Laden Guiding Plots Against U.S.," July 8, 2004, http://www.cnn.com/2004/US/07/08/ridge.alqaeda/index.html; and "Officials Discuss How to Delay Election Day," July 12, 2004, http://www.cnn.com/2004/ALLPOLITICS/07/11/election.day.delay.

89. Ibid.

90. Tom Ridge, Secretary of Homeland Security, "Threat Level Raised," Department of Homeland Security, Office of the Press Secretary, December 21, 2003, http://www.whitehouse.gov/news/releases/2003/12/20031221.html.

91. Press briefing by Scott McClellan, The White House, Office of the Press Secretary, May 26, 2004, http://www.whitehouse.gov/news/releases/2004/05/20040526–4.html.

92. CNN.com, transcript, "Ashcroft, Mueller News Conference," May 26, 2004, http://www.cnn.com/2004/US/05/26/terror.threat.transcript.

93. Remarks by Secretary of Homeland Security Tom Ridge regarding recent threat reports, Department of Homeland Security, Office of the Press Secretary, August 1, 2004, http://www.dhs.gov/dhspublic/display?content = 3870.

94. Dan Eggen and Dana Priest, "Pre-9/11 Acts Led to Alerts," *Washington Post*, August 3, 2004.

95. See David Yepsen, "Face It, Dean, We're at War," *Des Moines Register*, August 8, 2004, http://desmoinesregister.com/apps/pbcs.dll/article?AID = / 20040808/OPINION01/408080333/1035/OPINION.

96. Scott McClellan, "Press Gaggle Aboard Air Force One," The White House, Office of the Press Secretary, August 3, 2004, http://www.whitehouse .gov/news/releases/2004/08/20040803–5.html.

97. Eggen and Priest, "Pre-9/11 Acts Led to Alerts."

98. David Johnston and Don Van Natta, "Little Evidence of Qaeda Plot Timed to Vote," *New York Times*, October 24, 2004.

99. John Mintz, "Skepticism of Terrorism Alerts Cited," *Washington Post*, May 4, 2005.

100. Mimi Hall, "Ridge Reveals Clashes on Alerts," *USA Today*, May 10, 2005.

101. Falkenrath, "Grading the War on Terrorism," 124. A common response to this inference has been to point to the non-occurrence of attacks in the four years prior to September 2001, despite the absence of the War on Terror.

CHAPTER 6

1. Matt Bai, "Kerry's Undeclared War," *New York Times Magazine*, October 10, 2004.

2. "John Kerry in UCLA Address Promises More Effective War on Terrorism," text of speech delivered at the UCLA International Institute, http:// www.international.ucla.edu/article.asp?parentid = 8320.

3. As further evidence that Kerry's remarks to Bai reflected his actual views, Bai quoted Richard Holbrooke, the candidate's shadow secretary of state, as describing the idea of the War on Terror as flawed, as more of a metaphor than an actual war, and as needing to be replaced by an "ideological struggle so that people stop turning themselves into suicide bombers." Bai, "Kerry's Undeclared War."

4. CNN.com, "Bush Campaign to Base Ad on Kerry Terror Quote," October 11, 2004, http://www.cnn.com/2004/ALLPOLITICS/10/10/bush.kerry .terror/.

5. Susan Jones, "Kerry's Terrorism/Nuisance Remark Wasn't Even Origi-

nal," CNSNews.com, October 12, 2004, http://www.cnsnews.com/View Politics.asp?Page = %5CPolitics%5Carchive%5C200410%5CPOL20041012d.html.

6. Ibid.

7. Transcript of Bush-Kerry debate, October 14, 2003, http://seattlepi.nw source.com/national/04debate3.html. Kerry's tougher-than-thou message regarding prosecution of the War on Terror was echoed in early 2006 by a chorus of Democratic politicians who condemned the Bush administration's approval of a deal that would have given a Dubai-based company control over some operations in some American ports. Despite the president's protestations that national security was not put at risk by the deal and the virtual absence of expert opinion that it would represent a security threat, the arrangement was sidelined. In this episode, the enormous power of the War on Terror was on display in the irrelevance for public policy of any sober evaluation of evidence and in the irresistible impetus given to representatives of both parties to attack each other whenever possible for not prosecuting the War on Terror strongly enough. See, for example, Dick Meyer, "In Defense of Dubai," CBS News.com, February 22, 2006, http://www.cbsnews.com/stories/2006/02/22/opinion/meyer/main1335531.shtml.

8. Daniel Benjamin and Steven Simon, *The Age of Sacred Terror: Radical Islam's War Against America* (New York: Random House, 2002).

9. Daniel Benjamin and Steven Simon, *The Next Attack: The Failure of the War on Terror and a Strategy for Getting It Right* (New York: Times Books, 2005).

10. Ibid., pp. 113–18, 230–61.

11. Ibid., p. 263.

12. Ibid., p. 140.

13. In Robert A. Pape's widely cited book, *Dying to Win: The Strategic Logic of Suicide Terrorism* (New York: Random House, 2005), the author makes a similarly iconoclastic argument—that suicide terrorists from Hamas to al-Qaeda are motivated almost exclusively by their desire to drive Americans and others out of their lands. His recommendation is that the U.S. military presence be removed from Arab and Muslim lands, but even this analysis and recommendation is presented as the way to "win the war on terrorism" (p. 248).

14. For the argument that America's typical response to security threats has been fearful, and even hysterical, overreaction, see John Mueller, "Simplicity and Spook: Terrorism and the Dynamics of Threat Exaggeration," *International Studies Perspectives* 6, no. 2 (2005): 208–34. For an attempt to measure the objective scale of the post-9/11 terrorist threat to other security problems the United States has faced, see Joseph J. Ellis, "Finding a Place for 9/11 in American History," *New York Times*, January 28, 2006.

15. Speech on the floor of the Senate by Senator Joseph McCarthy, June 14,

1951. The full text of the speech is available at http://www.localvoter.com/ speech_jm2.asp.

16. X, "The Sources of Soviet Conduct," *Foreign Affairs* 25, no. 4 (July 1947): 575–76.

17. Ibid., p. 582.

18. Ibid., p. 572.

19. Ibid., p. 576.

20. Ibid., p. 581.

21. Ibid., pp. 575–76. In all these respects, of course, Kennan's policy of containment was the virtual opposite of the War on Terror.

22. The White House, "President Discusses War on Terror at National Endowment for Democracy," October 6, 2005, http://www.whitehouse.gov/ news/releases/2005/10/20051006–3.html.

23. "John Kerry in UCLA Address Promises More Effective War on Terrorism," UCLA International Institute, February 27, 2004, http://international. ucla.edu/article.asp?parentid = 8320.

24. Hope Yen, "Former 9/11 Commissioners: U.S. at Risk," *Boston Globe*, December 4, 2005, http://www.boston.com/news/nation/washington/arti cles/2005/12/04/former_911_commissioners_us_at_risk.

25. Statement by John D. Negroponte, director of national intelligence, to the Senate Select Committee on Intelligence, 109th Cong., 2nd sess., February 2, 2006, http://intelligence.senate.gov/0602hrg/060202/witness.htm.

26. The White House, "The National Security Strategy of the United States," September 2002. http://www.whitehouse.gov/nsc/nss.pdf.

27. Ibid. An updated version of the National Security Strategy was released by the White House in March 2006. The War on Terror remained the dominant theme, with 124 references to terror in the 49-page document compared to 94 references in the earlier 31-page version. President Bush's letter of introduction to the new NSS begins with the sentence "America is at war." The enemy is "terrorism fueled by an aggressive ideology of hatred and murder." The 2006 version, however, gives considerably more emphasis than its predecessor to the multilateral advancement of democracy in the battle against "terrorist tyranny." See http://www.whitehouse.gov/nsc/nss/2006/nss2006.pdf.

28. The executive summary of the National Planning Scenarios study explains the term as follows: "Because the attacks could be caused by foreign terrorists; domestic radical groups; state-sponsored adversaries; or in some cases, disgruntled employees, the perpetrator has been named, the Universal Adversary (UA)." The authors of the study justify this abstraction by stressing that the "focus of the scenarios is on response capabilities and needs, not threat-based prevention activities." What is instructive is the attempt to separate "responses" from threats. What could be more reinforcing for an ever-

expanding War on Terror than imperatives to prepare for dangers of any kind, whether threats are perceived to exist or not, simply because when dealing with the "Universal Adversary," anything is possible? David Howe, senior director for response and planning, *Planning Scenarios: Executive Summaries*, The Homeland Security Council, July 2004, http://cryptome.org/15-attacks.htm.

29. Mary R. Habeck, *Knowing the Enemy: Jihadist Ideology and the War on Terror* (New Haven, Conn.: Yale University Press, 2006), p. 162.

30. Ibid., p. 6.

31. Ibid., pp. 161–69.

32. Michael Scheuer, *Through Our Enemies' Eyes: Osama bin Laden, Radical Islam, and the Future of America* (Washington, D.C.: Potomac Books, 2006), p. x. On October 10, 2001, then national security adviser Condoleezza Rice summoned the heads of the five largest television networks in America to urge them (successfully) not to broadcast in full any al-Qaeda statements. Bin Laden mocked the administration's public rationale for this advice—that coded messages might otherwise be delivered to sleeper cells—wondering if the administration thought we were still living in the age of "carrier pigeons." Max Rodenbeck, "Their Master's Voice," *New York Review of Books* 53, no. 4 (March 9, 2006).

33. For insightful analysis that considers the intrinsic potential of war against terrorists to produce outsized opportunities for the terrorists to rally new support and accomplish other important objectives, see Clark McCauley, "Terrorism, Research and Public Policy: An Overview," in *Terrorism, Research and Public Policy*, ed. Clark McCauley (London: Frank Cass, 1991), pp. 126–53. For McCauley's use of "jujitsu politics" as a metaphor applied to the exploitation by al-Qaeda of the fury and resentment triggered among Muslims by the U.S. War on Terror, see Clark McCauley, "Jujitsu Politics: Terrorism and Response to Terrorism," in *Psychology of Terrorism*, ed. R. Wagner and C. Stout (Westport, Conn.: Praeger Security International, forthcoming).

34. "Arab Attitudes Toward Political and Social Issues, Foreign Policy and the Media," poll designed by Shibley Telhami of the University of Maryland and carried out by Zogby International. http://www.bsos.umd.edu/SADAT/PUB/Arab-Attitudes—2005weighted.htm.

35. Data released by the Pew Global Attitudes Project, June 23, 2005, http://pewglobal.org/reports/display.php?ReportID = 247.

36. For my own analysis of this kind of al-Qaeda intent with respect to an American-led war in the Middle East, see "America's War and Osama's Script," *The Arab World Geographer* 6, no. 1 (Spring 2003): 24–26, http://users.fmg.uva.nl/vmamadouh/awg/forum3/lustick.html. See also Richard A. Clarke et al., *Defeating the Jihadists* (New York: Century Foundation Press, 2004), 10–12.

37. Clark McCauley makes a very similar argument in "Psychological Issues in Understanding Terrorism and the Response to Terrorism," *Psychology of Terrorism*, pp. 16–17.

38. For a typical use of this quotation in the War on Terror, see Graham Allison, *Nuclear Terrorism: The Ultimate Preventable Catastrophe* (New York: Owl Books, 2004), pp. 12–14. Of interest in this particular case, and reflective of the general way that experts as well as politicians frame threats to correspond to the contribution to the War on Terror they personally wish to make, is that Allison provides several paragraphs of text from the Abu-Ghaith article and highlights the four-million-killed sentence while omitting the sentence that immediately follows: "Furthermore, it is our right to fight them with chemical and biological weapons, so as to afflict them with the fatal maladies that have afflicted the Muslims because of the [Americans'] chemical and biological weapons." Presumably, had Abu-Ghaith mentioned nuclear or radiological weapons, that sentence would not have been omitted. For a discussion of the series of articles including Abu-Ghaith's contribution, known as "In the Shadow of the Lances," see Ben N. Venzke and Aimee Ibrahim, "Lessons Learned in Afghanistan: al-Qaeda's Advice for Mujahideen in Iraq," *Military Intelligence Professional Bulletin*, January/March 2004, http://www.findarticles.com/p/articles/mi_moIBS/is_1_30/ai_n6123715.

39. William M. Arkin, "Early Warning," *Washington Post*, January 26, 2006. For advice to the administration from one of its former officials that the name of the War on Terror had outlived its usefulness, see Richard A. Falkenrath, "Grading the War on Terrorism: Asking the Right Questions," *Foreign Affairs* 85, no. 1 (January/February 2006): 127–28. Concerning the administration's decision to rewrite its 2002 "National Security Strategy of the United States," see Francis Fukuyama, "After Neoconservatism," *New York Times Magazine*, February 19, 2006.

40. For this distinction and useful background, see Quintan Wiktorowicz, "The New Global Threat: Transnational Salafis and Jihad," *Middle East Policy* 8, no. 4 (December 2001): 18–38. For a treatment that integrates the rise of the jihadi movement and analysis of the anatomy of its international network of cells, see Marc Sageman, *Understanding Terror Networks* (Philadelphia: University of Pennsylvania Press, 2004). For a detailed account and interpretation of bin Laden's thinking and purposes, see Scheuer, *Through Our Enemies' Eyes*.

41. Fawaz A. Gerges, *The Far Enemy: Why Jihad Went Global* (New York: Cambridge University Press, 2005).

42. On al-Zawahiri's metamorphosis, see ibid., pp. 89–96. See also Gilles Kepel, *The War for Muslim Minds: Islam and the West* (Cambridge, Mass.: Belknap Press, 2004), pp. 70–107.

43. Ibid., pp. 119–84.

44. From an interview with Osama bin Laden by Jamal Ismai'il, recorded at an unspecified location in Afghanistan in December 1998, as broadcast by Al-Jazeera satellite TV on September 20, 2001, monitored by the BBC Monitoring Service, September 22, 2001.

45. Ibn Taymiyya was an early fourteenth-century Muslim thinker who emphasized fanatical devotion to God, violent jihad against non-Muslims, and rigorous adherence to the original practices and beliefs of the first generations of Muslims. He is a commonly cited traditional source for contemporary Salafis partly because he sanctioned *takfeer* against Muslim Mongols.

46. Gerges, *Far Enemy*, p. 270.

47. Ibid.

48. Wiktorowicz, "The New Global Threat," p. 35.

49. Reuven Paz, "Global Jihad and WMD: Between Martyrdom and Mass Destruction," in *Current Trends in Islamist Ideology*, ed. Hillel Fradkin, Husain Haqqani, and Eric Brown, vol. 2 (Washington, D.C.: Hudson Institute, 2005), p. 76.

50. For the full transcript of bin Laden's speech, broadcast on Al-Jazeera on November 1, 2004, see http://english.aljazeera.net/NR/exeres/79C6AF22–98FB-4A1C-B21F-2BC36E87F61F.htm.

51. Reuel Marc Gerecht, "To Bomb or Not to Bomb," *Weekly Standard* 11, no. 30 (April 24, 2006); http://www.aei.org/publications/filter.all,pubID.24230/pub_detail.asp.

52. Seymour Hersh, "The Iran Plans: Would President Bush Go to War to Stop Tehran from Getting the Bomb?" *New Yorker*, April 17, 2006, http://www.newyorker.com/fact/content/articles/060417fa_fact.

53. See, for example, the extended discussions of this point by Benjamin and Simon in *The Next Attack*, pp. 81–95; and Kepel, *The War for Muslim Minds*, pp. 241–95.

54. In 2004 the total number of inner-circle al-Qaeda activists was estimated as 200–4,000 people, with 50,000–200,000 members of other jihadist groups in a Muslim world of 1.5 billion people. Clarke et al., *Defeating the Jihadists*, p. 17. In 2004 the Southern Poverty Law Center, which traces right-wing extremist groups in the United States, identified approximately 650 white supremacist hate groups in the United States, including the neo-Nazis, Ku Klux Klan, the Christian Identity Movement, Skinheads, and Neo-Confederates. In 2000 the FBI estimated that the Christian Identity Movement alone had up to 50,000 members. http://www.splcenter.org/intel/map/hate.jsp; Carolyn Tuft and Joe Holleman, "Inside the Christian Identity Movement," *St. Louis Post-Dispatch*, March 5, 2000. In 2006 the Bnai Brith Anti-Defamation League provided information on its Web site on dozens of similar and related groups. Total membership, in an American population of 300 million, is probably not much

more than 50,000. http://www.adl.org/learn/ext_us/default.asp?LEARN_
Cat = Extremism&LEARN_SubCat = Extremism_in_America&xpicked = 1&
item = 0.

55. Sageman, *Understanding Terror Networks*, p. 176. For a similar argument advancing law enforcement as the "treatment of choice for a chronic terrorist threat," see Clark McCauley, "War Versus Justice in Response to Terrorist Attack: Competing Frames and Their Implications," in *Psychology of Terrorism*, ed. B. Bongar, L. M. Brown, L. E. Beutler, J. N. Breckenridge, and P. G. Zimbardo (New York: Oxford University Press, forthcoming); and John Mueller, "Devils and Duct Tape: Terrorism and the Dynamics of Threat Exaggeration," paper presented at the Browne Center for International Politics, University of Pennsylvania, February 20, 2006. For the effectiveness of law enforcement as a counterterrorist strategy when terrorists do not have a state sponsor, see Daniel Byman, *Deadly Connections: States That Sponsor Terrorism* (Cambridge: Cambridge University Press, 2005), p. 72.

56. Sageman, *Understanding Terror Networks*, pp. 180–81.

57. Sean McCormack, Daily Press Briefing, Department of State, February 7, 2006, http://www.state.gov/r/pa/prs/dpb/2006/60618.htm.

58. Polling in the Muslim world shows that the United States and Israel vie for the top spot when respondents are asked to name the chief enemies of Islam. Benjamin and Simon, *The Next Attack*, p. 52.

59. Ian S. Lustick, "Through Blood and Fire Shall Peace Arise," *Tikkun* 17, no. 3 (May/June 2002): 13–19; and "Yerushalayim, al-Quds, and the Wizard of Oz: Facing the Problem of Jerusalem after Camp David II and the al-Aqsa Intifada," *Journal of Israeli History* 23, no. 2 (Autumn 2004): 200–215. See also Benjamin and Simon, *The Next Attack*, p. 206.

60. For how little jihadis cared about the Israel question and how little attention they gave to it *before* the bin Laden-engineered shift to the "far enemy," see Gerges, *The Far Enemy*, pp. 45–46. As bin Laden and al-Zawahiri shifted attention to the far enemy and their objective to "pit the ummah [all Muslims] against the leader of the Western world, the United States, and to unleash a clash of religions and cultures," their rhetoric increasingly emphasized Israel. Ibid., pp. 157–58.

61. Benjamin and Simon, *The Age of Sacred Terror*, pp. 140–41 and 147–48.

62. As Michael Scheuer has pointed out, "Bin Laden referred to the Palestinian struggle seven times in his 1996 declaration of war on the United States." *Through Our Enemies' Eyes*, p. 261.

63. Usama Bin Ladin, "Al-Qa'ida Recruitment Video," *Anti-American Terrorism and the Middle East: A Documentary Reader*, ed. Barry Rubin and Judith Colp Rubin (Oxford: Oxford University Press, 2002), pp. 174–83. The translation and analysis of the video were done by Fawaz A. Gerges and Richard Bulliet.

64. For the argument that the surfeit of volunteers for suicide bombing missions in the Muslim world is directly linked to Muslim fury at "foreign occupation," including both Israeli occupation of Palestinian territories and the presence of American forces in the Persian Gulf, see Robert A. Pape, *Dying to Win: The Strategic Logic of Suicide Terrorism* (New York: Random House, 2005). On Muslim hostility to the United States as stoked by a perceived double standard regarding Israel, see Rami G. Khouri, "Politics and Perceptions in the Middle East after September 11," *Contemporary Conflicts*, September 2002, http://conconflicts.ssrc.org/mideast/khouri/; Craig Charney and Nicole Ya-katan, *A New Beginning: Strategies for a More Fruitful Dialogue with the Muslim World* (New York: Council on Foreign Relations, 2005), pp. 3, 33, 44–45, 58.

65. Mueller, "Simplicity and Spook," p. 220. Mueller's discussion is excellent and wide ranging. He quotes the toilet statistic from John Stoessel, *Give Me a Break* (New York: HarperCollins, 2004).

66. W. J. Burns and P. Slovic, *Predicting Public Response to a Terrorist Strike*, Report No. 06–02 (Eugene, Oreg.: Decision Research, 2006).

67. U.S. Environmental Protection Agency, http://www.epa.gov/ttn/atw/nata/natsafaq.html#B3.

68. See especially "First Annual Report to the President and the Congress to Assess Domestic Response Capabilities for Terrorism Involving Weapons of Mass Destruction" (December 15, 1999). This and four subsequent reports were prepared by what is most commonly referred to as the Gilmore Commission. All five reports may be accessed at http://www.rand.org/nsrd/terrpanel/.

69. See James Risen's critical account of one such operation, code named MERLIN, in *State of War: The Secret History of the CIA and the Bush Administration* (New York: Free Press, 2006), pp. 193–218.

70. On the thinking within al-Qaeda circles about weapons of mass destruction, and in particular nuclear weapons, see Paz, "Global Jihad and WMD."

INDEX

9/11 attacks, 59–60; effect on airline industry, 84–85, 162–63 n.30; effect on bureaucratic foreign policy battles, 60–65; exploitation of, 50; irrational government response to, 1–2; strategic reasons for, 132–34; tips from the public concerning, 1, 2; as the work of al-Qaeda, 62–63, 132–33
9/11 Commission, 8, 61; and dangers of the political marketplace, 74–75
24 (Fox), 27

Abbas, Mahmud, 157–58 n.32
Abrams, Elliott, 51, 52
Abu Ali, Ahmed Omar, 41
Abu-Ghaith, Sulaiman, 128, 173 n.38
Abu Ghraib prison scandal, 108, 132
acquired immune deficiency syndrome (AIDS), 87, 164 n.39
al-Adl, Seif, 133
Afghanistan, 5, 15, 54, 66, 103, 157–58 n.32; anarchic conditions in, 87
AFL-CIO, 85
Africa, 164 n.39
Age of Sacred Terror, The: Radical Islam's War against America (Benjamin and Simon), 118
Agency, The (CBS), 27, 94–95, 165 n.52
"Agenda for Action, An: Veterinary Medicine's Crucial Role in Public Health and Biodefense and the Obligation of Academic Veterinary Medicine to Respond," 80–81
Ahmadinejad, Mahmud, 135
Alaska, homeland security funds received by, 76
Albright, Madeleine, 55
"All Hazards National Preparedness Goal," 96
Allen, Charles, 12

Allison, Graham, 173 n.38
America Prepared campaign, 8
American Academy of Pediatrics, 81–82
American Association of Colleges of Pharmacy, 81
American Insurance Association, 80
American Patrol, 98–99
American Pharmaceutical Association, 81
American Psychological Association (APA), Subcommittee on Psychology's Response to Terrorism, 82
American Society of Health-System Pharmacists, 81
Anderson, Jeffry, 152 n.21
anthrax. See bioterrorism, and anthrax
Armitage, Richard L., 51, 59
Aryan Nations, 99, 137
Ashcroft, John, 33, 36, 37, 40, 47, 108, 109
Association of American Universities, 91
Association of American Veterinary Medical Colleges, 80
"asymmetric" war, 127–28. See also "Al-Qaeda Organization and the Asymmetric War"
Atta, Muhammad, 124
avian flu, 87
"Axis of Evil," 6, 48, 62, 65
al-Azdi, Abu Jandal, 134

Bah, Adama, 153 n.36
Bai, Matt, 115, 169 n.3
Baker, James, 55, 56
Barnes, Fred, 155 n.3
Baucus, Max, 81
Beers, Randy, 159 n.52
Benjamin, Daniel, 118
benzene pollution, 143
Berger, Sandy, 55
Bilmes, Linda, 23

bin Laden, Osama, 43, 57–58, 84, 107, 125, 141, 172 n.32; and the genesis of al-Qaeda, 129–32; inability to capture, 103; "October surprise" videotape of, 106, 134–35; and the Palestinian problem, 141–42, 175 nn. 60, 62, 175–76 n.63; political problems of and his brilliance in solving, 132–33; "UBL" acronym for, 158 n.33

bio-security, 22, 82–83, 87, 92, 166 n.67. *See also* Center for Biosecurity

bioterrorism, 22, 87, 92; and anthrax, 94; and botulism, 97; and hoof-and-mouth disease, 80–81; rationale for, 173 n.38; science research in the context of, 93; and smallpox, 94–95

bird flu. *See* avian flu

Bolton, John, 51, 52, 53, 56, 69; on regime change in various nations, 157 n.28

Bosnia, 129

botulism. *See* bioterrorism, and botulism

Boyle, Brian D., 32

Brady Center to Stop Gun Violence, 83–84

Bremer, Paul, 157 n.28

Brzezinski, Zbigniew, 54

British Broadcasting Corporation (BBC), 26

Brooklyn Bridge, 41, 112

Brooks, David, 106

Brown, Michael, 86

Bruey, Judith, 47

Bulliet, Richard, 175–76 n.63

Bush, George H. W., development of foreign policy under, 54, 55

Bush, George W., 5, 32, 36, 46, 47, 110, 117; approval ratings of, 62, 135, 167 n.75; belief in Saddam Hussein/al-Qaeda connection, 63–64; and the "Churchillian" definition of his leadership, 62; and the controversy over Dubai-based company's control of U.S. ports, 170 n.7; decline in support for, 20; definition of those responsible for 9/11 attacks, 64–65; immigration policy of, 100; invasion of Afghanistan and Iraq, 157–58 n.32; jokes concerning Iran and Cuba, 157 n.28; pragmatism of, 62; presidency as a sacred mission, 62, 157–58 n.32; response to 9/11 attacks, 60; scientific research budget of (FY 2006), 92; speeches concerning terrorism, 10–11, 13, 148 nn.6–7;

views on foreign policy, 55; and the War on Terror, 102–3, 123–25, 164 n.39; weekly radio broadcasts of, 13. *See also* Bush administration, foreign policy battles within

Bush administration, foreign policy battles within, 55–56; effect of 9/11 on "supremacists'" position, 59–60; post-9/11 supremacist policy of, 61–62; pragmatist faction of, 56, 58, 59, 61; and the "supremacist" faction, 56–68 passim, 71

Bush vs. the Beltway: How the CIA and the State Department Tried to Stop the War on Terror (Mylroie), 58

cabal, 5, 135, 155 nn. 2, 6; makeup of, 49–53; power exerted by, 53–68 passim; tactical success and strategic failure of Iraq War policy, 68–70

Carter, Jimmy, 54

Cassandra, 27–28

Celtic Knights of the KKK, 99

Center for Biosecurity (University of Pittsburgh Medical Center), 163–64 n.37

Center for Survey Research and Analysis, 19

Centers for Disease Control (CDC), 92

Central Intelligence Agency (CIA), 35, 56, 148 n.13

Chalabi, Ahmad, 59, 157 n.25

Chechnya, 129

Cheney, Dick, 5, 11, 51, 52, 66, 110, 155 n.2; influential power in George W. Bush's administration, 53–54; views on 9/11 attacks, 104

Chertoff, Michael, 100, 112; criticism of, 78; triage approach to counterterrorism funding, 78–79

China, 15, 16, 18, 58

Christian Identity Movement, 174–75 n.54

Christopher, Warren, 55

Ciluffo, Frank, 93

Clancy, Tom, 95

Clarke, Richard A., 57–58, 118, 159 n.52, 168 n.81; conversation with George W. Bush concerning Saddam Hussein, 63–64; focus on bin Laden and al-Qaeda, 61

Clinton, Bill, 50; development of foreign policy under, 54, 55; and failed insurrection in Iraq, 157 n.25

CNBC, 106
CNN, 91, 105–6
Cohen, Bernard, 102
Cohen, Eliot, 56
Cold War, x, 11, 55; compared to the War on
    Terror, 14
Collins, Susan, 76, 77
Committee for the Liberation of Iraq (CLI),
    67
"Communicating the Principles of Prevention
    and Protection in the War on Terror"
    (Luntz), 104
Confidence in U.S. Foreign Policy Index,
    16–17
Congressional Research Service, 24; investiga-
    tion of terrorist threats from 2002 to 2004,
    112
Convertino, Richard, 39
Council of Conservative Citizens, 99
counterterrorism, funding for, ix, 20–24, 149
    nn. 19, 25; budget for State and Local
    Homeland Security, 76; budget for Urban
    Area Security Initiative, 76, 79; compared
    to the budget for education, 24; FY 2006
    budget compared to FY 2005 budget, 76;
    and health-related government agencies
    (biodefense funding), 82–83; high-risk tar-
    gets as basis for allocation of funds,
    77–78; new guidelines concerning, 78–79;
    relation of experts to, 91–92; and requests
    for proposal (RFPs), 93–94; in rural ver-
    sus urban areas, 76–78; of scientific re-
    search, 91–93, 165 n.46; at universities, 95;
    use of funds to advance pet projects by
    professional organizations, 79–83; use of
    funds by special interest groups for politi-
    cal purposes, 83–88
"Crusader-Zionist" alliance, 141
Cuba, 18, 157 n.28

David, Steven, 93
De Niro, Robert, 101
Dean, Howard, 111
democracy, domination of by the War on
    Terror, 101–12
Democrats/Democratic Party, 104, 117, 170
    n.7
Deshong, Debra, 117

dirty (radiological) bombs, 97
Dirty War (2004), 26
Dobriansky, Paula J., 51, 52
Dying to Win: The Strategic Logic of Suicide Terrorism
    (Pape), 170 n.13

Ealy, Michael, 27
Edwards, John, 109–10
"effects-based" operations, 127
Egypt, 129, 131, 132
El Al Airlines, 41
"enemy combatants," 32
Enterprise Foundation, 85
entertainment industry, 24–25; exploitation of
    terrorism plot lines in films, 25; television
    networks, and broadcasts of bin Laden
    videotapes, 172 n.32; terrorism threat as
    portrayed in made-for-television movies,
    25–26; terrorism threat as portrayed in
    novels, 25; terrorism threat as portrayed in
    television series, 26–27
Environmental Protection Agency (EPA), 143
ethnic profiling, 44

Fallows, James, 55, 63, 158 n.33
Far Enemy, The (Gerges), 175 n.60
Faris, Iyman, 40–41; mental competency of,
    153 n.29
Federal Bureau of Investigation (FBI), 1, 2, 3,
    31, 107; allocation of agents to counterter-
    rorism activities, 34–35, 151 n.10; authority
    to investigate American citizens, 33; count-
    erterrorism funding for, 21; Field Intelli-
    gence Groups, 25
Federal Emergency Management Agency
    (FEMA), 86
Feinstein, Dianne, 77
Feith, Douglas, 52, 56, 66, 69, 159 n.50
Foreign Affairs, 50, 57
foreign policy, presidential development of,
    54–55
Foreign Policy Association (FPA), 15
"Four Years after 9/11, War on Terror Slogs
    On" (Jenkins), 14
Fox News, 91
France, 139
Franks, Tommy, 106; endorsement of George
    W. Bush for president, 168 n.82
Frum, David, 155 n.3

Gafney, Frank, 52–53
Garner, Jay, 157 n.28
Garrett, Laurie, 87
gay marriage, 102
Gerecht, Reuel Marc, 155 n.3
Gerges, Fawaz, 131, 133, 175 n.60, 175–76 n.63
Gillespie, Ed, 116–17
Gilmore Commission, 176 n.68
Goldstein, Joshua S., 14–15
Gonzalez, Alberto, 35, 37, 71
Goss, Porter J., 12
Gregg, Judd, 77
Guantanamo Bay Naval Base, 32, 132

Habeck, Mary R., 124
Hadley, Steven, 11, 51
Hamas, 41, 170 n.13
Hamdi, Yasar Esam, 32
Hamilton, Alexander, 72
Hamilton, Lee, 27, 123, 125
Hannity, Sean, 107
Harvey, F. Barton, 85–86
Hayat, Hamid, 43–44
Haydar, Tashnuba, 153 n.36
Hayden, Michael V., 12
Helms, Jesse, 64
Heritage Foundation, 11
Hersh, Seymour, 57, 64
Hezbollah, 135
High-Threat City Joint Working Group on Homeland Security, 77
Hitler, Adolf, 103, 128
Hoffman, Dustin, 101
Holbrooke, Richard, 169 n.3
Home Box Office (HBO), 26
Homeland Security Act (2002), 32
Homeland Security and Terrorism (ed. Howard, Forest, and Moore), 166 n.67
Homeland Security Appropriations Act (2005), 21, 77
hoof-and-mouth disease. *See* bioterrorism, and hoof-and-mouth disease
Howe, David, 171–72 n.28
Hughes, Karen, 67
Hurricane Katrina, 86
al-Hussayen, Sami, 40
Hussein, Saddam, 5, 49–50, 53, 54; and linkage with the 9/11 attacks, 59, 63–64; and weap-
ons of mass destruction (WMD), 51, 52, 66

Ibn Taymiyya, 132, 174 n.45
immigration, 166 n.70; presumed threat of illegal immigration, 98–101
Immigration and Nationality Act, 100
Immigration Reform Caucus, 99–100
Independent Insurance Agents and Brokers of America, 80
Indonesia, 126–27
Institute for Advanced Strategic and Political Studies, 52–53
International Association of Fire Investigators, 161 n.11
Iran, 54, 60, 65, 69, 157 n.28; terrorist response to any attack on by the United States, 135–36; U.S. response to uranium enrichment program of, 135
Iraq, 5, 12, 65; terrorism in, 13, 36
Iraq Liberation Act, 51
Iraq war, 6–7, 11, 53, 68–70, 103; casualties of, 145; costs of through 2005, 24; plan to seize oil fields, 59; planning for, 63, 158 n.33; political preparation for, 65–68; projected total costs of by the Stiglitz-Bilmes study, 23; reasons for, 65–67, 159 n.49; as serving al-Qaeda's purposes, 17, 36, 126–27, 132; strikes against Iraq's command and control centers, 55–56, 156 n.14; support for, 67–68
Islam, 134; "American/Christian/Zionist" threat to, 131–32; distinction between Islam and Salafist movement, 130; transnational culture of, 129–30
"Islamo-fascism," 52, 122
Israel, 53, 56, 132, 175 n.58, 176 n.64; policies toward the Palestinians, 141

Jenkins, Brian Michael, 14
Jewish Institute for National Security Affairs (JINSA), 52
jihadis, 130–32, 173 n.40, 175 n.60; "heroism" of, 133
judo politics, 126

Kagan, Robert, 50–51, 67; on George W. Bush's foreign policy thinking, 59–60

Kashmir, 129

Kean, Thomas, 27

Keating, Frank, 77–78

Kelley, William, 93

Kempthorne, Dirk, 40

Kennan, George F., x–xi, 120–22, 129; and the "Long Telegram," 120, 147 n.1; on the Soviet Union and U.S. policy toward, 120–22

Kennedy, Edward M., 82

Kenya, 134

Kerry, John, 105, 108, 111, 125, 169 n.3; on George W. Bush's anti-terrorism strategy, 116, 170 n.7; categorization of terrorist threats as a law enforcement problem, 115–17; as Democratic Party nominee for president, 109–10, 168 n.80

Khalilzad, Zalmay, 51

Kissinger, Henry, 54, 56

Knowing the Enemy: Jihadist Ideology and the War on Terror (Habeck), 124

Koran, 130

Krar, William, 47

Krauthammer, Charles, 56, 155 n.3

Kristol, William, 50–51, 56, 67

Ku Klux Klan, 137, 174–75 n.54

Kwiatowski, Karen, 159 n.50

Lake, Anthony, 55

Lebanon, 129, 135

Lemann, Nicholas, 64

Lenin, Vladimir, 136

Letterman, David, 105–6

Libby, I. Lewis ("Scooter"), 51, 56, 67; resignation of, 69

Libya, 157 n.28

Lieberman, Joseph, 77, 111

Limbaugh, Rush, 107

Los Angeles, 41; targeting of the Library Tower by al-Qaeda, 46, 154 nn. 46, 48

Luntz, Frank, 104

Luti, William, 56, 159 n.50

Madison, James, 72

Maine, homeland security funds received by, 76–77

Malaysia, 154 n.48

Maples, Michael D., 12

Marx, Karl, 136

Mass Immigration Reduction Act (2003), 100

Massachusetts, 76–77

Matalin, Mary, 67

McCarthy, Joseph, 119

McCauley, Clark, 172 n.33

McClellan, Scott, 109, 111

McFarlane, Robert, 54

Medicaid, 22

medical malpractice insurance, 88

Medicare, 22

Mehlman, Kenneth, 102

Mein Kampf (Hitler), 128

Miller, Judith, 67, 105

Minetta, Norman, 84–85

Minutemen, 99

al-Moayad, Mohammed Ali-Hasan, 41–42

Muhammad (the Prophet), riots after cartoon depiction of, 139

Mohammed, Khalid Sheik, 45, 154 n.48

Mote, Dan, 91

movies/film. *See* entertainment industry

MSNBC, 91

Mubarak, Husni, 131

Mueller, John, 142

Mueller, Robert S., 12, 21, 41, 106, 108

Mullin, Leo F., 84–85

Muslim Brotherhood (Muslim Brothers), 130, 131

Muslims, 126, 131–32; American, 139–40; Egyptian fundamentalist, 129; in Europe, 136–37; relationship with Christians and Jews, 139, 141–42; seventh-century, 130; Sunni, 129. *See also* Islam; jihadis; Muslim Brotherhood (Muslim Brothers); Salafist movement

Mylroie, Laurie, 57, 58, 156–57 n.23

National Abortion Rights Action League (NARAL), 97

National Advisory Committee on Children and Terrorism, 92

National Alliance, 99

National Association of Chain Drug Stores, 81

National Association of Insurance Commissioners (NAIC), 79–80

National Association of State Universities and Land Grant Colleges, 91

National Counter-Terrorism Center, 36

National District Attorneys Association, 80, 161–62 n.18

National Endowment for Democracy, 11

National Institutes of Health (NIH), 22, 82–83

National Institute for Mental Health (NIMH), 91

national laboratories, 91–92; Argonne, 91; Lawrence Livermore, 92; Los Alamos, 95; Sandia, 91

"National Planning Scenarios," 86, 96–97, 124, 163–64 n.37

National Rifle Association (NRA), 97, 162 n.28; NRASafe program, 84

National Science Foundation (NSF), 91, 95

National Security Agency (NSA), 2, 34, 35, 151 n.7

National Security Council, 156 n.12

"national security letters," 33–34

"National Security Strategy of the United States" (White House, 2002), 123–24, 171 n.27, 173 n.39

National Socialist Movement, 99

natural gas freighters, bombing of, 97

Negroponte, John, 12–13, 32–44, 123

Neo-Confederates, 174–75 n.54

neoconservative cabal, 5, 135, 155 nn. 2, 6; makeup of, 49–53; power exerted by, 53–68 passim; tactical success and strategic failure of Iraq war policy, 68–70

neo-Nazis, 137, 174–75 n.54

Netanyahu, Benjamin, 53

New Jersey, 77

New Orleans, 86

New York, 77

New York City, 8–9

New York Times, 2, 42, 67, 151 n.7; assessment of terrorist threats to 2004 presidential elections, 111–12

Next Attack, The: The Failure of the War on Terror and a Strategy for Getting It Right (Benjamin and Simon), 118–19

Nigeria, 15

Nixon, Richard M., 54

No Child Left Behind program, 13

North Carolina, counterterrorism expenditures by, 78

North Korea, 65, 157 n.28

Nuclear Terrorism: The Ultimate Preventable Catastrophe (Graham), 173 n.38

Office of Domestic Preparedness. *See* U.S. Department of Homeland Security (DHS), Office of Domestic Preparedness

Office of Special Plans, 67, 69, 159 n.50

Office of Strategic Initiatives, 106

"Officials Worry of Pre-Election Attack," 107

Oklahoma City, 79, 142

Packer, George, 157 n.28

Padilla, Jose, 36–37

Pakistan, 126–27, 132

Palestine/Palestinians, 56, 129; U.S. policies toward, 140–41. *See also* al-Qaeda, and the Palestinian problem

Pape, Robert, 170 n.13

Paz, Reuven, 134

Pentagon. *See* 9/11 attacks

Perle, Richard, 51, 52–53, 56, 57, 64, 67; on the need for regime change in various nations, 157 n.28; resentment of the intelligence community, 58; resignation of from the Defense Advisory Board, 69

"persons of interest," 35, 151 n.14

Pew Research Center for the People and the Press, 17–18

"Pharmacy Involvement in Preparedness for and Response to Public Health Emergencies and Terrorism Attacks," 81

Pillar, Paul R., 64

Plame, Valerie, 105–6

Poindexter, John, 54

political marketplace, 73; and the expansion of the War on Terror, 74–75; and "negative externalities," 73–74; poor information and failure of, 74

Post Terrorism Mental Health Improvement Act, 82

Powell, Colin, 5, 54–55, 155 n.2; Iraq policy of, 59; loss of influence to supremacist hawks, 66

presidential elections (2004): Republicans' attacks on Kerry's view of terrorist threats,

116–17; speculation on terrorist attacks preceding, 106–12
Project BioShield, 21
Project for the New American Century (PNAC), 50, 60, 62; and the Iraq Liberation Act, 51; key documents of, 50–51; letter of to President Clinton, 51–52
Property Casualty Insurers Association of America, 79
Public Agenda surveys, 16
Public Discourse Project, 8
public opinion, 13–14, 102; attentive public level, 9, 10; levels of, 9–10; mass level, 9–10; political elite level, 9, 10
public opinion polls: ABC News/*Washington Post*, 19; Arabic, 126–27, 175 n.58; CBS News, 19, 20; CNN/*USA Today*/Gallup, 19; Fox News/Opinion Dynamics, 19, 20; Lexis-Nexis, 18; National Opinion Ballot, 15–16; NBC News/*Wall Street Journal*, 19; *Newsweek*, 19
Purdue University, Homeland Security Institute, 95

al-Qaeda, 5–6, 32, 41, 59, 65, 109, 170 n.13; alliance with the Taliban, 68; attacks on American embassies in Africa, 134; base in Afghanistan, 62–63; disruption of plots by, 45–46; genesis of, 129–32; justification of for massive attacks on America, 128–29; and nuclear terrorism, 144–45; number of members, 174–75 n.54; and the Palestinian problem, 141–42, 175 nn. 60, 62, 176 n.64; recruitment video of, 141, 175–76 n.63; responsibility for 9/11 attacks, 60, 62; short- and long-term objectives of, 125–27; simplistic view of on the part of the United States, 122–25; sophistication of, 134; targeting of the Library Tower of Los Angeles by, 46, 154 nn. 46, 48; transnational subculture within, 129–30; visibility and stature in the Muslim world, 137–38. *See also* 9/11 attacks
"Al-Qaeda Organization and the Asymmetric War, The" (al-Azdi), 134

Racicot, Marc, 116
Ranch Rescue, 98–99

RAND Corporation, 14
Reagan, Ronald, development of foreign policy under, 54–55
Real Guest Act (2005), 100
"Red menace," 119–20
"red-teaming," 94, 96
Reducing Immigration to a Genuinely Healthy Total Act (2005), 100
Republicans/Republican Party, 5, 104–5, 135, 167 n.75; attacks on Kerry during presidential elections (2004), 116–17, 168 n.81
Rice, Condoleezza, 11, 51, 61, 66, 99, 172 n.32; role in foreign policy development, 55–56; view of Saddam Hussein as "chump change," 56; view of terrorism, 107
Richardson, Bill, 117
Ridge, Tom, 108, 110, 111, 112
Risen, James, 144
Rodgers, William, 54
Rodley, Carol, 12
Rodman, Peter, 51
Roosevelt, Franklin D., xi, 103
Ross, Mike, 161 n.11
Rove, Karl, 67, 167 n.75; as architect of George W. Bush's administration policies on terrorism, 102–4
Rumsfeld, Donald, 5, 11, 29, 51, 57, 66, 155 n.2; on Iraq's presumed connection with al-Qaeda, 63; and regime change in Iran, 157 n.28; signature theme of, 12
Russert, Tim, 104

Sadat, Anwar, 129
Safire, William, 64, 106
Sageman, Marc, 138
Salafist movement, 130, 131, 133–34
San Diego Union-Tribune, 14
San Francisco Chronicle, 43
Saudi Arabia, 16
Schmitt, Gary, 67
Schneider, William, 167 n.75
Schultz, George, 54
Scowcroft, Brent, 55, 56, 117; realism of, 156 n.15
Securing the Homeland, Strengthening the Nation, 103
Sha'ath, Nabil, 157–58 n.32
Sherman, Roger, 72
Shilton, Henry, 134
Shinseki, Eric, 66

Shulsky, Abram, 159 n.50
Simon, Steven, 118
Singer, Phil, 117
Skinheads, 174–75 n.54
Sleeper Cell (Showtime), 27, 38, 152 n.21
sleeper cells: the discovery of al-Qaeda
    "sleeper cells," 38–47; lack of evidence for,
    46–47
Small Business Administration (SBA), 75–76,
    160 n.5
smallpox. See bioterrorism, and smallpox
Snyder, David, 80
Southern Poverty Law Center, 174–75 n.54
Soviet Union, x–xi, 11, 61, 129; assessment of
    by G. F. Kennan, 120–22; first detonation
    of atomic weapon by, 119
Stabenow, Debbie, 88
"stabilization and reconstruction" operations,
    128
Sternberg, Michael, 162–63 n.30
Stewart, Jon, 168 n.81
Stiglitz, Joseph, 23
Strategic Plan for Biodefense Research (NIH), 82–83
Sudan, 134
Sum of All Fears, The (Clancy [movie version,
    2002]), 95–96
Supplemental Terrorist Activity Relief
    (STAR) program, 76
"supremacists." See Bush administration, for-
    eign policy battles within
Sweeney, John J., 85
Symington, Charles E., 80
Syria, 53, 60, 69

Taiwan, 15, 16
takfeer, 130, 131
Taliban, 5, 32, 65
al-Tamimi, Ali, 41
Tancredo, Tom, 99–101
Tannenhaus, Sam, 159 n.49
Tanzania, 134
television networks. See entertainment industry
Tenet, George, 58–59, 61, 66
"terror porn," 29
"terror talk," 10
terrorism, ix, 160 n.1; American obsession with
    threat of, 29–31, 89; Americans' beliefs
    concerning, 9–27 passim; entertainment

industry's portrayal of, 24–27, 95–96;
    "false negative" versus "false positive" ap-
    proach to threat of, 31; fear of, 8–9, 97,
    119, 166 n.63, 170 n.14; as a law enforcement
    problem, 115–17, 138–39, 175 n.55; nuclear,
    144–45; right-wing extremist, 47, 137,
    174–75 n.54; vulnerability of America to,
    96–97, 166 n.67. See also terrorism, legal is-
    sues concerning; War on Terror
terrorism, legal issues concerning, 80; case of
    Abu Ali, 41; case of Sami al-Arian, 42; case
    of Iyman Faris, 40–41; case of Hamid
    Hayat, 43–44; case of Sami al-Hussayen,
    40; case of Jose Padilla, 36–37, 45; case of
    Mohammed Ali-Hasan al-Moayad,
    41–42; case of sixteen-year-old "suicide
    bombers," 42–43, 153 n.36; Detroit, Michi-
    gan, sleeper cell, 39; and the discovery of
    al-Qaeda "sleeper cells," 38–47; Lacka-
    wanna, New York, sleeper cell, 38–39;
    number of charges filed, 37–38; number of
    convictions, 37, 44, 151–52 n.19, 152 n.27
Terrorism Implementation Working Group,
    80
Terrorism Risk Insurance Act (TRIA), 79, 80
terrorists, 139, 176 n.64; "Christian," 137; as ex-
    istential threat, 137–38; right-wing extrem-
    ists, 47, 137; simplistic image of held by
    U.S. policy makers, 122–25; types of at-
    tacks possible by, 95–97; as "Universal
    Adversary," 124, 171–72 n.28. See also "per-
    sons of interest"; al-Qaeda
Thompson, Tommy, 83
triage, 2; definition of, 3
Turkey, 126–27
"Two Girls Held as U.S. Fears Suicide
    Bomb," 42

United Nations Security Council, 66
United States, 132–33, 140, 175 n.58; cultural
    trends within and relations with Islam,
    118–19; democracy of as envisioned by the
    founding fathers, 72–73; fears of its citi-
    zens, 30–31; military power of, 61, 68; poli-
    cies concerning the Palestinians, 140–41;
    and the reconstruction of "failed states,"
    87; response to Soviet atomic threat,
    120–22; toleration of domestic deaths

within, 142. *See also* "National Security Strategy of the United States" (White House, 2002); terrorism

"Universal Adversary (UA)," 124, 171–72 n.28

"Universal Task List," 96

Urban Area Security Initiative, 76, 79

U.S. Congress, appropriations for funding the War on Terror, 22–23

U.S. Department of Defense (DOD), 12, 32, 129, 147 n.2, 148 n.13; consultation of with Hollywood filmmakers, 95; counterterrorism funding for, 22

U.S. Department of Education, 150 n.32

U.S. Department of Health and Human Services (HHS), 83

U.S. Department of Homeland Security (DHS), 32, 107, 110; cancellation of airline flights by, 108; disaster scenarios (National Planning Scenarios) of, 86, 96–97, 124, 163–64 n.37, 171–72 n.28; funding for, 21, 22, 24; guidelines for counterterrorism funding, 78–79; Office of Domestic Preparedness, 93; suspension of oil shipments by, 108; threat warning system of, 8–9

U.S. Department of Justice (DOJ), 32, 37, 107, 151–52 n.19

U.S. Drug Enforcement Agency (DEA), 35

U.S. Election Assistance Committee, 107

U.S. Office of Management and Budget (OMB): and counterterrorism funding, 22–24; substantive program categories of, 21–22

U.S. Senate Committee on Commerce, Science, and Transportation, 84

USA PATRIOT Act (2001), 19, 32–33, 34, 39, 100

USA Today, 107

Uzbekistan, 132

Vance, Cyrus, 54

Vietnam War, xi

"wag the dog," 87, 104, 159 n.52; *Wag the Dog* (1997), 101–2, 159 n.52

War Against America, The: Saddam Hussein and the World Trade Center Attacks (Mylroie), 58

War on Terror, ix, 3, 47, 53, 66, 70, 71–72, 160 n.1; compared to the Cold War, 14; "cover your ass" (CYA) response mechanism, 88–90; editorial opinions concerning, 18; failed strategic policies of, 126–27; and imagination in fighting, 93–94; influence of experts on policy concerning, 90–97; lack of criticism of, 118; as the "long war," 129; mechanisms of, 72–75; media influence on, 90–91; opinion polls concerning, 16–19; opportunities for the outlandish in, 98–101; perceptions and treatments of by the attentive public, 13–18; perceptions and treatments of by the masses, 18–20; perceptions and treatments of by the political elite, 10–13; and "red-teaming," 94, 96; and the riddle of absent attacks, 112–14, 169 n.101; and simplistic views of the enemy, 122–25; strategies for success of, 127–36; terminology issues concerning, 148 n.13, 160 n.54, 173 n.39; as a threat to Americans, 6–7, 48, 72, 115; understanding and clarifying threats of, 3–4; vortex theory of, 48–49; willingness of the public to sacrifice for, 19–20, 160 n.6. *See also* counterterrorism, funding for; democracy, domination of by the War on Terror; War on Terror, dynamics of; War on Terror, entrapment in; War on Terror, solutions and new strategies for

War on Terror, dynamics of, 75–88 passim; and the influence of experts in self-powering the War on Terror, 90–97; and low-interest counterterrorism loans to small businesses, 75–76

War on Terror, entrapment in, 4; cynical explanation for, 4–5; generous explanation for, 4

War on Terror, solutions and new strategies for, 136–45; and accepting terrorism as a chronic problem, 143; example of European approach to, 136–37; importance of a rational approach, 142–43; political acknowledgment of the problem, 136; positive work on nuclear terrorism, 144–45; and reducing the "temperature" of the Muslim world, 140–41; thought experiment concerning, 137–38

Washington, D.C., 110, 145

Washington Post, 33, 37, 40, 45, 93, 111

weapons of mass destruction (WMD), 29, 51, 52, 57, 67; and evidence of "specialized aluminum tubes," 66

Weekly Standard, 50, 64, 155 n.3

White House Iraq Group (WHIG), 67

White Revolution, 99

Wiktorowicz, Quintan, 133–34

Wilkerson, Lawrence, B., 155 n.2

Wolfowitz, Paul, 51, 56, 57–58, 63, 66, 69; as advocate of the war on Iraq, 59, 156–57 n.23; ambitious idealism of, 156 n.15; on reasons to invade Iraq, 159 n.49; on regime change in Iran, 157 n.28; on state terrorism policy, 64

Woodward, Bob, 55, 105

Woolsey, R. James, 51, 52, 56, 67

World Affairs Councils, 15

World Islamic Front for Jihad against Crusaders and Jews, 130–31

World Trade Center (WTC), attacks on (1993), 57, 58, 142. *See also* 9/11 attacks

Wurmser, David, 53, 56

Wyoming, homeland security funds received by, 76

Yankelovich, Daniel, 16–17

al-Zawahiri, Ayman, 43, 125, 130–31, 141

Zeman, Robert, 79